CW00670328

HIGHBURY
Memories

Edited by TONY McDONALD

First published by Football World
in June, 2021

© Football World

All rights reserved.

Without limiting the rights under copyright reserved above, no part of this publication may be reproduced, stored in or introduced into retrieval system, or transmitted, in any form or by any means (electronic, mechanical, photocopying, recording or otherwise) without the prior written permission of the copyright owner of this book.

ISBN: 9780992742775

Football World, 9 Nursery Close, Glossop, Derbyshire, SK13 8PQ, England.

Design & Production: Jack McDonald

Sales & Distribution: Susie McDonald
Tel: 01708 734 502

Email: arsenalmemories@gmail.com

Web: www.footballworld.co.uk

Facebook: Highbury Memories

Twitter: @arsenalmemory

Instagram: @highbury_memories_book

Printed by Premier Print Group (London)

Cover images: We hope the various items of memorabilia on our cover rekindle fond memories of past times. We would particularly like to thank: Pat Rainsford for sending us the knitted scarf; Eileen Collier for the red silk/satin scarf; Ian Castle for the newspaper cutting; Les Easterbrook for the pennant; Lorraine Haugh for the Herbert Chapman bust photo; Lee Hisscott for the rosette; Roberto Puzzi for the final game ticket; Andy Bullen for the Peter Simpson coin; Marc Silvester for the holdall; and Steve Carey for the Subbuteo team and rattle.

Previous page: Thanks to Anne Grange for the rosette.

CONTENTS

INTRODUCTION

THIS book is for Arsenal supporters who treasure special memories of the Highbury years – from the club's move from Woolwich to the N5 district of north London in 1913, to the switch to Emirates Stadium in summer, 2006.

What makes this nostalgic package unique is that it is written by the fans, for the fans.

More than 100 avid supporters – from a handful of Octogenarians who first stood on the terraces in the late 1940s to much younger Gooners who got their first glimpse of the all-seater Arsenal Stadium in the noughties – share personal anecdotes in response to our questionnaire.

They begin by explaining why they chose Arsenal over nearest rivals Tottenham Hotspur and other clubs and recall their first visit to this great bastion of the game with its fabled marble halls; nominate their favourite players, greatest goals and most memorable matches; standout North London Derbies; cult heroes; highs and lows; and their emotional final pilgrimage to the famous ground that was home for 93 seasons.

Many of the photographs and evocative images we've used were taken by our contributors or belong to them. The collectible souvenir items represent some of what being a football fan was like before the beautiful game became cynically driven by money, greed and sold its soul.

This is most definitely not intended as an historical record laden with stats and facts and the views of authors and journalists who have covered Arsenal – plenty of other books written about this great club have already fulfilled that purpose. However, the glory of League and Cup doubles and triumphant first European trophy, won at Highbury in 1970, inevitably feature through the eyes of fans who can proudly say 'I was there'.

Supporting any football club is a roller-coaster ride, so their views also re-live shattered dreams of more trophies and Champions League success. One or two recall being among just 4,554 dejected die-hards for a top-flight game against Leeds United. The gamut of emotions experienced by the people who have Arsenal ingrained in their DNA are laid bare in these 264 pages.

I hope it is an entertaining lasting legacy not only for generations of the 'Arsenal Family' to enjoy, but one that will resonate with the wider football community who remember the days gone by with equal affection.

Tony McDonald, Editor/Publisher
June, 2021

1 WHY ARSENAL?

FIRST-EVER VISIT TO HIGHBURY

WHY support Arsenal? It's a question the majority of supporters have asked themselves on plenty of occasions over the years. For most, following the club was not a conscious decision or a deliberately chosen path. It's simply in the blood, a family tradition passed down through the generations with inextricable links to this area of North London. For others, a quirk of fate or a random event may have led them towards the Gunners.

Our contributors span the last eight of 10 decades of football at Highbury, from the 1930s right up to the final game, and they still follow the club from all parts of the world – in Australia, America, Africa, Asia and across Europe.

Q1: What, and who was it, that led you to Arsenal and what do you recall from your first visit to Arsenal Stadium?

Richard (Dickie) Boyes: I was born in 1931. My parents, Richard and Catherine, lived at St. Paul's Road, near Highbury Corner, in an area called Mildmay Park. Needless to say, Dad and his brothers were all mad Arsenal supporters. I saw my first game at Highbury in 1936, on Dad's shoulders at the South Bank end. We beat Everton, 3-2 (29/8/1936), and I was hooked for life.

In those days Islington was working class and very tribal, which was reflected in the great atmosphere inside Highbury. No singing, just a great roar of cheering and booing and no yuppies to ruin the mood.

I met my wife Gwen in 1955. She was also Arsenal-mad, as was her dad, Frank Brinkman. We married in 1959 and moved to Romford, where our three children – Angela, Richard and Peter – were born but we still never missed a home game.

Gwen Boyes: The evening of May 29, 1955 was the night I met the man of my life. I was a very shy 17-year-old and Dick Boyes (see above) was a complete stranger of 23 years but after a dance and him apologising for stepping on my toe, he told me that he was awaiting a knee cartilage operation, so started a conversation on football.

I have always been an Arsenal supporter. I used to go with my dad Frank Brinkman and always stood under the clock, so our conversation started to get interesting. Dick had also watched Arsenal sitting on his dad's shoulders. In those days, not many girls were interested in football, let alone go to watch games – it was a boy thing.

I think Dick may have been doubtful and asked me a question that he thought only a true supporter would be able to correctly answer: 'What colour socks do Arsenal players wear?'.

A trick question but one I had no problems with. 'White with navy rings, of course!' I answered, not imagining then just how important my response would turn out to be.

We have been married for 60 years in March (2019) and still support Arsenal. In fact, there is not one non Arsenal supporter in our large family.

Dave Nathan: My great-grandfather, Wally Dale, was groundsman at Highbury in the 1920s. He and my grandmother Doris used to live on Gillespie Road, behind the North Bank, and that's the reason I always stood at that end.

Wally was out doing the pitch one day in the pouring rain in the late 20s. He had to be carried home ill and died over the weekend from pneumonia. Arsenal then paid my great-grandmother – helped by Doris and her seven brothers and sisters – to wash the Arsenal kit twice a week in their back garden of Gillespie Road, using her washboard and mangle.

Doris grew up and went in to the Army, where at one time she was the youngest serving British sergeant in WW2. That's where she met my grandad, Captain Eric Nathan, an Islington lad and Arsenal fan. So I could have been born in Timbuktu and would still have had a red-and-white scarf for Christmas.

Philip Ashman: I followed a tradition set by my parents, Phil snr and Lilian, and uncles Jim, Jack, Glyn and Roy Ashman and Petros Iatrou (Mum's brother). In a 1950s *Gunflash* you can see my parents and uncle Jack marked out in the crowd at the semi-final replay v Chelsea at WHL.

Dad came up from Wales in 1938 and looked for a club that wore red, like Wales, hence we all became Gooners. I saw my first game in 1949, when I was only three-years-old.

Tony Porter: I was drawn to Highbury by my father. He was called the Revd Charles Porter, and he had studied for a year at the London College of Divinity, the original owners of the field that the football club transformed. He was lucky enough to be there when Herbert Chapman was in his pomp.

There were free seats for the ordinands at home matches and they even sometimes trained with the players. The seats were in the West Stand, so that's where we always sat, my father keen to protect me from the crowds – and perhaps some of the language?

I was eight when he took me to my first game, v Sunderland (11/11/1950). It was magical – the bright colours, the excitement, the drama being played out. But I'd heard quite a bit about Arsenal before being thought old enough to actually be there and at half-time it was only 1-1. I remember turning to my dad, puzzled, and asking: "Shouldn't Arsenal be winning?" "Just wait and see," he replied. "They've had a good look at them and things will be different in the second-half."

They were: we won 5-1 I remember Sunderland's one more than any of our five. Someone put up a steepling kick – what rugby players call a Garryowen – and Ted Platt in goal misjudged the catch, spilled it, and their centre-forward popped in the loose ball. Platt was

Highbury from the Clock End, 1950.

6

the reserve keeper to George Swindin, so he was probably a bit rusty.

Tony Fisher: I grew up in Hackney, so my team had to be either Arsenal or Tottenham. In the late 40s there was no TV, only sketchy reports on the wireless and old newspapers if you could find them. So my only knowledge of football was from school mates who were lucky enough to have fathers. My dad was lost in the Second World War and I had no uncles who were interested in football. I first learned about Arsenal as a young boy from my best friend Brian whose uncle was Len Wills, the Arsenal right-back.

With Brian having moved away, I went on my own as a nine-year-old in 1952. I remember the great adventure I had getting the 236 bus from London Fields to Blackstock Road. Walking with the crowd before turning into the top of Avenell Road to get my first sight of Highbury looking down the hill. I think I paid 1/3d to get in to the Clock End and made my way to the front, just to the right of the goal which became my permanent spot for some years until moving round to the standing enclosure in front of the West Stand. I was filled with awe looking at this vast arena and sea of people, having never seen anything like it.

To my right, in front of the East Stand, there was suddenly music playing – my first encounter with The Metropolitan Police band and their singing PC, Alex Morgan. This felt like being at the Hackney Empire and I felt very special. Looking above them, I saw what seemed like thousands of rich people in big coats smoking cigars.

I can't remember anything of the game other than thinking how massive the players looked. Goalkeeper Jack Kelsey (right) became my immediate hero, because I was looking up at him for a whole half. I know I cast covetous eyes over to the enclosure by the tunnel, as I couldn't afford the 3/- to get in there. In later years I have been fortunate enough to witness that same first time wonderment on the faces of my children and grandchildren.

J. Kelsey

I often wondered why I found such a joy and comfort going to Highbury. Perhaps the Club was like a surrogate father figure. I had no real male role models or close male family and being in this world of men fulfilled my need for a feeling of belonging and sharing.

Chris Welstead: I was born and raised in Hornsey, about two-and-a-half miles from Highbury. Neither my dad nor my older brother were particularly interested in football. However, my uncle Sonny and one of his sisters, my auntie Phyllis, were both season ticket holders. Sonny vowed that there would be another member of the family to carry on the tradition of supporting the Gunners.

He took me to my first and several subsequent games until I was old enough to attend by myself. At the age of six, my first game was a league match against Middlesbrough (22/3/1952) which we won 3-1. I don't really remember anything about the game but I do recall catching my first glimpse of the pitch from the West Stand Upper. The view from the upper tier was breathtaking. I had never seen anything like it in my life. I think I was hooked from that moment.

Andy Strouthous: The Korean War is why I am an Arsenal fan. In 1951 we were living in East Sheen near my father George's restaurant. A slump followed the war and the restaurant went bust (1951), so we fled north to near The Arsenal to live with my mother's parents. My pa went to work at the Park Lane Hotel, the owner one Bracewell Smith. Smith gave free Arsenal tickets to staff who wanted them.

I was so young when taken to the Arsenal that I cannot remember my first game, although I know it was 17 years before I saw a trophy, and by then on the North Bank. I am a season ticket holder who has supported the club for at least 65 years. I went to both legs of the final with Anderlecht and was there for that first trophy.

Bernard Chaplin: My first recollection was watching the 1950 FA Cup Final on our nine-inch black and white TV. I studied the history and became hooked, although most of my school mates at that time supported other London teams.

I vividly remember my first match, v Middlesbrough (24/4/1954). It is difficult to put into words but the experience was very emotional. Non-football fans simply do not understand. I was actually watching my heroes in the flesh. A school friend took me and we stood in one of the corners behind the scoreboards. Just after half-time a man would come and put the scores up. Nothing electronic.

One of my favourite players at that that time was Jack Kelsey (right), the goalkeeper, as I also played in goal at school. He would often have friendly banter with the crowd behind his goal.

John Bowles: Dad John – not a Londoner or a fan himself but he encouraged me to support my local team – took me to my first game, a 1-0 defeat by Burnley (26/11/55). We went to 15 or so games until I was old enough to go on my own. Few memories of that first trip to Highbury apart from disappointment and chestnuts after.

Graham Lister: If I didn't imbibe Arsenal with my mother's milk, then I certainly absorbed Arsenal sat on my father's knee as he enthralled me with tales of his own Highbury heroes from the Chapman and Allison eras. As a seven-year-old, Mick Lister had listened on a tinny wireless when underdogs Arsenal took on then-mighty Huddersfield Town in the 1930 FA Cup Final and beat them to lift the first major trophy in the club's history. Mick was hooked for life; now as a father of two sons he was ensuring that my older brother Dave and I would be similarly smitten.

I was not yet four when my mum Eileen bought Bernard Joy's newly-published club history, *Forward Arsenal!*, as a Christmas present for Dad from his two boys in December 1954. The book's atmospheric cover photograph showed Joy in action with one of Highbury's imposing stands behind him, and the next logical step was a trip to the iconic stadium.

So we were taken to a reserve game against Luton Town's second string (2/3/1957). I was a five-year-old overawed by the sheer scale of Highbury. We were perched high in the East Stand, the sward of green laid out below us like a magic carpet. I recall being struck by the way the net billowed when a goal was scored. Arsenal rippled that netting three times as they won by the odd goal in five.

But my next visit to the stadium, by now aged six, was more significant as Gunners' first team took on Leeds United in a Division One match (28/9/1957), and Dad took the whole family to see it. We four stood on the terracing, fairly close to the pitch, among a crowd of 39,347, as David Herd scored twice in a 2-1 win. Some years later I read (in Geoffrey Mowbray's book *Gunners On The Target)* a review of the 1957-58 season in which that Leeds match was described as 'tepid'; yet nothing could dim my shining memory of the occasion. The grandeur and excitement of what to me seemed a packed, palatial Highbury was enhanced by the smells and particularly the sounds within the stadium and in the teeming streets around it.

And then there was the sight of those heroes in bright red and white shirts, with the distinctive white-and-navy blue hooped socks, passing that ball around, in between and beyond Leeds players in blue and yellow. I had no doubt I was in the Home of Football, the one genuine theatre of dreams; nor that I would be back just as often as I could possibly get there.

I was so captivated by that Highbury experience that as soon as we returned home I drew and meticulously coloured in on a large, discarded sheet of Dad's draughtsman's paper, a depiction of the match that included all 22 players, the officials and the crowd. Highbury had me hooked.

To a small boy, of course, Highbury was always going to seem huge but in those days the sweep of the open Clock End terrace and the carrying capacity of four uncovered corners gave the ground a majestic scale that threw the two symmetrical Art Deco stands along either side of the pitch into monumental, imposing relief. To my eye, the capacity reductions of later years forced on Highbury by the requirement for all-seater stadia diminished its scale and detracted from its visual glory, even though the changes were mostly implemented tastefully and maintained much of the integrity of the 1930s design.

The Arsenal team v Leeds Utd in 1957: Con Sullivan; Len Wills, Denis Evans; Cliff Holton, Bill Dodgin, Dave Bowen; Danny Clapton, Ray Swallow, David Herd, Jimmy Bloomfield, Mike Tiddy.

I should add that my love of Highbury was heightened when, on the first day of the following season, I was treated to a free, impromptu tour of the stadium – years before such tours became a staple of football clubs' commercial initiatives. And my guide was an Arsenal legend, George Male.

It was August 23, 1958, and the first team were opening their campaign up at Deepdale against Preston North End, from whom Arsenal would sign Tommy Docherty the following day. But Arsenal reserves were at home to Fulham in the Football Combination, and match referee Ray Pipe was a friend of Dad's. I travelled to Highbury with Dad and Ray, whose status as a match official allowed us access that we would otherwise never have enjoyed.

George Male, by now a coach at the club, took us under his wing while Ray prepared for the game. Male and Eddie Hapgood had been the star full-backs of the great 30s teams, and one of Dad's boyhood heroes. So it was a thrill for him, then 35, to be in the company of George (48) as he showed us round the marble halls, boardroom, players' dressing rooms and tunnel and the training pitch that was then behind the south terrace at the College or Clock End.

Dad saw me gazing up in awe at Male and told the great man that he'd looked at him in a similar way when he was a lad and George was wearing the No.2 shirt for Arsenal and England.

The only disappointment of that memorable day was that I'd been so starstruck I'd forgotten to ask for any autographs. It didn't help when Ray said if only he'd known he'd have got both teams to sign for me!

John Exley: My dad John used to take me to matches most Saturdays during the late-1950s – we always went to see Stan Matthews whenever Blackpool played in London. Saw them at Highbury and that was it for me. Also saw the Busby Babes' last match before the Munich air crash. We always stood on the Clock End. Took my son Robert when he was about eight. He is now a regular attendee and has articles published in *The Gooner*.

Bernard Kiernan: I was two-years-old when our family came over from Dublin in 1951. We initially lived in a very poor neighbourhood at The Angel Islington, which of course was solid Arsenal territory. My dear old dad, Barney, was a publican in King's Cross and Euston (also Arsenal territory). My brother Paddy is five years older than me and obviously Arsenal too. Those three very early influences inevitably make me cradle-to-grave Arsenal.

My first game was v Blackpool (29/11/1958). I was nine-years-old and Dad took me that day because Stanley Matthews was playing. It was an overwhelming and fascinating experience for a little boy who knew his place and was struck by how old the great man was (even though it turned out he was still good for a few more years, including a return to Stoke City). Even though at the time I had nothing to compare with subsequent games, I was also struck by how reverential the crowd seemed to be when Matthews came near us by the touchline. He paused over the ball, which I realised later was his style, before suddenly whipping it past one or more defenders.

It was all a blur to me on the day. When I looked it up now for these memories, I am reminded that we lost 4-1.

Paul Harris: I was blessed by having a football enthusiast for a father. Bill Harris was a Blackburn Rovers supporter but did not attempt to influence me. We lived in Edmonton, very close to the Tottenham border at the time of the famous Spurs Double team. My schoolmates all seemed to be Spurs fans and I felt them to be arrogant.

Dad took me on my bicycle to as many grounds as he could in the London area. We went to non-league as well as league grounds. I was unmoved by White Hart Lane, frightened of The Den, unimpressed by the Boleyn Ground.

I still remember my first trip to Highbury, for a FA Cup third round replay v Rotherham United (13/1/1960) that ended 1-1. Rotherham, whose home kit was similar to Arsenal's, had held us to a 2-2 draw in the first game at Millmoor and won the second replay, 2-0, at Sheffield Wednesday's Hillsborough.

I was blithely unaware of Rotherham's location or their lowly status, being totally captivated by the atmosphere on the North Bank. In those days young boys were carefully and cheerfully manhandled to the front and I remember then seeing the top of the terracing and a lot of legs. But there was an almost indescribable feeling of magic when the Arsenal team ran out of that old chicken run with their red shirts and white sleeves and – I may be wrong – but in the navy-and-white hooped socks which, together, made the kit unique. The noise was almost frightening. I also recall rosettes, rattles as well as scarves.

I recall the cycle home in the dark through the crowded streets and, later, my father asking me if Arsenal was now my team. He said to me that if I said 'yes', I could never go back, and that when you support a team it is forever, whatever happens. I agreed, so Gunners have

WITH THE COMPLIMENTS OF Ty·Phoo TEA LTD., BIRMINGHAM 5

ARSENAL F.C.
Back row, L to R : Court, Sammels, Furnell, Armstrong, Howe, Baldwin
Front row, L to R : Storey, Ure, McCullough, Neill, Simpson. Insets : (L) Baker (R) Eastham

The 1964-65 squad (back row, l to r): Court, Sammels, Furnell, Armstrong, Howe, Baldwin.
Front: Storey, Ure, McCullough, Neill, Simpson. Insets: Baker and Eastham.

been my team ever since that joyous winter day of discovery.

Keith English: My father, Samuel, was an Arsenal supporter all his life and he took me to my first game v Everton (20/2/1960). The two things that stood out that day were, I wasn't sure if Arsenal were in red or blue and John Barnwell, although I'm not sure why I remember him.

Jeremy Doltis: My dad, Sid, took me in about 1960. But, Jesus, I was only four-and-a-half and can't remember a thing from the game or even who we were playing against!

David Hillyard: I still vividly remember that my first Highbury game was v Blackburn Rovers (6/2/1960). On a cold day, I was sitting on my dad's shoulders in the North Bank wearing my red and white scarf that my nan had knitted for me. I remember my uncle Ken feeding me roasted peanuts because I had mittens on and couldn't open them. We won 5-2 (a Mel Charles hat-trick, plus a goal each from Joe Haverty and David Herd). I fell in love with Arsenal that day.

Mel Charles

Jeff Owens: It's difficult to pin down the exact reason why I support Arsenal. It's really down to a number of factors. I was born and raised in Islington and attended Hanover Junior School and Highbury County Grammar. My mother Dorothy Owens (nee Wright) and her father (my grandfather – Thomas Wright) supported the Gunners. Incidentally, my Dad's family came from south-west London and he was a Chelsea supporter, although he never pressured me to support them. My school friends supported Arsenal, they were my local team, so who else would I support?

My first visit to Highbury was as a nine-year old in April 1961 I went with two friends from my street, John Emery and Terry Knott. I recall that we got there very early – not long after the gates opened –having got the tube from Essex Road to Drayton Park. We stood right against the hooped metal railings behind the goal at the Clock End. Arsenal's first division opponents were Blackpool (8/4/1961) who were at that time regarded as a 'big' team

Clock End v Wolves, 1963.

11

because Stanley Matthews played for them. I don't recall that he did much in the course of the match – possibly because big Billy McCulloch kept a close watch on him.

The player who sticks in my memory was Blackpool's goalie, a young Gordon West. During the first-half my heroes in red and white mounted attack after attack towards the Clock End. We were expecting Arsenal to score at any minute but West threw himself around the goalmouth making save after spectacular save. I couldn't believe that we hadn't scored.

At half-time it was nil-nil and we spent the interval staring up at the (to nine-year-olds) amazingly tall grandstands and watching the Metropolitan Police band.

In the second-half, Arsenal defended the Clock End, so Jack Kelsey stood in the goal right in front of us. He wasn't nearly as busy as Gordon West had been. He seemed like a giant in his bright green jersey and was a bit scary the way he shouted at his team-mates. In the end, Arsenal scored down at the North Bank to win 1-0.

Tom Badger: My family's loyal support of Arsenal, spanning three generations, was mentioned in the home programme v Sheffield United (11/9/1973). The letters page included one from my dad Bill, who wrote the following about 'The Badgers at Highbury':

After reading on this year's programme cover that we have been at Highbury for 60 years now, it urged me to write to you about my father (Bill, aged 72).

He has been supporting the Gunners for these 60 years since the kick-off against Leicester Fosse in 1913. Unfortunately, owing to ill health, this year he can only make reserve and youth team games, but as he says, who can complain after seeing eight League championship wins, eight FA Cup Final appearances (missing only one), one Fairs Cup win and two League Cup Final appearances.

I myself have been supporting Arsenal for 27 years, my eldest son (Tom) for 11 years and my youngest son (Brian) for two years, so the Badgers have been at Highbury for 100 years!

Yours truly,

WJ Badger

17 Gillett Street, Dalston, London, N6 8JH.

P.S. If you could publish this letter in our splendid programme it would be a great thrill to my father.

We beat Sheffield United 1-0 with a goal from Ray Kennedy. By strange coincidence, Len Badger played at left-back for the Blades – no relation but I always told my mates at school that he was my uncle!

Sadly, three months after my dad's letter appeared in the programme, grandad died. His funeral cortege was detoured from the route between his home in Dalston to the crematorium in Enfield to enable it to stop outside the entrance to the marble halls. His floral tributes? Red and white flowers, of course.

The class of The Arsenal shone through our darkness, however, when they posted a tribute to him in the programme for the match v Everton (22/12/1973, left).

My father died in 2007, wearing his Arsenal shirt right to the very end. Arsenal songs were included in his funeral service, too.

I was eight when I went to my first game at Highbury, a 3-1 defeat by Manchester Utd (25/8/1962). I don't remember much about the game (Eddie Clamp scored for Gunners) but recall approaching the ground down Conewood Street, towards Avenell Road, and seeing the magnificent stadium looming in front of me. Then entering the stadium, into the Clock End, the sight of the pristine pitch, the clock, the stands . . . it was overwhelming. Who cares if we lost. I wanted to come back again.

Lester Allen: My late father John and elder brother David both took me to my first game, v Sheffield Utd (10/11/1962). My first memory as an eight-year-old was the green pitch. The stadium seemed so full even though only 25,503 attended our 1-0 victory courtesy of Geoff Strong. We stood in the Clock End, to the right of the clock, and as a small boy I was lifted up and rolled down to the front, so any spending money fell from my pockets!

Peter Lewis: As a six-year-old, I moved with my parents into a new area of North London. Another kid, Connie Barrett, was a few doors from us and we got chatting. He revealed he was an Arsenal fan and, in order to make a friend, I said I was as well. I went to my first game with him and his dad and it all followed from there. I can't remember anything from the game other than it was against Blackburn Rovers (23/3/1963), Arsenal won 3-1 and their goalie was someone called Fred Else, which made me laugh when he saved a shot and someone called out 'Flippin' Else!'

John Blair: I was born in 1954 and If you had asked me at the age of three who I supported, I would have said (I feel like throwing up) 'Spurs'! But my older cousin Mike was having none of that. Mike who was a staunch Gooner and had been going to Arsenal since the mid-50s, decided to steer me and my cousin Ronnie away from the dark side and show us the light.

My first game was v Bolton Wanderers (7/9/1963), when we sat in the lower East Stand, just behind the players' tunnel. To this day it remains one of the most amazing matches I have seen in nearly 60 years.

Arsenal were 1-3 down with minutes to go, when we pulled one back to make it 2-3. Bolton then missed a penalty in the last minute. Straight from the goal-kick, we went up the other end and scored the equaliser (3-3). In the last minute of injury-time Ian Ure scored the winner.

Jacqueline Cooper: Both sets of grandparents and my parents, Jack and Joyce, supported Arsenal. Dad took me to my first match – an evening game in 1963 – at the age of nine. We had a flask of tea and sandwiches and I loved every minute of it.

Robert Thaine: My father, Edward Thaine (Ted), first took me to Highbury in 1963, to a night match (I think it was v Charlton Athletic). I was five and remember getting the train to Highbury and Islington, then the long walk through Highbury Fields and coming out at the top of Avenell Road. The first thing I noticed was the glare from the stadium, the smell from the vendors and the buzz from the crowd. I'd never seen so many people.

The match itself is still a bit of a blur but I do remember the noise of the crowd when Joe Baker scored twice, as if the roof was coming off. I was kind of scared but, at the same time, I loved it and have done ever since.

Lee Pritchett: My dad John and his three brothers, Jim, Jeff and Ray, were all fanatical Arsenal fans and went to every game. From the age of five, I had been pestering them to take me. The first game Dad let me go to was the FA Cup fifth round tie v Liverpool (15/2/1964), I loved every minute of the day, although we lost 1-0. It was a drab game apart from Joe Baker knocking out Ron Yeats in the centre-circle and both being sent-off.

Richard Stubbs: My divorced mum was introduced to Arsenal's legendary (1935-53) goal scorer Reg Lewis when I was five. They married, so that might have been a big influence. Very aptly, he took me to my first Highbury game, v Liverpool (15/2/1964), the team against whom he scored both goals in our 2-0 FA Cup Final victory in 1950. Despite losing 1-0, I have been to virtually every home match since.

John G. Bugden: I'm a third generation Gooner. My grandfather, Harold, took my dad, Harry, to Highbury in the 30s, when the love affair started. He kept going after the war, taking my brother Michael in the 50s, then me and my twin Vincent in the 60s. It's been a fantastic journey.

My first game was our 3-2 victory v Sunderland (12/9/1964), with George Eastham scoring

SO PROUD OF DAD

WINGER George Armstrong made his Arsenal debut in 1962 at the age of 17 and went on to make 621 appearances – then a club record, exactly 500 of which came in the League – before he left Highbury in 1977. He spent a season each with Leicester City and Stockport County, and then took up coaching. After a year as Kuwait national team manager, Armstrong returned to Arsenal as reserve team coach in 1990, a post which he held for the remaining 10 years of his life. George's daughter, JILL ARMSTRONG, reflects on her father's Highbury years with immense pride . . .

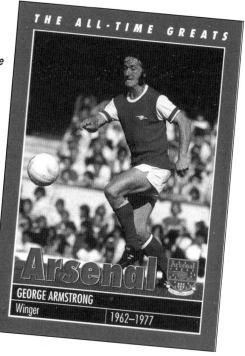

THE ALL-TIME GREATS

GEORGE ARMSTRONG
Winger   1962–1977

I was only young, a baby in fact, when Mum (Marjorie) would take us to watch Dad play. I was born in March 1967 and, sadly, only remember the last couple of years of his playing career.

We would always get a lift from Dad to the ground on match day. He would drop us off – Mum, my brother Tom and me – and we would have a meal and then wait in the main entrance foyer. It was an amazing experience for a young kid. Very grand with the Herbert Chapman bust and the amazing marble hall entrance, which was very special. I would watch out the windows at the fans pouring in. Incredible memories.

When I was still young, I remember the sound of the fans . . . cheering, chanting and, of course, my favourite song being 'Geordie Armstrong on the wing'. The sea of red and white scarves made me so proud to feel part of this great club.

Our family always felt so proud of Dad. A more Arsenal man you would never meet. The Arsenal was in his blood. The fans would always stop him for autographs and he never turned one away. He would sign one after another and as a young child, it would cause such annoyance to my brother and I. 'Oh no, Dad, not more!' But he would ignore our moans and continue to sign away 'till the last autograph was done. And this went on until his death in 2000.

Tom and I would also collect autographs after the game. Week after week we got them but I've no idea where they went.

I loved watching the games and as I got older I enjoyed it even more. When we lived in our first house in Winchmore Hill, Liam Brady and Wilf Rostron were in digs next door to us. Their landlady Mrs Cranstone was a very close friend of the Armstrong family. Liam and Wilf, along with Frank Stapleton, David O'Leary and Graham Rix, would often meet up after a home game in an Italian restaurant in Palmers Green.

Dad was always the last to leave the ground, chatting away until late. You would hear him coming – a roar of laughter belting down the corridor – and then, larger than life, he would burst through the tea room door while the tea room ladies would be stacking chairs and clearing cups. He would always bring a smile to your face. No-one was ever annoyed by him. The tea ladies would pour him a cuppa and listen to his stories.

My days at Highbury were special and I still find it difficult, emotionally, to recall the last game we went to, as guests of the chairman Mr Peter Hill-Wood soon after Dad had died. It was a great honour to be there but also so hard, because you kept thinking Dad would bounce in full of energy with his infectious laugh. So it was never the same again and that is why I never returned after the Arsenal v Chelsea match (13/1/2001).

The Arsenal and Highbury hold so many wonderful, special memories for me. Mostly they revolve around my wonderful Dad but also because of all the wonderful friends we made there.

twice and the other from Geoff Strong.

What I find incredibly sad is that there are a generation of Arsenal fans born in this century that would have never witnessed Highbury under the lights. I was lucky enough to have a season ticket in the West upper and those magical nights will never leave me.

Peter Coombs: My dad William was a chemist and worked on Saturdays. Living in Winchmore Hill, N21 in the early 60s, the majority of boys my age were glory-hunting Spurs fans, so friends and family would take me to see Tottenham perhaps half a dozen times.

One balmy late summer evening, probably in 1965, Dad took me to see Arsenal play under the lights. Can't remember the result but I was hooked. There was plenty of room in a beautiful ground (Arsenal only getting half the Spurs crowd then), the magical stands and majestic North Bank. After a few more evening games, by the following season I was a regular. Aged 11, I got the bus down to Wood Green and on the tube to Arsenal.

Mike Birch: My dad Charlie came from Forest Road, Walthamstow, so it was red or white for me. Fortunately, I chose correctly. First game was a 3-1 defeat v Chelsea (4/9/1965) and I've missed less than 10 home games since, and only then because of weddings and funerals.

Gary Lawrence: My dad Tommy was born at Culford Road, just off Balls Pond Road, and as a kid used to walk to Highbury to watch Herbert Chapman's great 1930s sides. There was no way me and my brother Tony were going to support any other team.

My first game was the dying embers of Billy Wright's reign. We lost 3-1 to Newcastle Utd (26/3/1966). All I can really remember is the all-red Arsenal shirts and the black and white stripes of Newcastle. Oh, a lot of moaning and groaning from the Arsenal fans frustrated under Wright.

I've had a season ticket since 1976. My son Neil, my brother, his son Billy and my sister's son Jonathan are also ST holders. My cousin Lonny also goes to a quite few games and is a Silver member.

David Roche: Dad got me to follow Arsenal and it was a purely geographical decision – we lived in Kentish Town at the time. We eventually went to a game, a 1-1 draw v Blackpool (17/9/1966), and attended regularly after that. Arsenal were on a bad run at the time and I didn't see them win until we beat Fulham, 1-0, some six games later.

John Powell: First match was the 1-0 defeat by Leeds Utd (5/11/1966). I can't say this was a 'Nick Hornby moment'. I was seven and a little bored. The result didn't help either. But something inside had stirred and I'm sure it was Highbury's magic spell.

We were with family friends, a father and son both named Trevor, from Mill Hill who subsequently became part of our Arsenal family for many matches and would always be there for the Boxing Day fixture armed with our 'tuck'; Heinz tomato soup and turkey sandwiches.

I was in the lower East Stand family enclosure and noted how low it was. It seemed the pitch was above my head. The on-field action was mainly a swirl of legs.

I remember going to the shop (I'm sure it was in the East Stand back then?) and thinking how basic it was, but also how enticing. I had a rattle, hand-painted red and white with 'ARSENAL' written in bold white capitals.

Half-time was a standout (it wasn't a

East Stand facade, 1967.

great match). Firstly, the men in white coats placing the scores against the corresponding letters from the programme. And also the marching band led by Major Williams. I'll always remember the crowd's "Wheyyyyeee" when he threw the large baton in the air. He once dropped it, much to the delight of the crowd.

We parked on the north side of Finsbury Park station and walked through the long tunnel. Turning into Avenell Road, I was more taken with the crowds, the hot dog vans and the programme sellers. It was only when I faced the East Stand properly did I notice its grandeur and formality, particularly the commissionaire standing by the front door.

Soon after this first experience, I was taken by my Dad, John, to a match when we sat in the upper West Stand for the first time and I truly had my Nick Hornby moment. I was hooked and it dawned on me that watching a match at Highbury, with the rolled tobacco smoke, the profanities, the chants and the smell of overcooked onions wafting in the air, was going to be a significant part of my life for the next 40 years.

I had spells in all parts of the ground. From the cheapest standing in the Clock End in the 70s, to corporate entertainment in the boxes built above it in the 90s. By 1969, my Dad had bought four season tickets for the East Stand lower tier (nearer the North Bank) for me and my two sisters, Sue and Sally.

My two stand out features of Highbury were its size and locality. It felt homely and comfortable. It also felt part of the community, like connective tissue to the local houses, cafes and pubs. Players and fans alike walking to the ground, as if it was home.

Keith Wilsher: I was born a mile from the ground and my grandad George lived at Highbury Barn. My uncle Arthur had a cobblers shop at 117 Blackstock Road and the sign is still there to this day. My auntie, Marie Lee, was the secretary to Bob Wall (assistant to Herbert Chapman and later ticket office manager), so I was born with Arsenal in my veins.

My father Peter took me to my first game a reserve match) and we sat in the West Stand. Two things stick in my mind about that game. Firstly, Ian Ure, an Arsenal player with white hair coming back from injury, who went on to win Quiz Ball; and the noise coming from one end of the stadium.

Mark Wilson: My father Spencer said he would take me to an evening game in 1966-67. I was seven-years-old. I came home from school, ate my tea, did my homework and waited for Dad. Being a London cabbie, he came home at different times and on this evening he arrived at 6.30. "Let's go, let's go," I kept saying but Dad insisted on eating his supper first.

I ran to the taxi but he said: "No, son, we are going on the tube." I thought we'd be late because I had looked up the game and knew it started at 7.30pm.

So we walked to Arnos Grove tube and arrived at the ground at 8.20. The big green gates were opened to enable men to go out to smoke. Or go home. We walked in and we saw Arsenal score one goal I went home ecstatic. A magical evening, it could have been the League Cup game v Gillingham (13/9/1966) in which Tommy Baldwin scored.

Imagine how depressed and agitated I was, though, when I went to school the next morning and found out we had drawn 1-1 . . . and that I'd missed a whole half of football!

It took three more visits before we saw the full 90 minutes.

Highbury was like a palace to me.

Ian Castle: My father Arthur worked on Saturdays, so taking me to football had never really been an option. But on the Bank Holiday Monday he was free and offered to take me to Highbury for the first time, for the first division match v Liverpool (28/8/67).

To be honest, I don't remember the details very clearly, other than my first view of the pitch and the final score. We sat in the East Stand lower; Dad just paid at the turnstile – no advance ticket required – and I pushed hard against a heavy revolving turnstile that clanked loudly as it reluctantly turned before depositing me inside the stadium. I felt I had entered another world.

Dad may have bought me a drink or something to eat, I don't remember, but I do recall my first incredible sighting of that lovingly tended luminous green sward. My only previous experience of football pitches were the muddy battlefields in my local park, dotted with the odd spot of dog mess. This was something completely different; it was an unforgettable moment.

I always found sitting in the lower tier at Highbury a rather strange experience. Because of the upper tier seating above, the 'ceiling' – if you can call it that – was low and I would come away at the end of a game feeling I'd watched the match peering through a letter box. If anyone hoofed the ball up in the air, and I can assure you they did – often – it would disappear from view for a few moments, leaving you to watch the players jostling for position as though they were part of a life-sized spot-the-ball competition.

As I said, I don't remember any details of that first game other than the fact that Arsenal won 2–0 (Jon Sammels and own-goal). My lack of memories bothered me and I wondered why that was. I decided to investigate and I think I found the answer; one newspaper report unenthusiastically described it as 'a generally poor game'. But I had no comprehension of good football or poor football back then, just football – and Arsenal had won. I was hooked.

Extracted from Ian's book, *Arsenal – The Agony & The Ecstasy*, published in 2012.

Richard Storey: v Man City (23/9/1967), we won 1-0 and John Radford scored. It was my birthday the week before but my dad couldn't get tickets for the Spuds game, which we won 4-0.

Dad moaned at me for watching the crowd in the North Bank instead of the football. We were in the upper West Stand and, at half-time, I remember how noisy and smoky it was, and that there were only a handful of women there.

Paul Robertson: First home game of the season (13/8/68), we beat Leicester City 3-0. Bobby Gould scored two and David Court the other. It was a night game and I remember the floodlights along the East and West Stands lighting up the pitch. I was eight-years-old.

James Miller: Father Freddie took me to my first match when I was three-years-old, back in 1966, and I don't remember a thing about it. However, the first match I really recollect was our first home game of the season v Leicester City (13/8/1968). We won 3-0 with goals by David Court and Bobby Gould (two).

Steve Birch: My dad Johnny went to Highbury as a lad in the 1930s and took me when I was eight, to see the 1-1 draw v Liverpool (17/8/1968). We used to get the tube from Holborn and he made me a little chair to stand on in the North Bank.

Bob Varney: My dad, Don (aka 'The Don'), lived in Bletchley all of his life but when all the other kids were supporting Luton Town, he supported Arsenal. The Arsenal. The mighty Arsenal of Herbert Chapman and the dominant team of the 30s. How many times have I heard him recite that team: Moss, Male, Hapgood . . .

In 1937, for his 10th birthday, The Don and his dad went down to London on a steam train, walked from Euston to Highbury, queued up to get in and watched HIS mighty Arsenal lose his first match! But his love of Arsenal Football Club stayed with him until the end and it was only the day before he died that he was asking me for transfer gossip.

It was August 1968 and I can only imagine how much The Don must have been hurting inside. A Leeds United poster had gone up on my bedroom wall. I was a football-mad eight-year-old and a budding goalkeeper. The Don kept calm and told me I could support any team I wanted; it didn't have to be Arsenal.

In December he took me to Highbury for the first time to see us play Everton (7/12/1968) and introduced me to his friend Eric. Eric said I should put my Leeds United poster up in the "smallest room in the house". I took a while to work out exactly which room was the smallest in the house.

The Don took me into the club shop and introduced me to the shop manager, Jack Kelsey, the ex-Arsenal and Wales goalkeeper. Jack was cool. He had a stud mark in his forehead. The tide was turning.

We walked down past the marble halls, the aroma of fried onions in the air and through a small narrow turnstile into the darkness. Pushing through a mass of people smoking, drinking, laughing and swearing, we eventually climbed a small flight of stairs towards the bright shining light. Suddenly we were out into the early season sunshine, the Highbury pitch before us, huge and so, so green.

Bob Varney (aka The Don) and grandchildren.

The teams ran out, Arsenal in red, Everton, a "proper football club", in blue. The Don clapped the away team onto the pitch, as he would do for many decades to come. "Without them we wouldn't have a game," he once said. 'We' won 3-1. It was the best day of my life. Thanks to The Don there would be many more 'best days of my life'.

The Leeds United poster was down within the hour. The Don knew stuff . . .

John White: v Coventry City (12/10/1968). Aged eight, I went with older boys from my flats in Hackney, who plonked me on a barrier in the North Bank. David Court and John Radford scored in a 2-1 win. I remember the Met Police band and its leader throwing his baton in the air. Pure class. I fell in love with the place.

Peter Gregory: My grandfather Herbert Button started going to watch The Arsenal in the 1930s and became a season ticket holder after the war. He then took my mum Jean. When I was about five, grandfather and mum took me and my older brother Robert to see them beat Manchester Utd 3-0 (26/12/1968). Although Robert supported Man U, grandfather made sure I was Arsenal.

Dave Randall: I was taken to Highbury for the first time by Ian Squires, a friend of my mum, to see the 1-1 draw v Nottingham Forest (1/2/1969). He told me that from that day forward I would be an Arsenal fan – and he was right!

I remember walking into the West Stand, rather like Nick Hornby, and being captivated by the green pitch. Most of the day was a blur to me – I was only eight-years-old – but it was to lay the foundations of my life from that day to this. Not sure where Ian is now, or indeed if he is still alive, and I would love to find out the answer to either question.

Marvin Berglas: My dad, David, took the 10-year-old me and my brother Peter to my first game at Highbury, a 1-1 draw v Leeds Utd (19/8/1969). It was an evening game and I remember vividly the purposeful approach through the throng of the crowd to the stadium, the unfamiliar sounds of grown men chanting and swearing, the smells in the air of the smokers, the police horses, hot dogs and roasted chestnuts, the cries of the colourful rosette and souvenir stalls and programme sellers. That first precious sight of the resplendent manicured Highbury oh-so-green pitch under the floodlights was something else.

The distinctive Arsenal shirts with the brightest, most vivid red I can remember, with the famous little canon emblem and the whitest sleeves with red cuffs adorned by the heroes I knew so well from their pictures all over my bedroom wall. Radford, Armstrong, Wilson, a very young Pat Rice, the blond hair of Ian Ure but, alas, my favourite Frank McLintock was missing that game. Amazingly, I spotted him outside on the steps leading to the marbled halls before the game and although I was starstruck, I awkwardly mustered the courage to enquire if he was playing, and he actually told me himself that he was injured.

Nick Stephens: My father, Sydney Wicks-Stephens, took me to my first game. We lost 1-0 to Coventry City (4/10/1969). Dad was no football fan and spent as much time in the bar as he could but I was hooked.

Wayne Flatman: I went three times in the 1969-70 season with Nick McAllen ,who was a 22-year-old Arsenal fan, while I was a football-mad 10-year-old. My first visit was Arsenal v Ipswich (25/10/1969), attendance 22,458 ("dull and dismal" according to *Gunflash*).

I remember my dad taking us to Diss train station and I had a £1 note in my pocket for the day. I entered the ground to the North Bank from the Avenell Road turnstiles. The climb up the steps to reach the top of the terracing seemed to go on forever. And then the view: the North Bank roof, the East and West and, lastly, the Clock End.

For the home games v Ipswich Town and Man City I sat at the back on a crash barrier, so I got a great view, and the atmosphere was an intoxicating mix of stale beer, smoke and noise of the chanting. My spending for the day excluding train and tube tickets 6d for a programme, a visit to the small shop at the side of the North Bank for a badge rosette, comb in a case or other similar item. I spent three shillings on food, mainly chips or a hot dog off mobile sellers.

I could come back home with a 10 shilling note and thought I was a rich man. Dad showed great trust in allowing Nick to take me and the next season we teamed up with John, Tony and Jenny Boyle – and to this day they are my Arsenal family.

Daniel Goldring: My grandpa Charles Greene first saw Arsenal in the 1940s. Then my uncles, Jon and Steven Greene, went in the 50s and at the start of the 90s my cousins Phil and Craig started going too. Grandpa used to sit in the West upper executive area and after he handed the doorman a bottle of whisky at the start of the season, my brother Nick was allowed to sit on his lap.

After Grandpa passed away in the early 80s, Nick and I got two season tickets in the West upper centre section (Block W, Row D). Now five family members sit in the East upper centre. We have carried the family tradition on and I take my kids, Charlotte, Libby, Alfie, Isabelle and Olivia, when possible.

Steve Kell: After my dad took me to Spurs for my first live match, the reason I became an Arsenal fan was because of Geordie Armstrong, the smallest player on the pitch, who scored the winner against Stoke City in about 1968-69.

Pete Mountford: Became an Arsenal fan because my dad Bill had supported them since the 1930s (although I had actually had a childhood dalliance with both Spurs and Man City prior to this). After watching the 1969 League Cup Final, my first Highbury visit was v Chelsea (17/1/1970). Dad took me and two friends of mine, Gary Moy and Paul Milsom, in the lower East Stand. It was a crushing 3-0 defeat, made worse by Paul being a Chelsea fan and celebrating every goal.

Mark White: Although I grew up in Marylebone, my mum's mother lived on the White City Estate in Shepherds Bush, near QPR's ground, which you could just about see from the top floor of one of the blocks. I'd just started learning about football, kicking a ball up against the wall of the garages with my aunt's boyfriend (and later my uncle) Brian.

Mum's brother, Len, used to go to QPR and, if I was visiting, he'd tell me that he'd take me to Loftus Road when I was older. I told my dad, Fred, what my uncle had said and he told me that life didn't work that way and I had to follow his team (Arsenal). He said he'd take me to see the Gunners when I was old enough. From then on I started following The Arsenal.

In 1969, Dad passed the Knowledge to become a London taxi driver and in return for taking our neighbours to Heathrow Airport, they gave him the use of their season tickets whilst they were away.

My first game at Highbury was a nil-nil draw v Stoke City (7/2/1970). 26,361 people, plus the Old Man and me, watched the world's best goalkeeper Gordon Banks keep a clean sheet for the visitors, while Bob Wilson did likewise.

I remember the sheer volume of people, the atmosphere and the match day smell – the mixture of onions and tobacco – and that Dad bought me a red and white silk rosette with a picture of my favourite player George Armstrong in the middle. The picture had been cut out of a football magazine and didn't last very long but it was a treasured memento of the day for several years. I had only just turned nine, so my memories are limited.

I wore it again a few weeks later, when Arsenal drew 2-2 with Wolves (28/3/1970). Over 32,000 people were there that Saturday, probably due to the better weather but also maybe because Gunners were doing well in the Fairs Cup – they went on to win it the following month against Anderlecht.

Ewan Drake: We lived in a little village called Hardington Mandeville, just outside Yeovil. Growing up in rural Somerset in the 1970s, I was given a hand-me-down shirt to play football in at school. It was red, with white collar and sleeves and red cuffs.

So I went to our local sports shop in Yeovil – think it was Marney's – and worked out which team it was. The shop had one of those simplistic maps of England with illustrative football kits marked on it along with the names of each team they represented. I've been a Gooner ever since.

Derek Barclay: As a nine-year-old, I was just getting into football when my sister Valerie developed a crush on Arsenal's new signing Peter Marinello – the much-vaunted, 'new Georgie Best'. Val had a friend called Penny who was a regular at Arsenal, so she decided to go along with Penny to see her heart-throb in the flesh. And of course, as her kid brother, I insisted on tagging along.

The opponents were Stoke City (7/2/1970) and Jon Sammels immediately became my first favourite player (a view not shared by many at Highbury, who around this time adopted him as their whipping boy). Rather disappointingly, the result was 0-0 and Peter Storey missed a penalty right in front of us at the North Bank end. I can't recall if Gordon Banks saved it – I think Storey shot wide without intervention from the world's greatest keeper. I'll forgive Peter, as he was to convert a far more important penalty against Banks just over a year later.

John Williamson: My dad Bill was born at the Angel in the 1920s. I was born 1960 in South London; I was an Arsenal fan from day one. Dad was a ST holder pre and post war.

My first home match was v Manchester Utd (22/8/1970) and I've since attended over 1,000 matches at Highbury.

Paul O: In 1970-71 I had to pick a team at school that no-one else supported. So I watched a TV highlights show and saw a team win 9-0, and I was delighted that no other kid already had them. Only later did I realise that the final score was in fact 3-0 – I'd been misled by seeing multiple replays of the same goals! – but I was hooked on Charlie George and Arsenal was now my team. I was six, by the way.

Tony Daisley: I became an Arsenal fan for a couple of reasons. Firstly, my dad John had supported the club since the 1930s. Secondly, after we lost 3-1 to Swindon Town in the League Cup Final of 1969, I must have felt sorry for them but it shows I was no glory-hunter! Arsenal hadn't won anything for 16 years and, because they were against a third division team, were expected to win a long-awaited trophy. But a combination of mud and flu conspired against us.

My first Highbury match was the 2-0 win against West Ham Utd (9/1/1971) in the Double year of 1970-71. However, my outstanding memory is from my second match, v Chelsea (3/4/1971), which I attended with my best friend at the time, Ian Mellor, and his father Richard. The crowd was 62,087 and being a 13-year-old little 'un and the North Bank being particularly crowded, I was passed down to the front over people's heads so I was able to watch the game alongside the pitch with all the other young children. Won't ever forget that experience. Won 2-0, with Ray Kennedy grabbing both.

Nobby Ralfe: It was John Radford that made me start following Arsenal. My uncle Jack took me to my first game, v Newcastle Utd (17/4/1971). We sat in the East Stand (posh seats) for my one and only time (apart from Martin Keown's testimonial). To mark this special occasion, Jack took me – dressed in red and white scarf and bobble hat – to a photo booth on Waterloo station. I would love to find that pic.

Nigel Evans: My first game was in the Football Combination, v Reading in October 1970. I sat in the East upper and, as I recall, we won 6-0 or 6-1 and I'm sure Peter Marinello scored a hat-trick. My first 'proper' game was v Newcastle Utd (9/10/1971). This time I was in the East lower to see us win 4-2 with goals from George Graham, Ray Kennedy, George Armstrong and Eddie Kelly.

Emilio Zorlakki: My father Alex was an Arsenal supporter from his younger days growing up in Cyprus. In Cyprus he told me you were either an Arsenal or United fan. He immigrated to the UK in 1961 – not a great year for Arsenal supporters.

He started taking me in the late 60s, when I was five or six, but I was not that interested at the time. I remember going to a few North London derbies (the first, I believe, was in August 1968 at WHL) and also, we brought my Greek Cypriot cousin George, a couple of years older than me and supported Spurs. I think Dad was trying to change his allegiance but it didn't work.

I caught the football bug thanks to the 1970 Mexico World Cup in Mexico and collecting Esso coins at petrol stations. We also had my Spanish uncle, auntie and two cousins (from my mother's side) coming to live with us temporarily and they were really into football. They got me interested in doing the pools (Australian matches).

I took a keen interest in Arsenal at the start of the 1970-71 season. Unfortunately, I had missed the Fairs Cup triumph but got excited when I saw the results of our 2-0 and 6-2 victories over Spurs and WBA respectively. I was devastated at our 2-1 defeat at Chelsea, after mistakenly thinking that we had drawn 1-1. I saw the game in black and white the next day on *The Big Match*. John Hollins' Golden Goal was shown ad nauseam in the titles for weeks on end.

Everton were our visitors (17/10/1970). A sunny day, my father was shaving and I asked him: "Where are you going?" "To football," he replied. "Can I come?" "No, you'll only want to go home at half-time!" "No I won't! I really want to go to Arsenal." My father was eventually persuaded and though this was not my first match by some distance, this was the first time that I really wanted to go with enthusiasm.

We queued in Gillespie Road to enter the West Stand Lower Tier seats and father bought me a hamburger with onions and sauce, plus a copy of the *Evening Standard*, which had a glossy cover. I started to read it from cover to cover while we waited for the turnstiles to open. I saw a cartoon of a man in a Spurs rosette trying to sabotage an Arsenal car with a caption that read: 'You won't stop Big John Radford that way, mate!'.

As we took our seats I started to absorb all the surroundings, the architecture of the East and West Stands, the big clock and the roof on the North Bank. I felt a sense of reassurance when I saw quite a number of kids of similar age to me, wearing rosettes and scarves.

When the sides took to the field, I was struck by the colours of both teams. Our distinct red shirts with white sleeves; Everton's dark blue shirts and Alan Ball's white boots. Ray Kennedy scored two first-half goals and father picked me up to stand on my seat, which had never happened before. I liked this. What a buzz! We went on to win 4-0 against the reigning champions and I loved watching the recorded highlights of the match on Match of The Day that evening. I was totally hooked and have been going ever since.

Yasir Matloub: I went to London with my parents at the beginning of July 1966. World Cup fever had already arrived and there were posters and flags of St George all over the place. We were at the Cumberland Hotel, Marble Arch, which was one of top hotels in that period. One day I was using the lift when I was joined by someone I thought I recognised.

That person turned out to be the one and only Muhammad Ali. He introduced himself and asked me if I was Egyptian, so I told him that I came from Iraq. To my astonishment, he invited me and my parents to his suite. I was 12-years-old and felt incredibly excited that I had been talking with one of the world's most famous people and a boxing legend.

Ali told us that he was preparing to fight an English boxer called Brian London, having six weeks earlier fought the very popular Englishman Henry Cooper, at a London football club (21/5/66).

He told me he had enjoyed the location in 1966 more than their first fight at Wembley in 1963.

That London football club was the Arsenal.

He showed me two football shirts – one for the England team and the other was The Arsenal. I was so immediately bewitched by the Arsenal shirt that I asked my father Jamil to get me one. He, in turn, asked my cousin Mazin, who was studying at Kings College, London, to take me and buy me the shirt.

A few days later we arrived at Arsenal, the only London Underground station named after a football club. We went to a small shop on Gillespie Road, where we were greeted by a lovely gentleman. He talked to us for nearly an hour about the Arsenal and from that moment I was committed and besotted. My cousin told me the man's name was Jack Kelsey, who had a distinguished career as Gunners' goalkeeper.

I had to go back to Iraq with my family but every summer from 1969 I used to come to London in mid-August to watch the Arsenal before going back home for school.

My first recollection of attending a match at Highbury was also with my cousin. It was a joyful occasion as the Arsenal triumphed 4-0 over Manchester Utd (22/8/1970) thanks to a John Radford hat-trick and another goal from George Graham. The Man U side included their great trio of Bobby Charlton, George Best and Denis Law.

Because of Arsenal, I came here to do my postgraduate studies in June 1980 and continued attending matches as much as I could, even though I was living in Cardiff at the time.

John Morley: My dad Ted supported Arsenal throughout his life until he died in 2008. He was born and bred around Clissold Park and used to walk to Highbury to watch The Arsenal as a teenager. Needless to say, I inherited his allegiance, even though I was born and bred in south London when he moved there after marrying Mum. There was only one team I was ever going to support.

My first vivid recollection of a game at Highbury was v Man Utd (22/8/1970), although I don't think this was my first-ever Highbury match. We stood in the Clock End (where we always stood thereafter) and I remember how impressed I was of the imposing, magnificent art deco-style East and West stands and also, with the sheer size of the ground and amount of people.

The other outstanding memory of that match was George Best being clean through on goal at the Clock End, only for the brilliant Bob Wilson to dive full length at Best's feet to deny him a certain goal with one of his trademark saves. We went on to win 4-0. Great memories and I was hooked.

I now have two sons who have also spent their whole lives to date following the Arsenal, having come up through the Junior Gunners ranks.

Cecil Smith: My father and I were in the East upper seats, nearer the North Bank, for my first game, v Wolverhampton Wanderers (12/12/1970). John Radford and George Graham got our goals in a 2-1 victory. I was glued to the game for the whole time. For a nine-year-old it was quite an experience. Then we went to every home game and watched from the same seats. After a while I asked Dad: "What did they call the ref?"

At 14, I started going by myself in the North Bank and later advanced to the Clock End to welcome the visitors. But we would go in the North Bank for London derbies.

Dave Heath: Frank McLintock visited my school, St John of Jerusalem, in Hackney when I was six. He signed autographs and left. The year was 1971, he had just captained Arsenal to the Double. From then on I was an Arsenal fan. I believe my first game was v Southampton (or possibly Sunderland), a 0-0 draw, when I was aged 11 in 1976.

John Hickford: Arsenal v Benfica in a pre-season friendly (4/8/1971). Gunners had lost 2-0 to the Portuguese champions in Lisbon four days previously. They exacted sweet revenge by thrashing Benfica 6-2 in front of nearly 45,000 at Highbury. I went on the pitch at the end and shook hands with their legendary striker Eusebio, who at that time was probably second only to Pele in the ranks of world greats. I was 12, dodged all the police and stewards and made a beeline for him. We didn't speak, just shook hands. I was made up. For the record, the Arsenal's scorers were: John Roberts, John Radford, George Armstrong, George Graham (2) and Peter Storey (pen).

Del Sharkey: I was six when my dad Johnnie and uncle David took me and my cousin Danny. They dumped us at the front of the North Bank with two young women and went and stood further back. George Graham, Ray Kennedy, George Armstrong and Eddie Kelly scored in a 4-2 win v Newcastle Utd (9/10/1971) and I was hooked. Saw precious little of the game, as I was too short to see over the advertising boards, but I fell in love with the whole atmosphere and aura of the place.

Tony Bateman: Cousin Alan Coyne got me hooked on Arsenal in 1972, after making me watch the FA Cup Final win against Liverpool the previous year.

Nick Jackson: Walking up the stairs to the East lower and seeing a green carpet, I was in awe as a nine-year-old. Charlie George and Alan Ball scored in a never to be forgotten 2-0 victory over Derby County (12/2/1972).

Michael Deasy: Although I was from south London, my family had moved from Cork in Ireland and lived on Highbury Hill, so my older brother John was a massive Arsenal fan and regularly went to games since the mid-1960s.

I started going to reserve games at Highbury with my brother Denis in 1971 and remember Charlie George playing. There would be loads of young kids at those games and I remember everyone running on the pitch and mobbing Charlie after we'd scored – even though he hadn't scored. Charlie told us, in no uncertain terms, to get off the pitch so the game could continue!

Mum was happy for me to go to see the reserves – crowds were small – but I was always nagging to go to a first team game. I finally got my way on the day we beat West Ham Utd 2-1 (22/4/1972). I went with my parents, Bridie and Denis, and sister Brenda. I don't know why the two females in the family were there because they had no interest in football.

We stood on the Clock End and it was my first taste of the match day excitement. Alan Ball scored twice that day and I think I'm right in saying it was the first time he'd scored for Arsenal at Highbury. That was just before my ninth birthday.

A couple of weeks later I watched us lose the FA Cup Final, 1-0, to Leeds Utd in a neighbour's house – they had a colour TV and it was the first game I'd seen not broadcast in black and white.

Nancy Wright: My dad Jimmy Rutherford was born and bred at The Angel and decided to support them up the road, just to be awkward I think. Thankfully, my older brother, also Jimmy, and cousin Bobby Irving took me over Arsenal in the 1971-72 season. I've never looked back.

Must add that Dad used to get me tickets for matches sometimes, including any at WHL – in with the Spurs fans – and the 1980 FA Cup Final. I was heartbroken that I didn't get a ticket via the voucher scheme but he got me one at the last minute – among West Ham fans. I look back at it now as a form of punishment!

Richard Holmes: v Manchester City (28/10/1972). Centre-half Jeff Blockley tipped one over the bar, keeper-style, but it wasn't seen by ref Gordon Hill and the game ended 0-0.

Mike Slaughter: Dad Norman – known to his friends as 'Todd' – came from near Clissold Park, so even though I was born and always lived in south-east London/Kent, Dad and I still went to Arsenal every week. I am told that I attended games in the 1970-71 season but do not recall them.

My first recollections are playing Bradford City in the FA Cup fourth round (3/2/1973). And the stand out memory was seeing my first black player, Ces Podd, who played right-back for Bradford that day. We sat in the East lower, just above the Metropolitan Police band.

David Marks: A 1-0 win v Crystal Palace (26/3/1973), with Alan Ball getting the winner.

John Skinner: Uncle Pete took me to see Arsenal play Leicester City (8/9/1973). We lost 2-0 but as a seven-year-old, coming through the turnstile, walking up the steps, seeing the pitch for the first time and all the people around me singing, it gave me an amazing feeling inside.

Pat Rainsford: My parents Patsy and Sheila emigrated from Ireland in 1956 and moved into Holloway Road. They first went to The Arsenal in 1956. My first visit was in '73 and I have been a season ticket holder for 35 years. Dad passed away in 2018 but Mum is still a fervent Gooner. She knitted me a scarf for the 1971 FA Cup Final.

Barry Smith: I lived in Kentish Town as a kid and you were either Arsenal or Spurs. Luckily, my parents, Derek and Maureen (nee Sullivan), were Arsenal and even up to the present time all members of the family follow The Arsenal.

First game was a 1-0 win v Birmingham City (6/10/1973), although the only memory of it is the view from the West side (North Bank end).

Neil Payne: As a very young lad I was very much in the open-minded bracket in terms of who I supported. I had spells supporting, among others, Leyton Orient (my grandad was a regular), Manchester United (whisper it) and of course Arsenal, which would have been solely down to my Dad, Brian.

Dad was a regular attendee of home matches. He had seen and lived through some dark times at the club. He is still proud to recall he never missed a home game in the glorious double season of 1970-71. I can often recall in our old Stepney home, as a kid, looking at programmes from that momentous season. I got to know very early that Charlie George's greatest-ever goal was the one-two he played off a Newcastle United defender before hammering home the only goal in a vital win en route to the Double.

Dad also likes to tell the tale of the Monday night the league was won at White Hart Lane (3/5/1971). Money was tight, so Mum (Vera) was out working while Dad was left looking after me and my brother Graham as the game evolved. Back in the day, with no TV or indeed 'live' radio commentary, he tried to get his two sons off to sleep while listening out for score updates on. Finally, when the news came through that Ray Kennedy had scored the late winner, he nearly screamed the house down, having just finally got his two boys to sleep!

My first visit to Highbury was for the 1-0 loss to Ipswich Town (20/8/1974). I recall very little of the game aside from us sitting in the East Stand upper as a family of four. Dad, Mum, brother and I had been to Hampton Court earlier, and a trip to Highbury was the order of the day on what, I think, was a Bank Holiday. It's staggering when I look back at the league table from that season; we finished just four points clear of the relegation zone. They must have been desperate times considering it was only three years since the Double.

Stephen Simson: It was my grandad Bert Horne, uncle Brian Horne and my dad Barry that made me a Gooner. My first game was v Derby County (16/11/1974) and we won 3-1 with a couple from Alan Ball and one from Brian Kidd. I remember the amazing atmosphere in the stadium. When your team scored, it was a magical moment your never forget and you can't wait for more. You automatically love the stadium, the players, the crowd and they become your team for life.

Andrew Whitnall: My father Keith took me to my first game, v Derby County (16/11/1974) from our home in Henfield, Sussex. I was nearly five and don't remember much other than being completely captivated by the whole experience. We used to park our car next to the flats in Aubert Park, overlooking the ground, and that first glimpse of the stadium was always exciting.

Malcolm Clayton: Started supporting Arsenal after watching FA Cup ties on TV in 1971 and seeing a young kid called Charlie George, my first footie hero. Made my Highbury debut when we beat Coventry City 3-0 (George Armstrong 2, John Matthews) in an FA Cup fourth round replay (29/1/1975) that had been postponed 24 hours.

I lived in Coventry and my mum finally allowed me to go on my own when I was 16. I actually jumped on one of the Coventry supporters' coaches – lots of them knew me, so I was OK, and they had seen me the day before at the coach station before we got the news that the game had been delayed until the following night. Being on the North Bank was a special moment.

Kelvin Meadows: I got to Burnt Oak tube one Saturday in September 1975. A few lads from school were gathering outside. Gary Stanton told me to drop what I was doing and go with them over The Arsenal. Eventually there were about 30 of us aged from 13 to 18, all running down the stairs onto the platform.

We went in the North Bank from the Gillespie Road entrance. I walked up the stairs and there before me was a huge expanse of concrete and the greenest grass I'd ever seen. We made our way to the very back of the terrace, directly behind the goal and police viewing step. This was in the days of the sliding doors at the back, not the huge refreshment stand (we had to make do with the green hut).

The ground filled up and the singing started a good 30 minutes before kick-off. Opposition that day (20/9/1975) was Everton. We got a late equaliser through Frank Stapleton to draw 2-2. I fell in love with it there and then. We went back on the Tuesday, when we faced Everton again in a League Cup replay.

John Reeve: My dad Reg made me a fan. He wasn't dogmatic. I could support Arsenal or live somewhere else – it was my choice. I took the same view with my own children and thankfully we all made the right choice. Family season ticket holders now for more than 60 years.

Richard Averillo: My dad Bill took me to the big match, v Liverpool (24/2/1976), having previously eased me in gently to the large crowds by taking me to a few reserve matches. The Liverpool game was three days after my ninth birthday and I can remember being overwhelmed with anticipation and excitement.

It was nil-nil until Liam Brady put in a perfect cross and John Radford headed home in the 90th minute for a 1-0 victory. In comparison to some attendances in the 70s, the crowd wasn't that big really, just over 36,000. To me it felt like the whole of north London was there at the game – I'd never been a part of such a large gathering of people.

We sat in the upper section of the East Stand and the view was fantastic. With about five minutes to go, Dad asked me if I wanted to leave to avoid the crowds but I opted to stay and it's lucky we did. Although Radford scored the first goal I had ever seen in a first team game at Highbury, the 20-year-old wizard on the wing called Liam Brady became my instant hero.

It's amazing looking back at the line-up: Alan Ball – World Cup winner; legends Pat Rice and George Armstrong; John Radford, fourth of all-time Arsenal goal scorers. A few of the players that day were coming to the end of their Arsenal careers: Armstrong, Radford, Terry Mancini and Brian Kidd.

Arsenal were in the depths of the first division at the time and talk of relegation was getting louder and louder but they managed to avoid going down and finished the season in 17th place.

Andy Selby: My grandfather David Selby, a staunch West Ham Utd supporter and season ticket holder at Upton Park, took me into the East Stand at Highbury to see us thrash his team, 6-1 (20/3/1976). He didn't try to convert me into supporting the Hammers because I was already a Gooner. My father hates football and we always said that if my grandfather had taken me to West Ham, I'd have supported them. But he never wanted to take us (my brother and I) and only did so because there was nobody else in the family who would do so.

I don't remember much about the game except the banter and back and forth chanting of "Uuuu-ni-ted", to which Arsenal fans responded with a short, sharp "Shit!" It was the first time I'd heard adults swear – and not just during the chanting but all around me and on the tube going to the game.

Obviously, I was taken in by it all and just like in *Fever Pitch* (film version), I wanted to go every week. Sadly, this only happened from 1978, when I was allowed to go unaccompanied by an adult.

Paul Manel: v Manchester City (4/9/1976). I was nine-years-old and not too interested in football. I was more into *Thunderbirds.* My uncle Michael was a season ticket holder and he had a couple of spare tickets as his friends were on holiday. As I came out of the Arsenal tube station tunnel with him and my dad, what astonished me was the crowd. I had never seen so many people in one place.

My senses were then struck by the sights and sounds of a first division football match: police horses, programme sellers shouting "programme, handbook", rosette sellers, scarf sellers and the smell of onions.

I recall seeing the lush green grass of Highbury for the first time (it was the second league game of the season). We were in the West Stand upper and there was a strange smell. At the time I didn't know what it was but I now associate cigar smoke with the West Stand upper tier.

We were high up, with the North Bank to our left. I was fascinated by the surges, the chants, the arms and the swearing. These people were actually getting away with swearing loudly in public. I wanted to be among them, swaying on the North Bank.

In the West Stand nobody seemed to be happy. Men kept on standing up and gesticulating angrily at players, the manager, the referee, anybody. Malcolm Macdonald had just signed for us and I remember one bloke constantly shouting: "Go back to Newcastle, Supermac, we're rubbish."

We drew 0-0 with Man City. Not a game that will be go down in the Highbury annals but, for me, it was a life-changing experience. I had been transported into a different world, rich with colour, noise and excitement. I wanted more.

Dave Button: It's very much a family affair. My great-grandparents, Frederick and Isabel Button, are from Islington and my dad John is from Hackney. He went to his first Highbury game in 1953 and took me in 1976, when I was aged seven.

A little story about my grandparents from my mum's side – her mum and dad, Dolly and Harry Ebbs – who also supported Arsenal. They moved from Hackney out to Romford in the early 80s. Anyway, one day Grandad went looking for a couple of bin-bags full of Arsenal programmes dating back to the 1920s . . . only to discover that Nan had thrown them in the dustcart even before they had left Hackney!

My sons, Joshua, Aaron and Liam, daughter Gemma and nephews Johnathon and Fabian Atlas, have maintained the family tradition as Arsenal supporters.

Robert Grainger: Arsenal were Double winners in 1971. My best mate at school, Richard Taggart, was a Gunners fan. He said: "You should support Arsenal, too." So that's how it started.

George Lampshire: My dad (Billy) and uncles (Terry, Harry and Lenny) were all mad Gooners. The family hailed from Islington and moved to Essex after the war. I was born in March 1971 and Dad named me after George Graham. That tradition has carried on my boy was named Charlie George in 2007.

My first Arsenal experience was in the photo (right) taken the day before the 1971 FA Cup Final v Liverpool. I'm told by family members that my little scarf was a thread the length of the room by the end of the game. Dad worked for the BBC at the time as a props supervisor and managed to get on the stage and sing *Good Old Arsenal* next to goalkeeper Geoff Barnett. Then he took Charlie George off to the BBC bar for some sneaky pictures with the Golden Boot that was displayed in the Highbury museum.

Dad took me to my first game as a five-year-old at Xmas 1976 . . . Spurs away. And then to my first game at Highbury in the New Year, v Leeds Utd (3/1/1977). The first time we drove past the snail picture on the estate at the bottom end of the Seven Sisters Road is a memory that I still have to revisit with each car journey I make to Arsenal. I remember Dad parking in Monsell Road and bumping the cars either side to get in, the first walk up Avenell Road and smell of fried onions from burger stalls, and Dad getting me my very first Highbury programme, which I still have today.

Then we went up the steps from the Avenell Road turnstiles to a world that just blew me away. I watched the crowd for most of the game while being in awe of what was going on around me. We drew 1-1 (Malcolm Macdonald), so, after the 2-2 draw at Spurs, I had not seen us win.

Who cared? I'd fallen in love with all things Arsenal.

David Pretlove: My love of Arsenal comes from Dad, Alec, who was an Angel Islington lad and his dad Bill before. My first game was a 4-1 defeat to Ipswich Town (5/3/1977) while sat in the West upper. I was hooked, though, and couldn't wait for the next game. Seated next to me was a big German man who loved Willie Young and he would taunt the away fans with his walking stick when we scored! Loved the walk to the ground and hearing the crowd singing as you approached. Great days at Highbury.

Alan Thompsett: It was the classic red shirt with white sleeves and the iconic badge that got me. As a four-year old, I had no idea that Highbury was easily reachable by train and underground from our home in Reigate, Surrey.

My first game, aged 10, was a 3-0 victory over Nottingham Forest (3/9/1977). Dad, Ray, and I sat upstairs in the East Stand, looking out onto a pitch bathed in brilliant sunshine. When Arsenal scored their first goal, I stood to cheer and, not realising my seat had automatically flipped up, as I went to sit back down I ended up on the floor! It was also the game in which Forest's Kenny Burns headbutted Richie Powling from behind. I slept with my programme and official handbook under my pillow for months.

Mike Hunt: My father Mikey Falco took me to my first game was I was aged seven. Got the No.4 bus from Goswell Road without telling me our destination. Only realised where we were going when we turned the corner of Elwood Street and saw Highbury for the first time. With tickets bought from Stan Flashman (a family friend), we sat next to in the directors' box amid the fog of Arsenal chairman Mr Dennis Hill-Woods' cigar. Whenever I smell cigar smoke I'm reminded of that night at Highbury. It was a drab 0-0 affair v Liverpool (4/10/1977) but I was hooked for life.

Family folklore has it that dad's cousin, Jimmy Falco, was the fan with the flag before

28

the 'Battle of Highbury' game in the 1930s. Family hail from Clerkenwell, of Irish-Italian parents, so could be some truth to this. Unfortunately, one distant relation (Mark Falco) decided to go up the road and play for the other side.

Ian Tredgett: For a decision that's had such an impact on my life, it's a pity that I can't really remember what it was that led me to support Arsenal. I do know I was about six or seven and at this time (mid-70s) most of the children at school supported Leeds Utd, Liverpool or Chelsea; the latter two being the most successful teams of the day, the former being the most local first division club. I do recall wanting to support a London team, and for it not to be the same one favoured by anyone else.

WILLIE YOUNG
ARSENAL

To be honest, I think Arsenal was the only other London team I had heard of. Dad was a Fulham supporter. In fact, the first few games I went to were at Craven Cottage but I think even he realised that, despite their 1975 Cup run, they weren't an attractive option for his seven-year-old boy. Dad was also a keen cricket fan – another love he passed on to me – and his own childhood hero was Denis Compton, so I guess there was an affinity with Arsenal too.

It took a few years before I was taken to Highbury – Mum eventually gave in after incessant requests. As a slightly belated 10th birthday treat we went to Highbury for the visit of Leeds Utd (10/12/1977). We sat in the West upper and if you recall the scene from *Fever Pitch* when the lead character gets his first view of the ground from this vantage point, my initial impression was almost identical. I was equally in awe.

I recall Mum being asked to sign a petition against a groundshare with Tottenham on a potential site at Alexandra Palace. The campaigner reasoned with her: "This is Highbury, this is our home", so even then a stadium move must have been mooted.

The game itself finished 1-1, Willie Young giving us the lead at the North Bank end, and it might not surprise you to know that we conceded a last minute equaliser to Gordon McQueen. I often wonder what became of the ground share idea, though.

Vince Pardoe: v Ipswich Town (2/1/1978), won 1-0 thanks to David Price. I was nearly eight-years-old and remember seeing the big police horses, the old man inside the ground selling roasted peanuts and the police band playing at half-time. It was magical. I was hooked.

Stefano Enepi: v Aston Villa (4/2/1978), lost 1-0. Someone scored an own-goal. It was raining. I was in the Clock End.

Richard Gosling: I was three-years-old when I first went with my dad Gerald to see us beat West Bromwich Albion (25/3/1978) 4-0. Supermac (Malcolm Macdonald) got a hat-trick and Willie Young completed the rout.

Barry Hughes: I was born In Belfast, where your Scottish and Northern Irish teams were rather pre-ordained based on your religion, so your English team was the one you could choose with your own free will. Most kids supported Liverpool or Manchester United. I chose Arsenal because they had a Northern Irish manager in Terry Neill, as well as three Northern Ireland internationals in Pat Jennings, Pat Rice and Sammy Nelson. Added to that were a strong contingent from the Republic Of Ireland, such as Liam Brady, Frank Stapleton, David O'Leary and John Devine.

After moving to England our first family visit to London came on a non-match day around 1978. My dad Peter and I walked up to the marble halls. On the steps Dad (despite Burnley being his English team) recognised Jack Kelsey, the former Gunners goalkeeper and now custodian of the club shop on Avenell Road. Dad explained my Arsenal obsession and, unbelievably, Mr Kelsey offered to give us a guided tour of Highbury. Now I have been on subsequent paid-for tours both at Highbury and The Emirates but nothing compared to this. We had access to the boardroom, both changing rooms and were even allowed to go onto the pitch. I have a picture of me leaning on the goalpost.

The hospitality Jack Kelsey provided made a lasting impression and I became even more hooked on all things Arsenal.

Paul Woodley: Dad Henry first took me when I was seven to see us against Bolton Wanderers (16/9/1978). There were balloons in the centre circle that were let off before the game, which we won, 1-0 (Frank Stapleton). It was the first trip for both of us, so still means a lot. All the family are now Arsenal but it started with us.

Barry Hughes

Gary Jones: Father Ray introduced me to Arsenal back in the early 70. My first game was the 1-1 draw v Aston Villa (7/10/1978) in which Alan Sunderland scored for us and John Kosmina was a sub. I was 12-years-old at the time.

The outstanding memories for me that day were the smells of the burger vans and the jostling of the crowd. I remember walking down towards the main entrance and just being blown away by the Art Deco facade and the flags flying outside. You knew the place was special and steeped in history.

Craig Pottage: I think I got into Arsenal through two brothers I went to school with, Mark and Gary Paulus, who I still go to games with today. My dad David was a big Brian Clough fan, so he took me to Arsenal v Nottingham Forest (13/1/1979). Brian Talbot's debut, highlights were shown on ITV's *The Big Match* on Sunday afternoon. It was a very cold day and the pitch so hard that I believe Tony Woodcock – then of Forest but a future Gunners striker – played in trainers. There were two Forest fans sitting near us but no trouble.

Mark Aughterlony: I am a fourth generation Arsenal supporter, my great grandmother, both sets of grandparents, my parents, aunts and uncles all being born and bred in Islington. I therefore had little choice in the matter of which team I would support. Not that my brother and I are complaining. Saying that, our dad never took us to see The Arsenal, despite the fact that up until the early 80s both sets of our grandparents still lived in Matilda Street and Sickert Court, Essex Road, respectively.

It was actually Chelsea-supporting friends of our family who took us to our first game at Highbury, v Chelsea (16/4/1979). We stood in the Clock End and watched us run out 5-2 winners.

My memories from that first visit number many, and are still clear to this day. I recall the Chelsea player Clive Walker strolling down Avenell Road, mingling with the fans – we were subsequently told (rightly or wrongly) that he lived locally and it was therefore far easier for him to walk to Highbury. I can still hear a female Chelsea supporter saying to her husband, as the teams warmed up: "Isn't that Mickey Droy big?" Also, my hero at the time, Frank Stapleton, scored twice, while Pat Jennings appeared absolutely massive in our goal, certainly 'bigger' than some average centre-half for the opposition. I recall my brother and I – aged 12 and 10 respectively – being amazed at the choice language being used by some of the opposing fans in their songs.

Tracy Sharpe: It was because of my dad Alan Abbott, who has been going to games since

You Are My Arsenal, My Only Arsenal

ALMOST 40 years after a father first took a son to Highbury, a new generation of Gooner is now accustomed to the comfort of Ashburton Grove. But in the words of LAYTH YOUSIF, the message is still the same, "Thanks for bringing me, Dad."

Highbury, North London

I am about to watch my first-ever Arsenal game. It is the early 80s. Islington is still predominantly working class. I clutch my dad's hand, fearful but excited at what is about to happen, unaware that my life will change forever.

Terraced houses veer into sight from the endless feet walking up the mottled grey pathway that leads from the subterranean tube train where grown men in red scarves and hats, smoke, drink and curse. It is gunmetal grey deep midwinter. Already the light is fading. We are minutes away from the 3.00pm kick-off. A kick-off time that seems as immoveable then as it will become anachronistic in the years to come.

My dad, an immigrant to this uncaring city, has taken his fair share of knocks but watching Arsenal gives him joy, gives him a release, even though the vintage he takes me to see are decidedly mediocre. Certainly in terms of the great teams of the past that are part of the rich folklore of his beloved club. Is this where I got my love of Arsenal Football Club from? Not the winning, certainly not the defeats – which left me grumpy and inarticulate with rage, despair, shame, or all of them – come to think of it they still do – but the simple, ridiculous pleasure of supporting my team through thick and thin.

A tall, wide building looms at me, white-walled with indents for windows. The lettering reads 'Arsenal Stadium'. Red flags are flying horizontal, ragged in the freezing wind.

Although it is cold I have time to marvel at the Art Deco East Stand, before I know what the phrase even means. I can't have been the only Gunners-supporting schoolboy who had heard of a 1930s architectural movement, along with the term "listed-building". And of course I knew that marble halls were the same as hallowed corridors.

We walk up substantial thick-set steps, my small legs aching with the effort. But what greets me when I get to the entrance is something that lives with me forever. My dad looks down at me with a kindly look, not just to make sure I'm OK but to also savour his son enjoying his first views of the pitch and the inside of this ground, that will become as familiar as the front rooms in the council estate flats I grew up in.

Pat Jennings is in goal in the darkening middle distance. He strides on cloying mud that seems to be encroaching on the entire penalty area. But what stands out for me, apart from the sheer size of the gentle Northern Irishman's hands, is the colour green. I had expected my vision to be engulfed in waves of red but the greenness of the pitch, coupled with our goalkeeper's dark green jumper, disorientates me. Even now, especially for the first home game of the season, I find myself staring at the sheer lush greenness of the turf at Ashburton Grove (and no, I'll never call it by a sponsor's name) and drift back to the days when mud was mud, astounded at how well kept our turf is.

We are seated in the East Stand, as dad has a bad leg. The crowd standing in the North Bank seems a vast amorphous mass. Indistinct chants that I would soon come to know by heart create a sound that amplifies under the corrugated iron roof. All around me are twisting whorls of smoke and grumbling. Grown men swear profusely. That, of course, shocks and attracts me. But it is the difference in tones of the swearing that intrigues. Some curse with real anger and aggression, others use it as a prop, more still use the words as nouns, adjectives and everything in between. But none are uttered without passion. Without caring. These Arsenal fans are loyal and long-suffering. They feel the pain of every misplaced pass, of every miscontrolled ball, of every bad pass and failed attack. I begin to understand that passion comes suddenly, even though it takes me a long time to realise it can last a lifetime.

The ball gets lofted high into the air, so high it almost reaches the upper tier. It drops again, thudding the soft, bald turf which absorbs the impact. Cold or not, I want to head the ball away so that my team can clear the danger. I am already infatuated with the game. With my team. With Arsenal Football Club.

Dad looks at me. "Enjoying it?" he asks me, already knowing the answer. I nod vigorously, to show him how much I really love it. "It's brilliant – but do you think we'll win?" I ask with genuine concern. He looks at me with a slight uneasiness, aware of the weighty responsibility that comes with investing a love of a football club into his young son, with all that it entails. "Yes, of course," he says slightly hesitantly. I don't think anything of it at the time, I am simply reassured because dads are never wrong, are they? "Thanks, Dad," I say. "Thanks for bringing me."

I must have attended nearly a thousand Arsenal games over the years; had a season ticket for 30 years; been to over 50 European away games and the same amount of reserve ones. I travelled home and away religiously for decades and have nearly as many stories. I have tried to spot future players at freezing cold South-East Counties youth games. My friends and I have spent New Year's Eve on the hard shoulder of the M6 after breaking down on the way back from Villa Park; drunk far more scrumpy than is necessary at a pre-season friendly in Yeovil; been chased by Millwall through Dickensian back alleys; slept on roundabouts in France on European away games; visited a mate in hospital in Copenhagen the day after a UEFA Cup Final – six years after we won the Cup Winners' Cup on our first trip there. The same city, completely different outcomes on and off the pitch.

I have been at the Parc de Princes and was part of the chorus that helped sing the first ever "1-0 to the Arsenal". I sat in the Stade de France, 17 minutes from eternal glory; I have also sat in a muddy field in Wrexham after one of the biggest shocks in FA Cup history. I have had riotous nights out in Cardiff and Bradford on the back of crushing defeats and I have been surrounded by Real Madrid fans in The Bernabeu – before a kindly soul, who couldn't speak a word of English, thrust out a friendly hand offering me a full plastic cup of rioja and a paper plate stacked with jamon. And when Henry scored one of the best goals in Arsenal's history, the same man shook my hand and simply said: "Muy bien."

I have been stranded on the motorway in deep snow attempting to get to Luton; got all the way to Middlesbrough on a National Express Coach, only to find our Tuesday evening game called off. Incidentally, not wanting to spend the night in a pub in a freezing deserted town, I went to the pictures and chose the longest film available – there can't be many people who can say they travelled all the way to Teesside just to watch *Lord of The Rings* before getting back on an overnight National Express Coach to London, which took a mind-numbing seven hours.

I have seen us win every trophy we've won since the 80s – if you discount the two years I spent travelling – and even then I managed to find BBC World Service in dusty Nicaragua to hear us win an FA Cup Final. I have been stood on top of a stunning Mayan ruin in deepest Yucatan and had a conversation with a Mexican about the need for a decent reserve goalkeeper; been on a black granite Buddhist stupor in Java, chatting to an Indonesian about our transfer policy; walked through Vietnam's DMZ while a man whose grandfather was in the North Vietnamese Army asked me my thoughts on Thierry Henry; been on a Roman fort in Sardinia and talked about the need for a back-up striker. I have been on a ferry in beautiful Sydney harbour with my back to the Opera House and Bridge, engrossed in talk about us beating Spurs.

While working for a charity in Kampala's biggest slum, I had the unsettling experience of a child with HIV asking me about Jack Wilshere. Unsettling because, although I had no way of understanding his suffering, I could empathise with his passion. With retrovirals in short supply, I just wondered how long he would be able to support our team.

David O'Leary

Arsenal Football Club has provided me with searing highs and crushing lows, and despite our form, the quality (or lack of) of our players, our transfer news (or lack of), scandalous ticket prices, and absentee chairmen, the fact is wherever I have travelled, Arsenal has been my *lingua franca*.

I have seen us lose finals in the flesh in six different competitions but supporting Arsenal is about the camaraderie, the sense of belonging, the dry humour, the gallows humour, the beers, the lock-ins, the joyous goal celebrations where you wonder if you'll ever breathe again, the crazy away days, the miserable away days, the fans you meet along the way (some of whom have become lifelong friends), the mishaps, the glory, the thrilling fightbacks, the crushing failures, the pain, the dedication involved, the guilt at seeing loved ones hurt at the amount of time you invest in such an unfeeling institution. Supporting Arsenal (or any club) is a lifelong addiction, one destined for as much sadness and regret as happiness and success. If that sounds like a family, I think you're right – a family is what it is for me and countless others.

For better or worse, it's in the blood.

I have seen most of the players fielded in the red and white of Arsenal over the last 30-plus years. From John Hawley and Lee Chapman to Dennis Bergkamp and Thierry Henry. From David O'Leary, Gus Caesar and Andy Linighan to Matty Upson, Igor Stepanovs and the worst centre-halves I have ever seen in Sebastien Squillaci and Mikael Silvestre.

I cried with David Rocastle and Paul Merson when they were forced out of the club, yet never forgave Ashley Cole; I have seen moments of skill that have burned into my consciousness, from Glenn Helder absolutely skinning Stuart Pearce to "Ian Wright Wright Wright" twisting, turning and lobbing the ball over various Everton players' heads before doing the same to that Big Nev Southall. From Patrick Vieira blockbusters to my original hero Charlie Nicholas lighting up "by far the greatest team", when to be fair there wasn't much greatness about; a Kanu hat-trick at Chelsea, where he was so near the line they should have shouted "Mind the gap!" at Fulham Broadway.

I have seen "Ian, Ian Allinson" and Rocky scoring at White Hart Lane to send us through to Wembley, which still remains my favourite Arsenal game ever. I have also seen us ship five at The Lane, and seen us win the league there. I actually sat in the home end that glorious day. Unable to move when we went 2-0 up early on, my cheek started involuntarily shaking. It was nice to know at least part of my body still celebrated outwardly.

I used to memorise the date of every fixture the day they were announced. I don't do that anymore, because they're not worth the paper they're written on. TV is not the only thing that is different. As I look back on more than three decades of supporting Arsenal Football Club I reflect on the changes that have occurred.

From a small shop counter run by Wales' greatest-ever keeper, the kindly Jack Kelsey, to a global money-making enterprise known throughout the world. From Terry Neill, Don Howe, Gorgeous George and one nil to the Arsenal, to the best attacking team that I have ever seen, which could also defend a bit – the 2004 improbable, immortal, Invincibles.

From the steak and chips pre-match staple to Arsène's steamed broccoli and stretching, which not only gave new life to our famed back four but revolutionised English football; from cramped but glorious Highbury to the shiny new ground on an old rubbish tip; from average players who mostly gave their all, to talented players who sometimes don't; from working-class heroes on the terraces to £25,000-a-year businessmen in Diamond Level who don't even re-appear for the second-half. In fact, the only constant I have known in that time is the sheer devotion, faithfulness, dependability – and let's say it, love – of the many loyal fans who are proud to call themselves Gooners and who give themselves up willingly to the cause. I salute you all.

Reading, Berkshire. Late October, 2012

A small boy is about to watch his first-ever Arsenal away game. He clutches at his dad's hand, fearful but excited, unaware of what is about to happen. Grown men in Arsenal scarves and hats, loiter, drink, smoke and curse outside. The father and son enter the away end at the new purpose-built ground on the town's outskirts. The boy's dad has taken his fair share of knocks but watching Arsenal gives him joy, gives him a release, even though the vintage he takes his son to see are decidedly mediocre. Certainly in terms of the great teams of the past that are part of the rich folklore of his beloved club.

Within 20 minutes Arsenal are 4-0 down. The boy looks up at his dad, crestfallen. The man takes a deep breath and tries to console his son, who is on the verge of tears. The best he can manage is a pathetic: "It's not over yet." The six-year-old nods uncomprehendingly as his eyes well up. Two hours later – two crazy, joyous, ridiculous, life-affirming, life-threatening, hours later – Arsenal win 7-5 in extra-time.

I stare at my son with a kindly look. "Did you enjoy it?" I ask him, already knowing the answer. He nods vigorously, to show me how much he really loved it. "It was brilliant," he replies. I look at him with a slight uneasiness, aware of the weighty responsibility that comes with investing a love of a football team into my boy, with all that it entails. "Told you we'd win," I joke. My son doesn't say anything but is reassured because dads are never wrong, are they?

"Thanks Dad," he says. "Thanks for bringing me." And I feel my throat catch.

Courtesy of www.theinsideleft.com

the 1930s. He finally took me to my first match, a 1-1 draw v Norwich City (28/4/1979). From that moment, walking up the terraces in the Clock End, I was hooked.

Tom Eldridge: My dad Alan (born 5/1/1945) is a lifetime Arsenal fan. His dad took him to Highbury to watch the great Stanley Matthews play (and beat) Arsenal in the 1953 FA Cup sixth round. But he decided he much preferred the home-side. He remains a season-ticket holder today. When there's a spare ticket available he now takes his grandson, my eldest boy, Johnny, rather than me. I was born in September 1971, apparently the second-best thing to happen that year, and he fought hard, but failed, to have me called Charlie or George, or both.

My first game at Highbury was with Dad against Middlesbrough (15/9/1979). I was eight. We had tickets in the East Stand upper tier and got there early. I will never forget walking up the really dark stairs, between the brick walls, into the bright white stand and looking down on that green turf and seeing the magnificent North Bank to my right and the grand old clock to my left. It is actually exactly how they recreated the scene in the *Fever Pitch* film for Nick Hornby's first game. A bit of a cliché, I know, but whenever I now walk into anywhere new that I've heard about, seen on TV or read in a newspaper, I remember walking up those East Stand stairs like it happened yesterday – and on most days I can't usually remember what I did the day before!

In terms of the game, my hero at the time, Frank Stapleton, scored, following an Alan Sunderland goal, and I am sure my other all-time XI hero, Liam Brady, put one on top of the North Bank roof and it got stuck behind one of the old cannon emblems (although that might have been against Derby County that same season, when we won 2-0 and Brady scored a penalty and Big Willie Young got the other).

Graham Price: v Middlesbrough (15/9/1979) with my dad Tony. He was an Arsenal supporter too. I was nine. We sat in the East upper but I only remember the pitch looking green and the atmosphere was buzzing. Won 2-0, with goals by Alan Sunderland and Frank Stapleton.

John Hilditch: I grew up living in Holloway, at 56 Holloway Road to be precise. My dad Brian used to look after me on Saturdays and took me to Highbury from about four or five years of age. It would have been late 70s/early 80s. I don't actually recall anything from my first game but the story goes that it was v West Ham Utd and we were seated in the West lower. Before kick-off, Dad explained to me that I should cheer when a goal is scored. West Ham scored, I cheered (as instructed) . . . and my old man had a bit of explaining to do to the Arsenal fans around us!

Paul Hemming: My grandparents were from Harlesden, Neasden, Willesden and one of my great-grandfathers ran off-licences, including ones in King's Cross and Caledonian Road. They started to "go over The Arsenal" in the 1920s. After WW2, my family had season tickets in the East Stand upper, Block B.

My dad died when I was four. He was a regular and proud to have been at the Leeds Utd game (5/5/1966) among the lowest-ever attendance for a senior competitive game at Highbury of 4,554, just before manager Billy Wright was sacked; he was at the Man Utd game before Munich in '58; went to the first leg of the '70 Fairs Cup Final away to Anderlecht; and danced a jig of delight on the pitch at WHL in '71.

I saw my first game, aged about eight, in 1979-80. I'd never been that high before and recall the smell of tobacco, fried onions and horse shit. The football? Can't remember!

Peter Norton: Both grandparents, Eddie and Margaret Dovey (nee Hodgson), were from North London. He was lucky to see the great teams in the 1930s and, as his first grandson, we had a special bond. I was always going to be a Gooner.

I was brought up on Eddie's tales of the 30s teams and then the first Double side. He took me to my first game in 1979 and I took him to his last game in the mid-90s.

I also remember phoning him slightly drunk from the phone box outside Finsbury Park station in May 1998 to celebrate the title. Lovely times. Sadly, I delayed phoning him in 2004 for the same reason until (I planned) after the WHL draw. He passed away a few days before that game.

Jem Maidment: v Coventry City in 1979 or '80, in the East upper (posh seats to start). We won. I spent the entire game in awe of David O'Leary (much to my big brother's annoyance). And I inexplicably remember holding onto a Mars bar for the entire game.

Paul Delaney: While at school, one of the helpers, Mr Bundy, happened to be an Arsenal steward and it was him who brought me to my first game, v Bolton Wanderers (23/2/1980). We won 2-0 with goals from Willie Young and Frank Stapleton. Never forget coming out of Arsenal tube station . . . the crowds, the smell of hot dogs, all the stalls. I sat in the West Stand lower that day. What a ground. I was hooked.

Stuart Pierce: Dad Bill, who was born on Highbury Hill (a son for my Arsenal-supporting grandad, William Pierce) and became a sports journalist, regularly covering Arsenal, claims to have played no part in my choice. Although I recall his delighted surprise when telling him of my life-changing decision, I can't think that Arsenal in 1980 was the obvious choice for a four or five-year-old living in Hemel Hempstead, so he must have had some influence.

I was taken to my first game v Southampton (19/8/1980) wanting a 1-1 draw and hoping to see my new team score and also Kevin Keegan – my favourite footballer who'd just signed for Saints – find the net. But once I saw the East Stand emerge from the hill on Avenell Road, having parked at Drayton Park, any neutral feelings were gone.

Dad, me and hundreds of others rushed up the stairs because the Tuesday night game had already kicked off following our delayed arrival in heavy traffic. The sight of the pitch as I got to the top of the few steps of our upper tier entrance was beguiling, and I'll never be articulate enough to do it justice.

Frank Stapleton

As it happens, the game did end 1-1, with Frank Stapleton scoring for Arsenal and Graham Baker for the visitors. By the next game I saw, against Man City a few months later, my knees were knocking in fear throughout the match.

Dad worked for the *Evening Standard, Daily News* (briefly), Extel and then the Press Association as a freelance journalist. I answered the phone to George Graham more than once. Dad considered him a friend and when Mum passed away in 2003, George took the time to phone Dad and have a chat with him. I was there in the hallway, suspecting who was on the other line, and when Dad got off the phone he said to me: "George Graham. Good lad, isn't he?" I forgave him for Tottenham after that!

Mike Green: No-one in my family supported Arsenal but I picked them for the 1978 FA Cup Final v Ipswich Town and stuck with them from that day. I am often asked why I support Arsenal and I was curious as to why I chose them when everyone else at that time supported the great Liverpool side who were so dominant in the early 80s.

I did some family research and it turned out that my great-grandfather, Morrison, was employed at the Woolwich Arsenal gun factory. Although he was of Scottish origin, he came down to London to work, so maybe it was fate and meant to be. I also had a great uncle Ken who once had a shop in Islington after retiring from the London Fire Brigade. When he moved back to the village where I was growing up he used to regale me with tales of The Arsenal and as a devoted fan at this time, it was great to hear. Many of the players who were around when he had the shop in the late 60s and early 70s used to go in there, so he often talked of the Double-winning side.

My first visit to Highbury was v Spurs (30/8/1980). Dad had promised that if I got a good school report he would take me to The Arsenal. We went to London for the weekend and spoke to Uncle Ken, who told Dad to get to the ground early to start queuing, as we had no tickets.

We arrived at 12.30pm and queued for what felt like ever to get into the North Bank. I was only just 10 at the time. My memories of that day are very vivid. Spurs had Ossie Ardiles and Ricky Villa, the 1978 Argentine World Cup winners, who were big signings for them. We had lost Liam Brady, my favourite player, to Juventus but fellow Irishman Frank Stapleton, my second favourite, was still at the club. It was a great game, and we won 2-0 thanks to David Price's header and Stapleton's lob over goalkeeper Mark Kendall.

The North Bank was so full and with all the swaying of the crowd, Dad was worried about my welfare. But I was lifted over the barriers at the front and sat on the gravel path to get a better view of the game. I was hooked on Highbury and what a majestic place it was. So full of noise and colour.

Alex Morrow: It's my dad Alan who is the man to blame for me becoming an Arsenal fan. His father, like a lot of people in the 1930s and 40s, used to go to lots of different games without really supporting anyone. If Arsenal were at home, he'd go there. The next week he would go to Tottenham, and another week Chelsea. As a boy in the 50s, and despite growing up a stone's throw from White Hart Lane, Dad decided to pick Arsenal as his team. I thank him every day for that choice!

He became a season ticket holder in the 60s, and took me to my first match when I was five-and-a-half-years-old. We were at home to European Cup holders Nottingham Forest (27/9/1980). The day did not start well, because our car broke down as we were about to set off. Thankfully, we were rescued by a friend, who went out of his way to pick us up and take us to the game with him. I remember thinking how much bigger his car was compared to ours.

I also remember climbing the steps up Block V from the back of the West upper, and looking at the pitch for the first time. We won the match 1-0 thanks to Graham Rix's goal and although I don't recall anything about the game itself, I do have my Infant school workbook which contains a picture of a football match that I drew on the following Monday under 'What I did at the weekend'. Leafing through, I can see that the effort I put in to that was far greater than any of the other pictures, so I was obviously hooked from the beginning.

Paul Donohoe: I became an Arsenal fan because of my grandad who was a commissionaire at Highbury from 1962 until 2002. His name was Nobby Clarke and the whole family was proud of him.

I went to my first game v Leicester City (4/10/1980), we won 1-0 (Frank Stapleton). I was only six at the time but I remember sitting in the East upper looking around Highbury in absolute awe.

Dave Ashby: Dad Allan grew up in Woolwich and had been watching Arsenal since the mid-1950s. He was at the United home game just before they went to Munich in '58, WHL '71, all of the 70s cup finals and then a ST holder from 1981 until he passed, just after the Invincibles season.

For my first game he bought a pair of tickets for the East upper and we beat Brighton & Hove Albion, 2-0 (1/11/1980). Graham Rix and Brian McDermott scored and I was hooked. Things that stand out for me were the peanut sellers – "all roasted" – outside the ground, the Make Money With Arsenal tickets (we didn't) and going to the club shop where Dad made a point of making sure I knew who Jack Kelsey – serving on the counter – was. We went once more that year before becoming season ticket-holders.

Kieron Pennie: Big brother 'Bam' took me to my first game, a 1-1 draw v Ipswich Town (27/12/1980). I remember him lifting me up to see over the wall so I could see the roof of the North Bank, then walking up the steps in awe as Highbury rose before me. Even John Wark's 77th-minute penalty equaliser – cancelling out Alan Sunderland's first-half close-range header – didn't spoil the day.

Simon Wadey: I remember my parents, Joan and Henry, taking me to my first game, a 1-0 victory (Alan Sunderland) v Liverpool (28/1/1981). Fell in love with Highbury as soon as I saw it. A magic place filled with so many great memories.

Kerry Smith: my Dad, Stewart Berman, was born and raised in Clapton. In those days (the good old ones) it was just a choice between two teams. Half of the school gave themselves a lifetime of misery while the other half (including Dad) chose to be Arsenal. It was therefore he who introduced me to football and, thankfully, The Arsenal. My brother Gavin Berman and cousin Scott Berman were also avid Arsenal fans, and together we would go to many games at Highbury and create special times that live long in the memory.

My first visit to Highbury would have been when I was about seven-years-old. I don't remember too much about it apart from the fact that Tony Woodcock scored and I bought a picture of him from the club shop. I just remember the pitch . . . walking up the steps and

Alan Sunderland leaves Liverpool's Phil Thompson grounded.

37

seeing it for the first time. So green and lush, it took my breath away and the love affair began.

Ian Mills: The red and white home colours attracted me to Arsenal as a five-year old. My best mate at school was a Liverpool fan and while they dominated football when I was growing up in the late 70s and early 80s, I liked how Arsenal's strip contrasted with their all-red strip – despite the Reds' dominance in terms of trophies. My support was further enhanced by a good work friend of my late father who brought me back flags he had taken to the three consecutive FA Cup finals we reached from 1978-80.

My first visit to Highbury was in 1982 with my aforementioned best friend and his dad (who was an Arsenal fan), which we won 4-3 v Aston Villa (27/3/1982). Check the records for that season – trust me, this was not the norm. My abiding memory is that of my friend's dad laying down the rules of the East Stand upper: "Politely applaud if and when we score but do not make a scene."

I was 10 at the time and disobeyed him for all four of our goals, by Alan Sunderland, Graham Rix (2) and Raphael Meade!

Paul Kelly: I followed William Kelly (grandad) and Michael Kelly (dad), both from Midleton, County Cork, Ireland, in supporting Arsenal. Now my son Robert is a fourth generation Gooner.

My first visit was for the final game of the season, v Southampton (15/5/1982). Sunny day, won 4-2 (Paul Davis 2, Stewart Robson, John Hawley). I had been to other grounds before and enjoyed each of them but Highbury was amazing. Standing on the North Bank, I was hooked. A group of between three-to-seven of us would travel up every home game from Worcester on the train, a 12-hour round trip.

John Lawlor: Having moved from Scotland to Dover in August '78 and not really following English football because I was a Celtic fan, my first real encounter with The Arsenal was the 1979 FA Cup Final, although it wasn't until '82 that I first went to Highbury.

My first game was a 1-1 draw on a warmish Tuesday night against Norwich City (31/8/1982). I went to the game with my school friend Paul Castle, his brother Ian Castle and his brother's mate Derek Butcher. We had travelled up from Dover on the train straight from school (me and Paul were only 14ish and his brother was a few years older). I remember being overawed at the size of the North Bank and how squashed it felt with so many people around us. I also recall asking how we changed ends at half-time, as that's what we had done at our local club. Then at the end of the game, having to rush back to Charing Cross to catch the last train back to Dover, otherwise we'd be stuck on the platform 'till the mail train left around 4.00am.

Colin Whitehouse: v Nottingham Forest (5/3/1983), I was aged 11 and travelled to the game by tube from Hounslow. On arrival at Arsenal station, as all the other Gooners got off and walked up the tunnel, I felt an enormous sense of belonging. As you exit the tube station onto the street, I can only describe it as a similar feeling like a footballer has walking out of the tunnel at Wembley. Seeing all the stalls selling anything from badges to burgers, then entering the North Bank turnstile and walking up the steps and seeing the pitch for the first time, I was in Heaven. From that moment on I was hooked and held a season ticket for the next 16 years.

The game itself was a boring 0-0 draw but I loved it all the same. Wonderful memories, especially for a young boy.

Gregg Lamb: Dad Terry took me to my first game, on the opening day of the season, v Luton Town (27/8/1983). I remember walking up the stairs of the East Stand lower and overseeing beautiful, majestic Highbury with its lush green turf. I was eight-years-old. Wonderful memory.

Mukhtar Khan: Earliest memory of Arsenal is reading the words 'Pat' and 'Rice' in a book

IT'S ALL ABOUT THE HIGHBURY FAMILY

PAUL PADFIELD wrote the following about what Highbury meant to him in September 2013 . . .

TODAY marks the 100th anniversary of Woolwich Arsenal's first game at Arsenal Stadium, Highbury. It marked the beginning of the club's association with Islington which endures to this day. As it is such a special anniversary I would like to share with you some memories of Highbury which I hope might convey what the old place meant to me.

One thing I will always be sure of is that the new place can never compare in the eyes of the generations that went there. My children will never know any different (although I was lucky enough to visit on a non-match day with my eldest shortly before the final game there and get a photo of him in my seat) and will come to regard Ashburton Grove as their 'home'. But to those of us old enough, and lucky enough, to have seen football there, Highbury will always be the most special football stadium in the world. More than that, it is the most special place in the world, full-stop.

It's 30 years since I first went to Arsenal. There are fleeting moments from that day. It was New Year's Eve and we were playing Southampton (31/12/1983). The game finished 2-2. I can remember Dad picking up two Southampton-supporting family friends as we drove out of Dover that morning. I also remember having to be 'persuaded' to actually go, as I had a late change of mind about seeing my first game and leaving Mum for the first time! We parked in Highbury Fields right up until a year or two before the old place shut and Islington Council made it difficult for people to get to games by car. We used to walk through the flats in Leigh Road and I vividly remember my brother telling me that I would be able to see the flags on the top of the stand as we got to the end of the road. As we got on to Aubert Park and turned towards Avenell Road, I saw he was right. It seems odd that my first memory of seeing the place is marvelling at the massive Arsenal flags fluttering on top of the East Stand.

As for the game itself, I remember virtually nothing, although the padded, green, theatre-style seats are an enduring memory. I've just looked it up and seen that I saw some top players that day, not all of them from Arsenal. On the pitch were Pat Jennings, Kenny Sansom, David O'Leary, Paul Davis, Tony Woodcock, Charlie Nicholas, Peter Shilton, Mick Mills, Mark Wright, Steve Williams, Danny Wallace and Frank Worthington. Both of Southampton's goals were scored by Steve Moran, while David Cork (with his only ever Arsenal goal) and Charlie Nicholas got Arsenal's.

Visits thereafter would be semi-regular. My brothers were becoming old enough (at least in Dad's eyes) to go on the North Bank together (they were 11 and eight in 1983, so I suspect Mum didn't quite appreciate what football terraces were really like).

Part of going to football as a small child meant having to get there early. As I said, my brothers would be going on the North Bank so would need to be as close to the front of the queue as possible in order to get their regular spot, on the corner of the barrier, on the East side looking straight over the raised shelf that stood about halfway up the terrace. This afforded them a perfect view, an easy exit at the end and a place where Dad could keep an eye on them from the East upper. Once or twice a season in the late 80s they would head to the very front of the North Bank in an effort to get themselves seen on the end-of-season video.

I reckon I must have paid more attention to them than to the matches, because I recall so little of the action. As a child I would watch the North Bank fill up (sometimes not quite so full if I'm honest) and there was always the regular vocal group who seemed to start the singing in the middle, right at the back, with the police keeping a close eye on them from behind. In those days each player seemed to have his own song from the supporters. In turn, they would respond to the North Bank as they warmed up on the pitch.

My first evening game was against Sheffield Wednesday and my abiding memories are of being told that there were two brothers playing for Wednesday – Glynn and Ian Snodin – and seeing BBC *Match of the Day* presenter Desmond Lynam walking in to the old bar in the East Stand. An evening game. I was only allowed to go to them when school was not on (my nephew has no idea how lucky he is – I was only allowed to go to night matches on a regular basis when I was 11-years-old).

Another evening game that really sticks with me was against Liverpool (25/10/89) in the League Cup. We won 1-0 and I can still see Alan Smith's goal now – the noise of the crowd is vivid to me. It's before the game that makes it stands out, however. As I said, we used to have to get there early, especially for a big game like Liverpool. Having seen my brothers safely on to the North Bank, me and Dad headed up to the main entrance of the East Stand. You could get really close in those days and we got talking to some people as we saw the likes of stand-up comedian Frank Carson and Southampton manager Lawrie McMenemy getting turned away by the commissionaires.

The people we (well, Dad really) were chatting with obviously were with the opposition but not all were scouse. Being so young, I took no notice of the fact that the old man with us was a Geordie. When Liverpool's coach arrived most of the players went straight in but Steve McMahon came over and gave tickets to some of the men we were stood with. Then Peter Beardsley came over to speak to the old man – his father. I'm fairly sure the old boy got Peter to sign our programme before he went in the changing rooms. Ever since then I've quite liked Peter Beardsley who always seems a very humble and underrated footballer.

Ian Wright

The years drifted slowly by and I would be taken along more and more regularly. My brothers invested in two season tickets in 1991, in the East lower, right beneath Dad's seats. I loved going and sitting down there, as there was a bit more of an 'atmosphere' in those seats. We were sat next to a man I knew only as 'John', who was a giant in terms of both his size and personality. I used to get dispatched to "get the teas in" shortly before half-time, when John would treat all the regulars within a four-seat radius and would then give me the change. I believe now that John may have been the much fabled Johnny Hoy, hero of the North Bank in the 70s and 80s. Part of me really likes to think that he most definitely was.

I was sitting there on the nights we beat Torino and Paris St Germain. The noise and relief at the final whistle of the Paris game was incredible, one of the greatest experiences ever, although John had moved on by then and been replaced by Andy Gibbons, who would move upstairs, and then down the road, with us all in the years ahead. My favourite game sitting down there, however, was a North London derby when Kevin Campbell and Ian Wright destroyed Spurs in a 2-0 win (1/12/1991). Big Kev ran right towards us after scoring a quite brilliant solo goal in front of the North Bank.

Later that season we'd say goodbye to the North Bank with Wrighty's hat-trick against Southampton (2/5/1992).
I have some great photographs of that day. Again, I remember the noise towards the end as he scored two in injury-time to claim the Golden Boot.

Only football can detach you from the world like that. In those seconds after a goal that means something so important to everyone present, there is seemingly nothing else in the world. Walking in to Highbury saw you turn your back on everything outside it. Its character and its history set it apart, and it had its own distinctive noise of crowd celebration.

My favourite Highbury day ever was against Everton (3/5/1998). Winning the League on the pitch at Highbury was actually a rare event considering the number of titles we won. It had been so unexpected at Christmas that the winning run was all the more special. When we blew Everton away and were 3-0 up with still ages to go, we knew we were champions.

Tony Adams would make the day, however, with that last-minute volley. If I close my eyes I can see him now. I can see it all. I remember the tears of joy it brought from the 19 year-old me. Tony Adams was Arsenal at that time, everyone's Mr Arsenal. What a goal.

I can see that trophy being brought on to the pitch by the commissionaires for the presentation, and Tony lifting it towards the North Bank – whose view had been slightly obscured by Carling's advertisements. That summed up how he knew The Arsenal, turning first to the North Bank before spinning round to all four corners.

40

In a perverse way, it was a moment that probably marked the beginning of the end for the old girl. Arsène Wenger saw the potential of the club, and knew that 38,500 was too small a crowd for a club of this stature. Whether we should have left is an argument for another day.

When it was time to leave, it was one of the saddest days I've ever experienced. You'd hoped it would never arrive, while knowing that it always would. Before home matches in those days, we used to meet up with the other Dover Gooners in the shadow of the East Stand. The usual meeting took place that day, although I was already welling up before I went in to the ground. Of course, we won and got in to the Champions League and all that was great, but this was the end.

Over the years we'd made lifelong friends with those around us. To Dad's right throughout my childhood was Bob Everett. Bob died in Summer 2001, and his son Glenn had taken over the season ticket from his father. Bob had been to the Cup Winners' Cup Final with Dad in 1980, and was with us (and Glenn) before the 1998 FA Cup Final. We'd met up at Derby before a League Cup tie on the road to Wembley in 1992. Bob was just always there at Arsenal when I was a boy. He'd seen me and my brothers grow up. He was the first person Dad phoned after Mickey Thomas won the title for us at Anfield – two old Arsenal fans sharing the most special moment in 18 years. When the club played a montage of the players we've lost in the closing celebrations, we were urged by Tom Watt to remember those around us that couldn't be there. Glenn put his arm round me and Dad and it was a moment that summed up Highbury for me – it was all about family. We were all one big Arsenal family.

I'm actually quite teary as I write this. To my left was Gary Goodson and his family, who have also become special friends. Gary stopped going on a regular basis a year after we moved down the road. The way the club had allocated the new seats meant it just wasn't the same for him, as we'd all been split apart. The new breed of 'fan' is something Gary seriously dislikes. A year or two ago he came with his son, Daniel, and sat with us as the boys won a Champions League tie. Sitting next to Dad, he said it was just like old times, and he wasn't wrong. Daniel, Laura and Nicola are still regulars, and occasionally take a ticket off our hands when one of us can't make it.

Family and friendship has endured despite leaving Highbury, and isn't that what it should all be about? Saying goodbye to Highbury was something I found so hard to do. I cried and cried as I walked out that final time. Block F, Row E, Seat 161. That was my season ticket. My home. My family. That's what Highbury meant to me. It was genuinely a cathedral of worship, The Home Of Football.

* Courtesy of Paul Padfield's www.myarsenalopinion.blogspot.co.uk

aged about four. It must have been a sticker album. After that, growing up in west and north-west London, I only heard Arsenal and Chelsea mentioned but, somehow, I always said 'Arsenal' when asked what team I liked. After moving out of London I found myself at a primary school where all the boys seemed to support Arsenal.

My first visit to Highbury didn't come until the game v Man Utd (6/9/1983) and because we had signed Charlie Nicholas, the excitement level was high. The buzz around the ground, the stalls selling merchandise & food. And then after entering the West Stand, the first thing that hit me was the green of the pitch. I had never seen that shade of green before in my life. It was intoxicating.

We started well and although we lost 3-2, I felt upset but still excited to have been to my first match.

Phil Murphy: A neighbour a few years older than me supported Arsenal. Aged nine, I was hooked. First Highbury game was v Liverpool (10/9/1983), lost 2-0. By then we were an average side.

Guy Thompson: My late stepmother's great-grandfather worked at the Woolwich Armoury and went to some of the first meetings when they talked about starting a football club. My uncles and grandfather had connections with Chelsea, Palace and Charlton but when I was a kid I was given an Arsenal crest on my first football shirt, so I became a true Gooner.

My first game was v Sunderland (5/12/1983), Tony Adams' debut and two weeks after my

16th birthday. Tony Woodcock scored in a 2-1 defeat. I wasn't allowed to go before I was 16 because of the hooliganism going on at the time and the fact that I was really small for my age.

I got the train up from Broadbridge Heath, a little village just outside Horsham in West Sussex, at the crack of dawn to Victoria and then made my way to Arsenal station. When I got off the tube and walked up what seemed like a tunnel that went on forever, I hit daylight and headed to Avenell Road to see the front of the stadium. Now I'd heard stories about it from my relatives and I'd seen pictures of it in *Shoot!*, *Roy of the Rovers* and on the TV, but to actually see it with my own eyes was something else.

As I made my way round the corner and it came into view, I looked up at the Art Deco façade, the huge cannon and the enormous red letters spelling out my club's name. I was in total awe. As I headed up towards the main entrance and the Marble Halls, the perspective of everything changed and the enormity of what I was looking at just blew me away. No pictures or stories could ever have properly prepared me for what I was looking at. I'd never seen anything like it in my life.

I remember thinking this was probably how Hercules must have felt when he first met Talos in *Jason and the Argonauts*. I felt not only on top of the world, but also quite invincible (yep, THAT word), because this was my club, and just look at her!

But I also remember feeling very, very small compared to what was in front of me. It really was everything I'd imagined. Only a million times better. It was the most amazing thing I'd ever seen. And I still knew the best was yet to come.

A couple of hours later I got up from sitting against the wall at the Gillespie Road gates as soon as I heard the stewards rattling the bolts behind them. I could feel my heart pounding as they opened them up and I started walking towards the turnstile. I paid my money and with an almighty clunk I pushed the thick red metal bar, the first thing I ever touched within the stadium (funny, the things we remember) and I was in. I hurried up past the old toilets on the right (Health and Safety would have a field day if they were still around) and up the steps at the right of the North Bank. The whole stadium just opened up in front of me.

With each step and the higher I got, the more I could see. The splendour of the East Stand came into view. Then the famous clock. And then the pitch. It was an unbelievable sight and feeling. I'm not a religious person but if there really was a heaven, then I'd just stepped right slap bang into the middle of it. I just stood there for a moment and took it all in. I'd made it. I was finally on the North Bank.

I was home.

Rob Griffiths: On the day of my first visit to Highbury (17/12/1983), we beat Watford, 3-1, and Raphael Meade scored a hat-trick.

Tim McCarthy: After nagging him for weeks, my brother David took me to our 3-1 victory v Liverpool (8/9/1984) but we didn't tell our mum! As an eight-year-old, I could not believe how amazing it was to stand on the North Bank (David hoisted me up) among the passionate singing, swaying fans. What also really struck me was how close the houses were to the ground – a proper community club.

Still remember the roar of the third goal (Brian Talbot scored two and Tony Woodcock the other) which put us top of the league. My expectation was set high from that day: turn up and beat one of the best teams in Europe! Took a while to realise Arsenal do things the hard way.

Gary Biggs: My dad, the late Dickie Biggs, wanted to call me Charlie George but Mum wasn't having any of it. My first game was v Aston Villa (5/10/1985). Arsenal won 3-2 with goals from Tony Woodcock, Viv Anderson and Chris Whyte. First memories always last. Walking up the steps of the North Bank, hairs standing up on the back of my neck, then viewing the stadium and pitch for the first time with tears in my eyes. I felt at home.

Priceless. Never to be forgotten.

Jamo Masterton: As a 10-year-old kid in 1985, just arrived from Glasgow, we settled in Grosvenor Avenue in Highbury. I joined the Junior Gunners and played in a few comps, gaining some medals on the way. By 1987 I was working on the pitch before games, at half-time and after the match helping Steve B and the rest of the guys get the pitch perfect. Afterwards we would go up the tunnel into the players' lounge and wait for our pay.

These were amazing times for me. Being from Glasgow, I was thrilled that Charlie Nicholas always took the time to chat and I became friends with a few players, like big John Lukic and Tony Adams. They were all great guys and a joy to watch every time they played at the famous Highbury.

A bit later on I went to work in the food kiosks for Richard, a nice guy in charge of all the catering at Highbury. My patch was up the North Bank. Wow! The place was always bouncing and swaying and the noise was incredible.

I have great memories of Highbury and the people who made it work.

Tony Woodcock

Paul Dargan: Won 2-0 v Liverpool (14/12/1985) in what was Niall Quinn's debut match and my first time in the North Bank.

Andy McGarry: v Man Utd (23/8/1986), aged 12. Went with my stepfather Anthony Bowen and mother's cousin Tony Kelly (we used to stay with him in Crouch End). Stood on the North Bank. Loved the Arsenal ever since. Both have sadly passed away, so that Arsenal connection means so much more.

Julian Kirkby: Started supporting Arsenal in the 1970s, as family on my mum's side were all from Islington/Essex Road/Hoxton way. Most of them moved away in the 50s and 60s but we didn't travel very far. I was born in 1972, brought up in Loughton but have lived in Wanstead now for more than 20 years.

First match I attended was an evening League Cup fourth round tie v Charlton Athletic (18/11/1986). We won 2-0, thanks to Niall Quinn and an own-goal. I remember the bright green of the pitch as I peered under the North Bank roof from the top side at the back of the terrace. A few mates from school were there and one of the older ones asked: "What are you doing here, I thought you were West Ham?".

"Be quiet," I replied, fearing I would get jumped upon by Gunners' fans, before telling him that he had got me mixed up with my elder brother Darron, who was a West Ham Chicken Run ST holder in the 80s and 90s.

The rest is history. I hardly missed any home matches from that night until we last played at Highbury.

Danny Young: My dad Bobby, his brothers Joe and Colin, and my grandad Fred Young, were all proper Gooners. Dad took me to stand on the North Bank when I was 11 and we saw us beat Southampton, 1-0 (27/12/1986), with a winner by Niall Quinn. I used to be shy and sung the songs quietly under the scarf wrapped around my face. Now my son James and I have season tickets.

Neil Davies: Two people are responsible for my love of the Arsenal: my dad Vic and grandad Fred Davies. From a very young age, I remember them either being happy or sad about their football team. Grandad would always have the latest season full-team poster on his wall in his hallway and I'd spend ages studying it, matching the names to the faces. He'd always dress up smartly for parties in his Arsenal club jumper and tie. I guess that it was his overt love for the club that swung it for me. Well, that and the fact that Dad shared an uncanny likeness to David O'Leary!

First visit to Highbury was for the visit of Coventry City (18/1/1987). It was a mightily unremarkable game, I suppose, but it was my first and that made it special. Dad said that I'd 'know' when I first saw the pitch and I wasn't sure what he meant until I saw it. I remember shaking with excitement as I climbed the steps towards the stand and the pitch slowly came into view. I stood, level with the halfway line in the West lower, and was instantly in awe – this place that I had built up to be some kind of mythical pantheon was there before me and I was hooked.

We drew 0-0 and it snowed sideways and all that happened was that Charlie Nicholas hit the post and I was fascinated by a bald guy in the Coventry ranks called Greg Downes. As we filed out of the ground, the men were grumbling about another toothless Arsenal performance but I was buzzing, asking when the next game was and when I could come again. An older guy behind me ruffled my hair, and said to my dad: "He's hooked – Arsenal for life." He wasn't wrong.

Stephen Orr: In 1948, my father Tom took ill in Belfast and spent a week in hospital at the age of eight. He was bought a book about Denis Compton and a love affair with Arsenal began. Now my 10-year-old Isaac is the third generation of passionate Gooners.

My first home game was our 4-1 victory v Leicester City (20/4/1987). We'd recently signed Alan Smith from Leicester but loaned him back to them, so he played against us that day. Our scorers were Martin Hayes (2 – 1 pen), Paul Davis and Charlie Nicholas.

James Smither: My Arsenal inspiration was definitely my grandad, Kurt Bromberg. As an Austrian refugee arriving in north London from Nazi-annexed Austria in the 30s, there was only one football team to support. The club became his consuming passion and he was a season ticket holder, a shareholder and a general obsessive for the remainder of his life – being among the fortunate few to be at iconic games such as both legs of the 1970 Fairs Cup Final, inside White Hart Lane for the 1971 title decider and at Wembley for the Charlie George and Alan Sunderland winners in '71 and '79.

He always said it was too close to call deciding between the Bertie Mee Double and the wedding of his only child, my mother, as the most significant event of 1971. My twin sister Sophie and I were taught to shout "Up the Arsenal!" for his benefit as soon as we could speak, and long before we knew what it meant.

The first FA Cup Final I can remember watching on TV, Manchester Utd v Everton in 1985, was watched on his new colour TV. He stopped going to games in the late 80s due to serious eyesight problems, so fretting along to matches on the radio replaced going to see them live as the centrepiece of his weekend routine.

It seemed somehow poetic that when he passed away, he was happy in the knowledge that we'd just completed our first Double since 1971, on the most significant Gooner date of all in the calendar: May 26, 1998.

Grandad will always be associated with Highbury in my mind – and leaving the old stadium was particularly bittersweet because so many of my memories there were tied up with my relationship with him. It was of course he who took me to my first game, a pre-birthday treat and a fairly straightforward 3-0 home win against Wimbledon (19/9/1987). Most of the game passed by in an excited blur for me, although I do recall my first live Arsenal goal being scored by my favourite player, David Rocastle (a Lewisham boy like me).

A Google search implies the attendance was only 27,752, although I remember it feeling packed and deafeningly raucous. The game also featured a Michael Thomas penalty – little did any of us in attendance that day know how important a figure in Arsenal's history he was shortly to become.

I also remember being warned in advance that a gentleman with a season ticket behind those of my grandad and his friend (whose space I was occupying) in the West upper was capable of some pretty fruity language for my innocent nine-year-old ears. But I was still surprised (and educated) by the torrent of invective he poured forth at great volume throughout the game (most of it aimed at our players and manager).

Other memories include being bought and handed the first of what would become a massive library of match programmes before kick-off and being taken for a greasy pre-match meal in a café somewhere near the ground and being the only child at a table full of

FROM CYPRUS WITH LOVE

George Stephanides: My father Michael Stephanides played a significant role in me becoming a loyal supporter of Arsenal. The Gunners visited Cyprus twice during the period 1967-70 and he attended both matches. The first time was in May 1967, when Arsenal visited the island for a tour and had a series of friendlies. One of those took place in Famagusta on May 31 at the GSE stadium. Arsenal won the match 2-0 and gave an impressive performance, despite the fact that their players were not used to playing on such a dry surface. That tour of Cyprus earned Arsenal a lot of new fans.

Soon after Arsenal won the Fairs Cup in April 1970 the club accepted an invitation from the Omonia Nicosia club to undertake another tour to Cyprus. Gunners played two friendly matches, one in Nicosia and the other in Limassol. The first match was scheduled in Nicosia on May 10, when the north Londoners won by 4-3 and received press headlines the next day. My father attended the match at the GSP National Stadium and was delighted by the tourists' showing. The other match, against Apollon Limassol, was played three days later.

George Stephanides with Charlie Nicholas

In this specific period of the late 60s and early 70s collecting card series of footballers' images was very fashionable among young fans in Cyprus. Almost every year a new collection of Cyprus footballers' card series was available to buy in shops, kiosks and sporting areas. But the trend got bigger since the arrival of Arsenal, the first-ever English team to play in Cyprus, and along with the local football card series, the English ones started appearing in my homeland. This made English football well known on the island, especially among young kids.

The first series to arrive was the yellow-backed A&BC gum cards of 1968-69. During the summer of 1971, the year that Arsenal won the Double, the A&BC gum cards of 1969-70, with orange backs, came to Cyprus. It was one of the best series ever produced. I was only five-years-old at the time and a cousin of mine, Memnon Hadjikyriakos, gave my father a big box with hundreds of the above mentioned series of cards as a gift to me. Once I opened the box, I was delighted to see that it was full of the new English gum cards with orange backs. "Look for the players with the cannon emblem on their shirts. It's the team that always wins," my father said to me. I started searching inside the box, exploring every single card, and I remember that the first Arsenal player I saw on a card was the image of Frank McLintock, immediately followed by that of Jon Sammels. My father told me that Frank was the captain of the team and the other one was a great player. I continued my search and soon I completed the full set of Arsenal players: Peter Simpson, Peter Storey, John Radford, Charlie George, George Graham, Bob Wilson, Bob McNab, George Armstrong, Ray Kennedy and Eddie Kelly. Great players from a great Arsenal team.

I was also very impressed by the club's uniform of red shirt with white sleeves, which meant they stood out from other clubs. Naturally, I demanded my father buy me the Arsenal playing shirt which was very

45

difficult to find.

That same year my godfather, Dinos Hasapis, went to London and I remember begging him to take me with him, in order to buy the famous Arsenal home shirt and of course take me to Highbury to watch Arsenal play. He refused and that made me cry. Eventually, when he got back home, he made me happy because he brought me a gift. I opened it and saw an all-red polo shirt of Arsenal with a huge crest. It was a symbolic commemorative shirt to mark achieving the League and Cup Double in 1970-71. There also was another small gift, a commemorative banner of Arsenal. These were added to my card collections, along with the two issues of sports newspapers covering the 4-3 win against Omonia Nicosia in May, 1970. Those were the only valuable Arsenal items I had at that time.

George Stephanides outside Highbury, 1988.

Ever since I became an Arsenal fan, I watched the English football highlights programme on TV every Thursday. But I always dreamed of going to Highbury and watching Arsenal playing live against any opposition.

After 16 long years Arsenal returned to Cyprus once more. This time they had won the League Cup (then known as Littlewoods Cup) thanks to two Charlie Nicholas goals. Arsenal took part in a Cyprus Super Cup tournament staged in Nicosia at Makarion stadium. along with Luton Town and the Cypriot clubs APOEL and Omonia Nicosia. Both clubs strengthened their sides by adding legendary players, Kevin Keegan and George Best respectively.

I remember the date of May 11, when Arsenal and Luton made it to the final. Three days later I walked into the stadium as an assistant photographer, helping the photo-reporter Kyriakos Andreou to take as many pictures as possible. On that night a combined Arsenal/Luton team played a combined APOEL and Omonia XI. Soon after the match Kyriakos took me to the stadium lounge to meet all the Arsenal players. I saw Tony Adams and Niall Quinn talking to the press but I went straight to my favourite Charlie Nicholas and had a nice little interview with him. Nicholas stated to me that he would stay at the club but hadn't yet signed a contract. He asked me not to believe any other rumours written about him in magazines and newspapers. That pleased me a lot and I told him that the next year I was planning a visit to Highbury to watch Arsenal and him play for the first time ever.

In the summer of the same year, 1987, I went to study in Thessaloniki, Greece. At the first opportunity I organised a trip to London the following year. In April 1988 I visited London for the first time to see my favourite team play and of course visit my relatives who lived there. My cousin Harry Charalambous, a loyal Chelsea fan, knew all about my plans and he organised some football activity. The first match I saw in England was a London derby at Stamford Bridge between Chelsea and Arsenal (2/4/1988). It finished 1-1 but what mattered most to me was the forthcoming one at Highbury.

And so it was, just two days later, I finally went to Highbury – a dream come true – to watch Gunners v Norwich City (4/4/1988), an 11.30am kick-off. Unfortunately, Charlie Nicholas had already left Arsenal to sign for Aberdeen the previous January but that did not prevent me from going to Highbury.

On our way Harry and I planned what to do. Once we had parked the car some distance from the ground and Arsenal tube station came into view, he told me to watch and absorb the whole area. When we made the turn into Avenell Road, Highbury stadium was just in front of me. I was truly amazed to finally be standing in front of a stadium that I had only seen in pictures and on TV.

After buying tickets and the official programme, we went straight to the Gunners Shop so that I could buy the new Arsenal shirt made by Adidas. I had the honour of meeting the legendary Arsenal goalkeeper Jack Kelsey, who was managing the shop at the time.

From there we quickly visited the marble halls and I had the chance to see the bust of the famous Arsenal manager Herbert Chapman. Then we entered the ground and immediately felt the unique Highbury atmosphere. Finally, I was inside Highbury, the Home of Football, sitting in the East stand upper tier, Block F, Row W, Seat 181.

Goals by Alan Smith and Perry Groves earned Arsenal a comfortable 2-0 win.

'adults" talking very earnestly about the team over their food and Woodbine cigarettes. I also remember learning that my grandad always left matches five minutes early to beat the rush (a habit I have not inherited): down the ageing stadium stairs, along Highbury Hill, into Arsenal Tube and onward to Caledonian Road, where he always parked his car in what I now realise are the back streets by Pentonville Prison.

Above all, I remember endlessly boasting about the experience afterwards to all my football-loving, Panini sticker-swapping friends at my south-east London primary school, none of whom were lucky enough to be taken to live matches by their families like I was – and whose jealousy only grew when I was invited back as a lucky charm the very next weekend to witness a second successive home win in another London derby, this time 1-0 against West Ham (26/9/1987). So tenuous was our playground grasp of North London geography that I seem to remember confidently claiming that my grandparents lived "just down the road" from Highbury, making such occasions particularly straightforward for our family. A bit of a stretch given that they lived in Stanmore, Middlesex!

Mark Briggs: I began supporting The Arsenal through my uncle, Tom Steers, a fan since the 70s, when he came to stay during a break from his missus. He took me and my brother Andrew to the 2-0 Boxing Day defeat by Nottingham Forest (26/12/1987). I fell in love with it all and haven't looked back. However, my brother didn't and loathes football.

Tom Leaney: It was thanks to my dad George, who had supported Arsenal since he was a boy. But my brothers, George and Oliver, followed Everton and Liverpool. When I was four Dad said to me: "If you support Arsenal, I'll buy you the kit." So I did. He took me to my first match, a 2-1 defeat v Man Utd (24/1/1988), and I got to take him to his last game in 2015, v Lyon in the Emirates Cup. He was an Arsenal fan for 68 years.

Robbie Jericho: My grandfather Tony Wakefield moved from Wales to north London as a child and had to choose between red or white. He always used to say how glad he was he went with red! So I have been a lifelong Gooner since I was born, travelling lots of miles from Barry (and now Swansea) in South Wales over the years to see the boys.

David McConachie: My grandma (Betty) and uncle (Gavin), both Arsenal fans, died in quick succession in the 1980s and I, a seven-year-old, decided to step in to fill the void rather than follow my dad Ian's team, Millwall.

For my first game, v Aston Villa (3/9/1988), I sat in the West upper with Dad and cousins Guy and Andrew. I remember being in awe at the sheer size of the ground, the magnificent circular pattern of the pitch and, most of all, seeing David 'Rocky' Rocastle live and being mesmerised. We came back from 2-0 down with goals from Brian Marwood and Alan Smith to level 2-2 but eventually succumbed. Tears were shed.

David Harman: My grandad Harold went to Highbury as a child and he took my dad Nick when he was a boy. Dad then went on to become a big Arsenal fan, going to games in late 60s and throughout the 70s. He then got married, so priorities took over and he couldn't go as often.

Mum is from a fanatical Spurs-supporting family. Actually, fanatical doesn't do them justice. Imagine the most stereotypical Tottenham fan, delusional with unrealistic grandiose beliefs and over-excitement at the smallest of achievements (you know what I mean).Then multiply that by 10 and you are somewhere near what they were like (and still are to this day).

As you can imagine, Dad had a pretty rough time dealing with them all throughout the 80s – one man versus an entire family. Quite frankly, he deserved a medal. So he made sure from an early age that I was an Arsenal fan (I had no choice) and I'm I glad he did.

The lead up to my first game was exciting. Despite being about seven, I remember Anfield 1989 very well. Mum and Dad had gone out for the evening (she had double-booked him and he wasn't happy), so my sister and I had a babysitter, which meant I wasn't allowed to

Clock End terraces and hospitality boxes.

stay up to watch the match on TV.

The game was recorded to watch the next morning (supposedly, without me knowing the score) but Dad had seen the game while out the previous night and was bouncing off the walls in the morning, so I knew it was good news. I remember not fully understanding the reason why Arsenal needed to win 2-0 but they did and it was good.

Anyway, following that, Dad took me to my first game next season at Highbury, when I was aged eight, to see us smash Sheffield Wednesday 5-0 (9/9/1989). Despite being from a football family, Mum never went to a game. Hillsborough had happened earlier in the year, so she was not too happy about me going, but she finally cracked and I went along.

I don't recall the game itself and couldn't tell you who scored (Paul Merson, Alan Smith, Michael Thomas, Tony Adams and Brian Marwood) but I remember watching the players arrive on the bus, then going to a chippie before the game. We sat in the West Stand and I clearly remember seeing the pitch for the first time and being utterly amazed.

Afterwards, we went to the club shop, where Dad bought me a full kit. The shop was tiny, absolutely nothing like it is nowadays. I remember getting home and listening to my parents having an argument about Dad buying me stuff I didn't need and that it wasn't fair on my sister, etc.

Amazingly, last year my brother found that same shirt when he going through some old stuff and gave it to me as a Christmas present. I was able to match the kit to some photographs of me wearing it, which I now have framed. The old man died in 2006, so rediscovering that kit was pretty special.

Kayne Goddard-Knell: With no father around and a mum that had no interest in football, no-one influenced me to follow Arsenal per se. But my friend Sean Ross had a sticker album and I chose my team, the wonderful Arsenal, based purely on the badge. I've been so glad of that day ever since.

Adam Pembrey: It ran in the family. My dad Albert took me to my first game the day before my eighth birthday, v Man Utd (28/11/1992). The mural was up at the time, I was in JG section, and we lost 1-0 to a Mark Hughes goal.

48

Chris Saltmarsh: My great-grandfather Albert Smith worked for Arsenal, although I'm not sure in what capacity. I tried to do some research but couldn't find much on him. I do know that later on he went on to work for the Rothmans tobacco company. My first game was a 4-3 victory v Southampton (20/3/1993). Our scorers: Andy Linighan, Paul Merson, Jimmy Carter (2).

Ben Sharpe: Mum Louise was an Ipswich Town fan and dad Pete was a West Ham supporter, so had no affiliation to Arsenal whatsoever. I've never really been able to answer the question of why I support The Arsenal but I'm led to believe that it was Ian Wright's goal scoring that did it for me.

Mum went to slimming club and there she met Pete – another one, not my dad – whom I still attend games with today. We used to go round his house and this is where I really got into Arsenal. Borrowing videos, reading programmes and just taking about it with him gave me the buzz before I'd even been to Highbury.

My first visit was v Newcastle Utd (18/9/1994) and I remember it as if it was yesterday. I even wrote a little book about the day and still have it!

I remember walking along Gillespie Road wondering where Highbury was. Then we turned the corner into Avenell Road and there it was, the famous East Stand accompanied by the smell of burgers and onions, which I still love because it always takes me back to that day.

We lost 3-2 but I remember being very intrigued by the amount of people that were there – I'd never seen anything like it before. I remember Ian Wright scoring in the last minute to reduce the deficit.

Daniel Coyle: Born in Camden, grew up in Finchley area. Went to Finchley High School, which was 90 per cent Gooners. My first game at Highbury was circa 1994-95, v Sheffield Wednesday or Bolton Wanderers (not sure which). My high school head teacher, Mr Hoare, was a Gooner and asked if I was an Arsenal supporter at my entrance interview.

Michael Cherrington: My parents were not keen on football when I was younger, so I started to support Arsenal because of a close friend at primary school called David Bower. My first visit to Highbury was to see us draw 1-1 with Leicester City (11/2/1995). It was a rainy day and Ian Selley broke his leg in what was not one of the greatest of games. But I still remember walking to my seat and thinking, 'wow!'.

Christopher Hylland: I was born in Oslo to a Norwegian dad and English mum but grew up in Burgess Hill, Sussex. First game, funnily enough, was v Spurs – mum Wendy thinking it'd be a good idea to take my brother Martin and I to see our teams play each other! She got lucky, it ended in a 1-1 draw (29/4/1995), with Ian Wright putting us ahead from the spot.

Living near Brighton, we were mostly surrounded by United fans. A lot of Gooners, too, but the oldest kid in the road where we grew up, where we played different sports every day, was a Spurs fan, so it spread down the ranks like wildfire. I've never been a sheep, a follower, and I must've realised that it would be a terrible existence – as it was for my brother for the first 20 years of his Spurs-supporting life.

I went home to Mum annoyed or disillusioned and she asked what was wrong: "I don't want to be a Spurs fan," I said to her. "This family is Arsenal," she replied. It was a shame she didn't foresee the need to push it on us earlier, I would've loved to have grown up sharing my love for The Arsenal with my brother – going to games, enjoying the wins, having a moan-up when we lose. As it is, we barely speak about football.

To this day I try and take Mum to a game once a season. I have lived in South America – initially Buenos Aires, Argentina and now Lima, Peru – for the last five years, so it isn't easy, but returning home it'll become something more regular.

James Seymour: I have never known a time when I didn't support Arsenal. From a very early age I apparently showed a likeness to the red JVC shirt. My uncle Gerald and grandad Percy jumped on this and I was indoctrinated in the Arsenal way. Fairly unremarkable other than the fact my dad Stuart is Spurs.

First Highbury match was a reserve game v Millwall, in 1992-93, when the murals were up behind both goals. My first team debut – again with uncle and grandad, plus Dad – was the 1-1 v Spurs (29/4/1995) with Ian Wright and Jurgen Klinsmann scoring.

Rhiannon Young: I was brought up in North Wales. My mother's father was an Arsenal fan and when my dad went to meet them grandad asked: "Do you know who I support?" When Dad replied "Arsenal", he asked how he knew. Dad pointed to the cannons by the TV!

My brothers, Aaron and Adrian, were Arsenal-crazy and I was always dressed in Arsenal shirts.

My brothers won a trip to Highbury by designing a cannon-shaped mascot after the club invited kids to design a club mascot. They came second to whoever designed Gunnersaurus!

Barry Davison: I got into football more seriously in 1994, just after USA hosted the World Cup tournament. Growing up in Deal, a small town in Kent, most of my friends and family supported Liverpool, Manchester United or Tottenham, so just to be different I choose Arsenal. That and the fact that I liked Ian Wright.

My first visit to Highbury didn't happen until a year later, when Arsenal signed Dennis Bergkamp from Inter Milan and the clubs played a pre-season friendly (10/8/1995). Not much to remember from the game – it was 0-0 – except Bergkamp and David Platt both making their debuts, while Paul Ince had just joined Inter from Manchester Utd, alongside an unknown youngster from Brazil called Roberto Carlos (wonder what happened to him). My trips to Arsenal were always with my non-football-supporting father Andrew, although later on he did grasp the history and ethos of the club.

Rob Macdonald: One of my best friends supported Arsenal and it felt like the right club for me. My dad Ronnie took me to my first match at Highbury, a 0-0 against Inter Milan (10/8/1995). Bergkamp and Platt were making their home debuts but I particularly remember Ian Wright hitting the bar twice. We watched from the North Bank seats and I always loved the atmosphere. After that we both became Arsenal members, and myself a Junior Gunner.

Daniel Marsh: I started supporting Arsenal because of my Nan, Mary Perry (nee Goldby), who passed last year (2019). She was from Hoxton/Shoreditch way and my great-grandad moved the family south of the river, to Peckham, in around 1939. All her brothers were Gooners and used to take her to Highbury – Jimmy Logie was a name I constantly heard growing up and her other favourites were Charlie George, Wrighty and Patrick Vieira.

First game for me was v Nottingham Forest (29/8/1995), Kevin Campbell's return to Highbury after being sold. A David Platt cracker in the Clock End and KC equalised for Forest in a 1-1 draw. I went with my stepdad Gary who didn't really care for football but took me after I continuously begged my mum Tracey to let me go.

Darell J. Philip: Growing up in a home where family members supported either Spurs or Liverpool, I was rather confused about which football team I should support. As most of my family supported Liverpool, I thought maybe I should support them.

That was until 1989, when I saw my first proper match on television, Liverpool v Arsenal at Anfield. I suddenly found myself being drawn to underdogs Arsenal and when Michael Thomas did the unthinkable, scoring in the last few seconds of the game to snatch the title away from Liverpool, I made my mind up that Arsenal was the team for me and I haven't looked back since.

My first memories of Highbury were during my time as a Junior Gunner, when I was chosen to be a member of the 1996-97 Ball Squad. It's difficult to explain the feelings of a young boy when you step out onto the hallowed Highbury turf for the first time. I was just awestruck.

Lorraine & Louise Haugh: We grew up in a house where two out of our three older brothers loved football and were mad Arsenal fans. Then there was the two of us, myself and my twin sister Louise, who hated everything to do with football.

I remember one summer we were all sitting around the kitchen table when our brother Paul said: "Yes, the football season starts soon." And our reaction was: "Oh, no." I think the amount of talk about Arsenal must have worn us down and eventually, in 1998, we asked our brother to take us to a game.

It was Arsenal v Port Vale in the FA Cup third round (3/1/1998), a sunny day and we sat in the North Bank. A boring game finished 0-0. But we both remember walking away from the ground and asking our brother when he would bring us back to see another match. From that day we were both hooked.

Roberto Puzzi: Growing up in Italy, I always loved English football but when I first visited London and Highbury I was as excited as a kid at the Luna Park. I remember everything from that day: it was Thierry Henry's first game in an Arsenal shirt, v Leicester City (7/8/1999).

I was there with my friend Matteo Tonna and we sat in the North Bank upper. I was impressed by the atmosphere around the Home of Football; all the street stalls, programme and fanzines sellers, this was what I was looking for and the right way to experience match day.

Edward Aiko'bua: I am a Ugandan cartoonist, born in 1984. I used to watch the English first division during the late 80s but mainly liked John Barnes (Liverpool). Then in the 90s, I fancied David Ginola (Tottenham), Ian Wright (Arsenal) and Eric Cantona (Man Utd); there was no team I supported besides Bayern Munich and Brazil but somehow I liked the JVC on Arsenal shirts. JVC is an electronics company with products in my country.

I loved playing football at school and near home but basketball legend Michael Jordan was my favourite sportsman; his athleticism was so inspirational that I followed his career through news coverage every week. However, when his second retirement was imminent, I decided to find another sportsman to follow with the same passion.

Arsenal's 2-0 victory over Newcastle United in the 1998 FA Cup Final enlightened me about the qualities of Emmanuel Petit and Patrick Vieira. I particularly liked their 'retreating defence' technique of winning the ball back. At the end of the game, I discovered that Ian Wright (an unused sub that day) was their team-mate . . . and so I never looked elsewhere again.

Tom Humphrey: My dad Gary is the reason I am an Arsenal fan. My full name is Thomas Charlie George Graham Humphrey (Michael Thomas, Charlie George and George Graham honoured in one name!).

Dad took me to all kinds of Arsenal games as a kid – from ladies, to youth and even celebrity XIs. My first visit to Highbury came in May 2000, a few months shy of my seventh birthday. Arsenal played Coventry City in the FA Youth Cup Final and my memories of that are cheering the youngsters' success like it was the first team and just falling in love with Highbury straight away. The place immediately felt like home to me and I was asking Dad to go back there ASAP.

Later that year he took me to two home first team games in back-to back weeks. In the first one we scraped past Southampton (2/12/2000) with a late Patrick Vieira winner (own-goal?) to beat them 1-0 and the following week I was treated to a 5-0 win over Newcastle

United (9/12/2000), a day that saw Ray Parlour bag a hat-trick as well as a goal each for Thierry Henry and Kanu.

Other than that fine memory, I remember eating too many sweets that day, causing me to be sick on the journey home!

George Pearson: Father Bill was (and still is but to a lesser extent) an avid Sunderland fan and having taken me to a few games at Roker Park when visiting family, he took me to see Arsenal v Sunderland at Highbury (30/12/2000).

I remember the smell of fried onions hitting me in the face as we emerged from Arsenal tube station and the buzz of many conversations as the crowd swept by. We were a bit early, so decided to walk around the stadium. I'd first seen the East Stand, with its red décor and massive Arsenal badges, the cannon and ARSENAL STADIUM written in huge letters just above it, but on match day it looked completely different.

All the people slowly piling into the gates, accompanied by this backdrop, was beautiful to me and I asked Dad to take me to as many games as we could following that game, just so I could see it again and again. At that age, I think I was probably more interested in the atmosphere surrounding the matches than the actual football itself.

I don't remember too much about the game, except we were winning and it finished 2-2 due to a Sunderland free-kick that went past Alex Manninger. The reason for my limited recollection was because of the position of our seats. Highbury had a few 'knock off' sections where the tickets were lower in price due to what they liked to call an 'obstructed view'. In this case, it was one of the poles holding up the roof of the stands and I could literally only see about a third of the pitch.

Andrew Stewart: Dad Derek and I remember that night at Old Trafford on May 8, 2002, when Arsenal needed a point against Man Utd to be champions. We were at home in Portrush, on the north coast of Ireland, watching the game on Sky. I was 16 at the time and can remember Sylvain Wiltord scoring that goal and Martin Tyler's commentary. Just, wow! . . . goosebumps is not the word.

The next day Dad handed me an envelope and said: "Happy early birthday." It was tickets to the 'coronation game' against Everton at Highbury (11/5/2002).

Filled with anticipation, once we landed at Luton airport on the Friday night I couldn't wait to walk around the stadium before going back to our hotel. I couldn't sleep with excitement.

On game day we met up with friends of my dad's who just flew over to join in the title celebrations. We went to the Blackstock bar, where there was a party atmosphere already, then to Highbury. I always loved the walk to the ground with the smell of burgers and onions filling the air. The sun was shining – Highbury had surely never looked better in all her glory, especially with the champions flags flying high.

Once inside the ground we got to our seats near the big screen in the Clock End. We won 4-3 and I can still see Thierry Henry's celebration, swinging his shirt above his head, the roar at the final whistle and then the trophy being lifted as Queen's *We Are the Champions* played. Tears of joy rolled down my face and I knew, there and then that day, that Arsenal were my team and I would support them come what may.

Sam Garrett: I was brought up by a family consisting of a divide – half supporting Arsenal, the other half supporting Chelsea. My household, though, was Arsenal and this was the team I was born into this world supporting.

I remember my first visit to Highbury as if it was yesterday. I was nine-years-old and saw the game v Bolton Wanderers (21/9/2002). Once I got on the tube, the excitement began to grow. I thought of all the memories I had witnessed from watching Arsenal at a young age on TV and this continued to increase my hunger to be there.

I emerged from Arsenal station, greeted by hundreds of Gooners in red and white along Gillespie Road, stalls for fans to buy merchandise from as an alternative to the club shops, the smell of fried onions and burgers wafting up the street – a smell we all are too familiar with in reference to our first experience football match. I looked to my left and started to walk and there was the famous North Bank filling the sky in front of me. I never forget my first glimpse of Highbury – it sent shivers down my spine and put butterflies in the stomach.

Despite this wonderful experience, I didn't go in to watch the game because I didn't have a ticket. Nonetheless, sitting outside the stadium was remarkable. Just to be there meant everything to me. I could hear the Arsenal crowd lifting every time we went on the attack in addition to the sound of thousands of seats lifting up – as they do whenever we go close to scoring. Out of everything on that day though, the best was yet to come.

As the game continued to unravel, I took a walk up to the marble halls and noticed a gate to the left which would be the entrance to the Clock End. I wish camera phones had existed back then, because what I saw was amazing. As a kid, I always played in goal and loved every minute of it – making a top drawer save brought me great satisfaction. After all, I was always one of the tallest in the class at school, so I was the right height for a keeper.

I approached the gate and peered through the gap to notice my all-time favourite goalkeeper, David Seaman, in between the sticks at the Clock End. This was all I could see but, for me, this was just the beginning of my Highbury memories. Thankfully, Kanu grabbed us a late winner in a frustrating game which saw Thierry Henry's opener cancelled out by Gareth Farrelly's equaliser that left Seaman blushing following his 47th minute blunder.

Four months later, I returned to Highbury for Arsenal v Farnborough Town in the FA Cup fourth round (25/1/2003). This time, I had a ticket which I treasured like a Willy Wonka Golden Ticket. Due to having two other siblings, money was tight, so getting to games wasn't always possible. I started off the day by arriving at the marble halls early to ensure I was at the front of the crowd to see the Arsenal team disembark from the coach and enter the stadium. This was magical and something I miss dearly since we moved around the corner to The Emirates. I saw Thierry Henry, Robert Pires, Freddie Ljungberg, Dennis Bergkamp, Sol Campbell, Arsène Wenger and many more, all up close in the flesh, which for me was the cherry on the cake. These were all people I looked up to as a young fan and to see this happen before my very eyes was incredibly exciting. (Unfortunately, Henry was given the weekend off from playing but still came to the game.)

With the players and staff now inside the stadium, I went towards the North Bank turnstiles. My heart began to beat faster and faster until the moment I had entered the stadium concourse. To be inside Highbury was a dream come true. My seat was in the North Bank upper, so a walk up the spiral staircases and taking in the views across London was a bonus. This was the moment every young fan experiences – entering through the walk-way into the stadium. Right in front of me was the hallowed Highbury turf. It was bright green and glistened in the sunlight. It had always been the best surface in the top flight.

I took my seat and looked around me to see where 35,000-plus other fans would soon be. I could see the Clock End, the West and East Stands, and the Arsenal players training ahead of the game. I was in my element and it is a breathtaking experience for any fan about to watch his or her first live game. This was a theatre of dreams and I cherished every second of being there.

I really had fallen in love with Arsenal Football Club and Highbury. Watching on TV previously was completely different to actually being there. In addition, this was two days after my 10th birthday and what a treat it truly was. I was blessed with a 5-1 scoreline – birthday boy Francis Jeffers netted two goals, while Sol Campbell, Lauren and the 66th minute substitute, Dennis Bergkamp, were also on the score-sheet. When the Iceman's goal went in, the crowd roared even more loudly simply because of his legendary status.

A male streaker then entered the pitch wearing just a pair of shoes and I remember seeing the stewards trying to tackle him to the ground. Why someone would discard all their clothes on a freezing cold Saturday afternoon in January is crazy. But it was an action-packed first Highbury game for me and, to this day, I still recall very fondly.

Dan Hill: I became an Arsenal supporter at the age of six. I was no doubt influenced by my uncle Gary and step-grandad Ron, who were Arsenal fans, and I was also attracted by the quality of football the team played at the time (1997-98 season), and from then on I was hooked. Sadly, because money was tight, it took quite a while before I attended my first game.

My first match was an FA Cup third round tie v Stoke City (9/1/2005), who were in the Championship at the time, aged 13. It was the season that we went on to win the Cup against Manchester Utd on penalties.

I remember stepping out of Arsenal tube station and smelling the hot food stands and seeing the stall-holders selling t-shirts. We made our way to the East Stand and watched the team arrive before heading into the ground. Once inside, I went to the front of the stand and remember being in awe of the players and the stadium. One memorable moment was during the warm-up, when a poor woman in the North Bank was hit in the face by a shot from Robin Van Persie, which knocked her glasses off. A few stewards rushed over to attend to her, although luckily she was all right.

Despite going 1-0 down before half-time, we fought back to win 2-1. Jose Antonio Reyes equalised and then when Van Persie sealed the win with 20 minutes to go, it prompted chants of 'You're not singing anymore' directed at Stoke fans in the Clock End.

Harry Clowser: Arsenal goes back to my great-grandad, so I didn't have much choice. I only went to one game at Highbury. It was midway through the last season at the ground, I was six-years-old and we beat Portsmouth 4-0 (28/12/2005) with two goals from Thierry Henry and one each by Dennis Bergkamp and Jose Antonio Reyes. I don't remember much apart from it being very cold and wondering why the ref was being called a w*****. But I was so happy just to have been there.

Sandra Thulambo: I went to visit my cousin Samalani Kazembe, who's an Arsenal supporter. I found him watching Arsenal v Liverpool (12/3/2006) on telly and Gunners won 2-1. I've been hooked ever since.

Looking towards the North and West Stands.

From the upper tier of the North Stand.

A much older and more elevated view from above the Clock End terracing.

ARSENAL FOOTBALL CLUB LTD.

No 10128

To be retained.

ARSENAL STADIUM,
HIGHBURY, N.5.

Friendly Match.

ARSENAL v. SPARTAK

TUESDAY, 9th NOVEMBER, 1954
Gates open 5.30 p.m.   Kick-off 7.30 p.m.
BY FLOODLIGHT.
It is in your interest to be at the Stadium early.

GILLESPIE ROAD
(OPPOSITE ARSENAL STATION)

WEST ENCLOSURE (STANDING)

TURNSTILE F
ADMISSION 5/- (including Tax)

Intact when presented at Turnstile.

ARSENAL FOOTBALL CLUB, Ltd.
This portion to be retained.

129

ARSENAL STADIUM,
HIGHBURY, N.5.

ROUND **3**

F.A. CHALLENGE CUP COMP.
SAT., 7th JAN., 1956.
IF DRAWN AWAY, VALID
FOR A RE-PLAY (For Date
and Kick-off see Press).

EAST STAND
AVENELL ROAD.
(See Map on back)

RESERVED SEAT 8/6 (including Tax)	BLOCK ROW SEAT	F E 160

ARSENAL FOOTBALL CLUB, Ltd.
This portion to be retained.

383

ARSENAL STADIUM,
HIGHBURY, N.5.

ENGLAND v. YOUNG ENGLAND

FRIDAY, 1st MAY, 1959
Kick off 7.30 p.m.

EAST STAND
AVENELL ROAD.
(See Map on back)

RESERVED SEAT 10/6	BLOCK ROW SEAT	F N

13

No 28

ARSENAL
v.
LIVERPOOL
SATURDAY, JANUARY 8th,

10/-

AVENELL ROAD

LOWER TIE
SEATING

...be retained throughout
...ced for inspection on

Arsenal   **CHAMPIONS**

Barclays Premiership

Arsenal v Middlesbrough

22 Aug, 2004 Kick Off 16:05

RTH BANK LOWER TIER

Block	Row	Seat	
3	M	67	£42.50

1P69538 Italy SC   O2

TO BE RETAINED

ARSENAL V RED STAR BELGRADE

U.E.F.A. CUP K.O. 7-30 PM.

BLOCK A EAST STND B/A 2

ROW SEAT

Y 21 £2.00 141110758

Arsenal
Football Club Limited

TICKET AND MATCH
INFORMATION
Telephone 01-359 0131
(24 HOUR SERVICE)

ARSENAL STADIUM HIGHBURY N5 1BU

Nº 3059

ARSENAL v.
LIVERPOOL

SATURDAY, FEBRUARY 1st, 1975

LOWER TIER SEATING £1.00
WEST STAND Including VAT

This voucher should be retained throughout the match
and must be produced for inspection on demand.
If today's Match is not played, this voucher must be
returned to the Box Office by post together with
addressed envelope, and the appropriate refund will
be made.

No refunds will be made after May 31st next, following
the date of the postponed game.

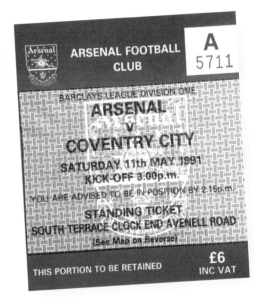

ARSENAL FOOTBALL
CLUB

A 5711

BARCLAYS LEAGUE DIVISION ONE

ARSENAL
v
COVENTRY CITY

SATURDAY 11th MAY 1991
KICK-OFF 3.00p.m.

YOU ARE ADVISED TO BE IN POSITION BY 2.15p.m.

STANDING TICKET
SOUTH TERRACE CLOCK END AVENELL ROAD
(See Map on Reverse)

THIS PORTION TO BE RETAINED

£6
INC VAT

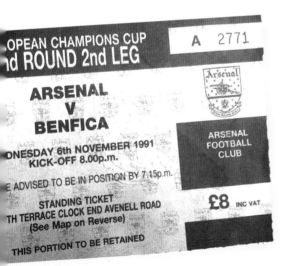

OPEAN CHAMPIONS CUP

A 2771

1d ROUND 2nd LEG

ARSENAL
V
BENFICA

DNESDAY 6th NOVEMBER 1991
KICK-OFF 8.00p.m.

E ADVISED TO BE IN POSITION BY 7.15p.m.

ARSENAL
FOOTBALL
CLUB

STANDING TICKET
TH TERRACE CLOCK END AVENELL ROAD
(See Map on Reverse)

£8 INC VAT

THIS PORTION TO BE RETAINED

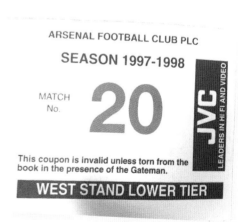

ARSENAL FOOTBALL CLUB PLC

SEASON 1997-1998

MATCH
No.

20

JVC
LEADERS IN HI FI AND VIDEO

This coupon is invalid unless torn from the
book in the presence of the Gateman.

WEST STAND LOWER TIER

JUNIOR GUNNERS

SEASON 1993·94

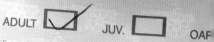

PEPSI JUNIOR GUNN
FAMILY ENCLOSUR

MEMBERSHIP CA
1994-199!

ADULT [✓] JUV. [ ] OAP

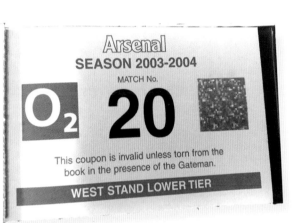

Arsenal

SEASON 2003-2004

MATCH No.

O₂ **20**

This coupon is invalid unless torn from the
book in the presence of the Gateman.

WEST STAND LOWER TIER

1

Nº 24

ARSENAL FOOTBALL CLUB, LTD
Arsenal Stadium, Highbury, London, N5 1B
Secretary: K. J. FRIAR

ARSENAL
v
WEST HAM UNITED
26 SEPT

Row....B........   Seat......64

ADMIT TO PRESS STAND
Entrance at Press Entrance in Avenell Road

ARSENAL STADIUM
HIGHBURY, N5 1BU

4 FEB 1989

EAST STAND
AVENELL ROAD
(See Map on back)

BLOCK *B*

GUEST ROW *F*

TICKET SEAT *57*

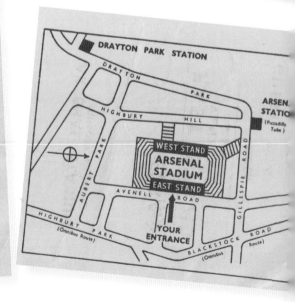

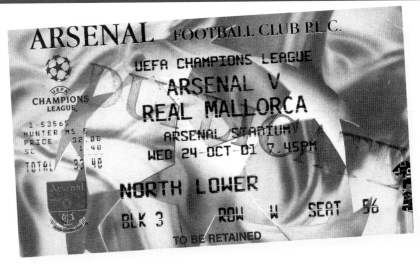

ARSENAL FOOTBALL CLUB P.L.C.
UEFA CHAMPIONS LEAGUE
ARSENAL V
REAL MALLORCA
ARSENAL STADIUM
WED 24-OCT-01 7.45PM

NORTH LOWER

BLK 3   ROW W   SEAT 96
TO BE RETAINED

Arsenal   uefa·com
V
PSV EINDHOVEN
TUE 14-SEP-04 K/O 19:45
WEST LOWER   O
BLOCK ROW SEAT PRICE
O   26   38   37.70

4-12622   REDWOOD/MR C

TO BE RETAINED

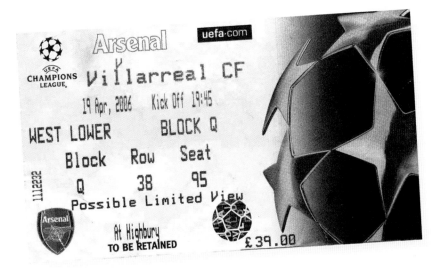

Arsenal   uefa·com
V
Villarreal CF
19 Apr, 2006   Kick Off 19:45
WEST LOWER   BLOCK Q
Block   Row   Seat
Q   38   95
Possible Limited View
At Highbury
TO BE RETAINED   £39.00

2 ROUTINES & RITUALS

FOR most, visiting Highbury wasn't just about watching a game of football. It goes much deeper than that. It was also a good opportunity to enjoy quality time and share a common bond with family and strangers, many of whom became life-long friends.

Whether it was pre-match pints in the local pubs or a fry-up in a favourite café you routinely frequented; the superstitions you followed outside and inside the stadium; or even the familiar journey by road, train or bus to that grand old stadium itself, supporters' personal rituals were as much a part of the match day experience as the 90-odd minutes sandwiched in between.

Q: Describe any rituals that you followed, or a favourite haunt that you usually visited on your way to or from Highbury?

Graham Lister: A somewhat nomadic existence meant that even when pre-match rituals looked like becoming established, they rarely had chance to set in stone. Travelling by train, car or tube to Highbury from, at various periods, Slough, Camberley, Sheffield, London or – since 1993 – Wetherby in Yorkshire, the one consistent pattern, when time allowed, was browsing the various stalls and garden walls in Gillespie Road displaying books, old programmes, photos and other unofficial Arsenal merchandise for some hitherto elusive gem of Gunners memorabilia.

Chris Welstead: In my adult years, the pre-match ritual would be to meet up at my mum's house in Hornsey for a bite to eat before leaving with my brother-in-law Tim, my nephew Richard and my younger son Nick. We would leave the house at around 2.00pm, catch a bus to Finsbury Park and then stroll down to the ground. In the latter years, evening matches would be preceded by a meal in the Arsenal Cafe in Blackstock Road. They had (and probably still do) the most enormous omelettes.

Tony Fisher: The Arsenal cafe in Blackstock Road became the must go-to for a pre-match fry-up in later years. Always had to use the same turnstile – fifth from the end on the right-hand side of the East Stand under the sign 'Blocks'.

Tony Porter: Our ritual was always . . . Liverpool Street (we lived in Essex), Circle line to Moorgate, Northern line to Drayton Park. A blind man used to sell matches on the corner of Aubert Park. At Christmas we would give him something – I probably would have given him a coin each time but begging was frowned upon.

Bernard Kiernan: We actually moved up to Highbury in 1961, when I was 12-years-old. Our old house at 124 Drayton Park was less than five minutes from Highbury Stadium and just around the corner from Arsenal tube station and, in fact, is now directly opposite The Emirates Stadium. Sadly, we moved away from Highbury to south London (ugh) in 1965. No local pre-match rituals to share.

Richard (Dickie) Boyes: I would have my hair cut at my barber in Hoxton, then catch the number 611 trolley bus at New North Road and get off at Highbury Corner, where I would meet my mates. We'd walk to the stadium, pay at the turnstiles and then stand in the same position at every game – on the South Bank behind the goal, a third of the way up. We knew everyone around us because they also stood in the same place come rain, snow or fog.

Jeff Owens: Pre-match rituals varied over the years. I don't recall any from my earliest visits but once I started work, I'd often rendezvous with friends in The Cock outside

Highbury & Islington station before evening matches. When I started taking my own children to matches, we'd visit the sweet seller's stall in Gillespie Road.

David Roche: I used to go straight to the match as a boy but when I got older I used many pubs in Highbury and Finsbury Park, including the George Robey, Plimsoll Arms and Bank of Friendship.

Dave Randall: Would park up by Drayton Park Library, then make our way to the Benwell Arms and off to the game. The chip shop on the corner would be a regular pre-match meal. Used to bump into Gary and Janet, who still go now, and Chris Hudson.

Jeremy Doltis: A group of us 16-year-olds, including Jem Dee, Andrew Beins and Ron Alonee, and later on Steve Maxwell and Howard, would all go for a fry-up in Blackstock Road and a drink at the Kings Head on the corner.

John Blair: Early years it was always pre-match fish 'n' chips at the Southgate Fish Bar.

Double fever at the local newsagent in 1971.

Keith English: When I was older I would meet my friends in the Robin Hood pub in Green Lanes before walking to the ground.

Lee Pritchett: My dad, John, and uncles would always have a beer in the supporters' bar in Gillespie Road and maybe pop in the club shop to see Jack Kelsey. But at 17, my only ritual was going in the Arsenal Tavern to watch the strippers before the game with my mate, Perry Griffin!

Peter Coombs: In the early years, coming out of the tube station before going into the North Bank, there was a little shop in one of the terraced houses, where I would buy a little white bag of Percy Dalton monkey nuts (cheaper than buying them from the sellers hawking them around the North Bank). At full-time you would be crunching your way out over the empty shells left on the terrace.

Peter Lewis: Always got the 253 bus from Bethnal Green to Finsbury Park and bought the evening paper on the way home to find out the other classified results in the 'stop press'.

John Skinner: Always wore an Arsenal shirt and used to go to Casey Jones burger bar at Victoria station.

Tony Bateman: No rituals but once I reached drinking age, I started going in The Gunners pub before games but later moved to The Blackstock.

Neil Payne: Typically over the years, when attending games with mates and in latter years with my dad, we were very much in the 'game only' contingent. Very rarely would we go for a drink before the match. Without fail, and no matter how big the attendance, we always seemed to find a car parking spot in the same area, Baalbec Road, just off Highbury Grove. From there it was just a short walk through Highbury Fields onwards towards Aubert Park before hitting Avenell Road. For standing in the Clock End, which I did in later years before all-seater stadia, it was perfect.

Mike Slaughter: As a kid I used to browse all the programme stalls and then head towards the main entrance to try and get some autographs. From 1988 onwards, I used to sell The Gooner fanzine before most games. It was then that I realised I had become part of fans' rituals. Many would say: "I always buy it from you" and one fan, in particular, would always sit near me, on the wall in Gillespie Road, eat his sausage and chips, drink his can of Coke and then finally come over to buy the fanzine. He did this for many years. He still goes to games and although we know each other to nod to, we have never spoken. However, I'm sure he will read this and realise who I am referring to.

Bryan Austin: Before every game we used to go to the same chicken shop in Blackstock Road (opposite Gunners Tavern) and, afterwards, would walk back to the train station along the same road.

Ian Tredgett: For a self-confessed creature of habit, it's surprising but I didn't really have any pre-match rituals. I guess as I grew up, left home, went to university, began working, etc, it meant my commute to the ground took different routes. Invariably, Finsbury Park was a more convenient station for my journey and I remember a photographic shop we used to walk past that had a (clearly posed for) portrait of John Devine. He wasn't in playing kit and it remained in the window long after he'd left us. It always struck me as a bit strange.

John Morley: As a kid attending with my dad, we always took the tube in those days to Drayton Park on the Northern Line, so as to avoid the crowds at Arsenal station. My big treat during the game was getting a bag of Percy Dalton's roasted peanuts (sixpence a bag). Dad always sat me up on the same crush barrier in the Clock End, where I could see all the action.

Barry Hughes: After becoming a ticket registration scheme member at Highbury in the 90s, my regular route to the game was via Finsbury Park tube. I would then walk up St Thomas's Road (while always thinking of Michael Thomas' goal at Anfield) and grab a burger from one of the fast food stalls.

Yasir Matloub: I used to go on the train to London Paddington, then take the underground to the Twelve Pins pub near Finsbury Park. Sometimes I used to go to the Bank of Friendship at the end of Gillespie Road. I also went to the Arsenal Football Supporters' Club and one of the shrewdest things I ever did was to become a life member of AFSC for a mere £25. The one and only Barry Baker was the cornerstone of the supporters' club and you would always find him at the AFSC, 154 St Thomas's Road.

I always liked the West upper and usually at 2.00pm, I used to buy two pints of lager in the stadium (drinking alcohol and smoking were allowed then). I liked this ritual and still miss it. Those days will never return.

Paul Manel: From the late 80s onwards, the ritual was always the same. Meet pre-match at the Plimsoll Arms. We all knew instinctively to make our way to The Plim whether it was Stevie P, Dino, Bobster, Donalan or any of the other boys. Highbury was a five-minute walk from the Plimsoll Arms. I used to love the walk down St Thomas's Road – you could see the back of the North Bank just waiting for you.

Alan Thompsett: I always bought two copies of the official programme from the first seller I encountered. I like to have one to read at the match and on the journey home, and the other to be kept nice and clean.

Andrew Whitnall: When I started going to games by myself I would always try and get up to Highbury nice and early to grab the same parking space in Highbury Quadrant – it was a bad start to the day if someone else had taken it! I always bought a programme from the first seller I saw and got a large frankfurter hot dog from the stall in front of the East Stand. Always used the same turnstile and grabbed my spot on the North Bank – near the column holding up the roof, just behind the goal on the east side.

Craig Pottage: Started off at the The Plimsoll Arms, then The Silver Bullet (opp Finsbury Park). The locals were always in there playing dominoes and getting very fraught with each other. It wasn't uncommon to see bar stools flying around the front bar. I then moved on to the Finsbury Park Tavern, Highbury Barn, Arsenal Tavern and Kings Head – our local when Highbury closed.

Derek Barclay: In the early 70s we used to get to Highbury so early that we were first onto the North Bank at 12.30pm. And then we'd position ourselves right behind the goal, so really only saw what happened at that end! As a grown-up, my routine was very different – one

Pre-match in Avenell Road, 1971.

season (1987-88) I recall I went to every game and never once saw kick-off because we'd stay drinking in the Highbury Barn as late as humanly possible.

Gary Jones: Turn left outside tube station, grab a bag of chips and then walk to The Woodbine pub or The Gunners bar, browsing the programme stalls en route.

George Lampshire: In my early years, when Dad used to take me with uncle Terry, it would always be the same routine. Dad would make up some tale as to why he couldn't take me, then about three hours before kick-off, with me disappointed, he'd say: "Grab ya scarf" and we'd be off.

After parking on the stadium side of Blackstock Road, Dad would grab me by the arm and tell me to "dodge the cracks" around the pavement slabs as I tried to keep up with him.

Once inside, we'd always head for a spot on the North Bank directly above the central walkway, so I could see. Dad would wait until I wasn't paying attention on the tunnel and say: "Here they come", leading me to spin around towards the tunnel with the old man laughing "got ya!". He 'got' me every week.

He'd also light a cigarette bang on kick-off and tell me we'd score before he had finished it. He would always buy a bag of roasted peanuts from the guy that used to roam the North Bank and by half-time I'd have a hoodie full of shells.

Really didn't have too many superstitions as a kid, they developed as I got older. If we were going for a trophy, I'd always repeat the same things I'd done prior to the last win, like walk home from work the same way. In 1998, when we were going for the League and Cup Double, I used to climb out the passenger side of the car, because the day we beat Man U away, I'd parked in a tight spot and the only way out was to climb over. So every game day until we'd won the title, I'd clamber over the handbrake to get out.

One thing above all was what happened in 1989. I'd broken my collarbone in September and started shift work, so had to take every opportunity to get to games after missing most of the first half of the season. Each time I did, we never won. The only game I watched us

win at Highbury that year was the 2-0 Tuesday night friendly victory v France (14/2/1989). I went to Aston Villa, Southampton, Sheff Wed, West Ham (FA Cup), Millwall, Nottm Forest, Charlton . . . and not seen us win one of them.

As our form dipped and Liverpool caught us, I decided I was a jinx and watched games on TV. My mates convinced me I was being stupid and so I went to Derby at home (13/5/1989). Another loss!

For the last home game of the season, v Wimbledon (17/5/1989), I was again persuaded to go by my friend Phil. I managed to climb onto the North Bank/East Stand corner toilets to watch the 2-2 draw. I was convinced it was me that was the problem.

The weekend before Anfield, the Michael Watson-Nigel Benn Commonwealth

Middleweight title fight was held in Finsbury Park. I was stewarding there, as my buddy Wesley had family in the Benn camp. Some Arsenal players were at the fight and in the VIP section I managed to tread on Mickey Thomas' right foot.

That was it. Despite possessing a ticket for Liverpool away that I'd retained from the postponed game in April, I was too much of a risk and decided not to go. I knew if I went I'd be the jinx to cost us and I'd never forgive myself. So although many Gooners claim to have been at Anfield to see Thomas score our winner on May 26, I'm one that should have been there too . . . but wasn't.

But that superstition of being a jinx paid off, and I felt like I'd played my part in our championship win by not going.

John Hilditch: We lived next door to The Brewery Tap on Holloway Road (now called The Lamb), so my Old Man would naturally take me in there. The landlord, 'Big' John Earley, would always fire a bag of Golden Wonder over the bar for me. Then we'd walk down to the junction of Drayton Park, into Burt's Café. Burt was proper old school, about two inches

of fag ash drooping from his Senior Service as he turned the bacon and fried bread below. After that, we'd walk down Drayton Park past the Drayton Park Hotel and the away coaches. Once we'd get into the ground, we'd pop into the bar under the West lower. It was a proper little pub with a commissionaire on the door.

Kelvin Meadows: We drank in many pubs around the ground: The Gunners, Arsenal Tavern, Plimsoll Arms, before eventually settling on The Montague (Benwell Road) in the 70s. We then moved to the Holloway Tavern which, was next door to the station back then, and drank there for a few years. By that time we'd progressed to the Clock End and approaching the ground from Holloway Road had the added excitement of bumping into the opposition. Different times.

We then went to The George in the 80s, until '91 when we moved to The Moynihan. When that shut we went over to Blackstock Road and drank in T-Birds for a few years.

Paul Hemming: After my dad died, different uncles took me and we always had fish 'n' chips while 'letting the crowd die down' in a cafe between the Arsenal Tavern and The Woodbine on Blackstock Road. One uncle always sat in the West lower because his dad had stood there when it was terracing and he liked to be opposite the tunnel. Another came up from Old Street on the bus and we'd pop in the Highbury Barn.

Started going with mates, as opposed to family, from about 1987. You could get served in the Tavern under age. We drank regularly at the Woodbine in the early-to-mid 90s, plus the Queens, Wig 'n' Gown, the Bailey, the George until recently. I've always liked to visit a few pubs. Sometimes I/ we'll drink at Finsbury Park or Upper Street, depends on the fixture and the company, and have a bit of a tour round.

Robert Grainger: Spent many years, pre-match, in the Arsenal Tavern, where I met the same friends for 15 years or so. We'd grab a burger from a box outside the East Stand.

Stephen Simson: Never really went to any places before a game, as I lived not far from the stadium. But one ritual I had during the game was to never let go of the crush barrier and, somewhat bizarrely, my left foot had to be just over the step until we scored! I don't know how this became a ritual but it stayed with me until we went all-seater.

Tom Eldridge: We lived, and still do, in South-West London, so Dad used to drive up to Highbury. We would go over Hammersmith Bridge, along the Westway and then take Euston Road past King's Cross, along Pentonville Road. We would park at the north end of Liverpool Road before the short walk to one of the chip shops on Holloway Road.

After the game we used to walk back to the car as fast as we could to listen to the five o'clock football results on the radio. I loved that. We did that pilgrimage for years.

Tony Daisley: In my early Highbury years, I went first to The Silver Bullet, opposite Finsbury Park. I then gravitated to The Bank of Friendship with fellow supporters, Ray Mallet and Tony Wills. In later years, my daughter Nicola and I always went to the little Greek/Turkish café on Seven Sisters Road, where we had our usual order of ham, egg and chips.

James Smither: I've never really been a big pre-game eater or drinker – I simply used to get too nervous as a younger fan during the 1990s to enjoy either activity properly, and would instead choose to arrive at the stadium quite early most match days, watch the coaches (and the odd off-duty player or glamorous partner) arrive at the Marble Halls before taking my seat at least an hour before kick-off, reading the programme and eating a pre-prepared sandwich or two waiting for the team to come out and warm up.

Once I got my season ticket next to a university friend in the East lower in 2000, things became a bit more settled and a Turkish-run café on Blackstock Road became the preferred pre-match haunt before that fantastic walk past the Gunners pub down Elwood Street, with the magnificent new North Bank rising above the terraced houses and the classic Art Deco exterior of the East Stand, which never failed to lift the spirits.

Around the same time, I got to know a well-connected Arsenal-supporting journalist through an old school friend and would from time to time be invited to join them at a post-match table of Highbury beat regulars at San Daniele, an otherwise unobtrusive-looking Italian restaurant on the Blackstock Road that just happened to be the preferred post-match dining location of Arsenal grandees. I was generally a little too tongue-tied and overawed (by which I mean, utterly unable to maintain my composure in the presence of my heroes) to make the most of the star-gazing opportunity this offered. Among the regular standing ovations offered to Arsène and his players when they took their seats after a successful evening's work, particular experiences I did enjoy were Liam Brady resting his hand on my shoulder while regaling the table with his view of the night's Champions League encounter, holding the bathroom door open for an unimpeachably polite Gilberto Silva, and being seated next to former S Club 7 member (and perennial high-placer in FHM's Top-100 Sexiest Ladies, and Arsenal fan) Rachel Stevens, who was at the time dating David Dein's son Darren, for one memorable pizza dinner.

Needless to say we barely exchanged a word all evening but that wasn't necessarily the version I regaled friends with afterwards.

John Lawlor: Rituals varied, although it was always the same train up from Dover, Kent and familiar route on the underground. I always wore my scarf from 1982. In later times, when I lived in London, I always wore the latest home shirt with the same jumper underneath, left home at the same time, took the same underground route and had a pint in The Gunners pub.

David McConachie: Dad and I would always go for a fry-up at a Turkish café a couple of doors down from the BlackStock pub.

Gary Biggs: Always got the tube to Finsbury Park. Couple of jars in the Twelve Pins, walk down to the burger bar outside the Auld Triangle, then head inside for a couple more jars.

Guy Thompson: When I was younger I always got off the tube at Arsenal, went and had a look at the front of the stadium, then grabbed a burger and a programme and sat down with my back against the wall at the North Bank entrance on Gillespie Road. About TWO HOURS before they opened the gates.

Ian Mills: Back in the 1990s I used to visit The Kings Stores at Spitalfields, where a few pints of Heineken Export and an individual Pizza Hut pizza were consumed on the premises (the pub had a small Pizza Hut on site) with my fellow Gooners, Belch and Bart.

As for a ritual, I used to visit the same hot dog stand, directly opposite the entrance to the North Bank. However, after a series of disappointing draws, I stopped going there and, guess what, we started winning again. But I missed the hot dogs so much, I sometimes visited after the game, safe in the knowledge that the three points were in the bag.

Marvin Berglas: As the football business evolved, match day hospitality became more

and more important and from 1993 onwards I became the first resident magician in the Premier League, performing magic to the VIPs and sponsors before each match in The Mezzanine in the South Stand.

There was a three-course meal with full entertainment and an interview with a past legend – usually Charlie George. Different celebrity guests appeared, including comedians such as Frank Carson, Rory McGrath and Matt Lucas (all Arsenal supporters). Me and my team would perform close-up magic which proved popular with the regulars, including Laurence Marks and Maurice Gran (co-writers of the BBC1

TV sitcom Birds of a Feather). It was a great atmosphere and the place to be.

Many of the players would pop their head in after the game on their way to the players' lounge next door. It was where I first got to meet my now good friend David Dein who was fascinated with magic.

Neil Davies: We had a couple of rituals. For a few perfect seasons, Dad, Grandad and I made the pilgrimage to the glorious old ground: three generations of Arsenal supporters, together. The earliest was to visit a Turkish restaurant on Blackstock Road called 'The Dream Restaurant'. We'd go in for a quick bite but the owners were all mad Arsenal season ticket holders, so they'd be urging us to hurry up and finish our kebabs so they could shut up shop and get to the game. The talk would be of the game: who had been picked? Who was injured? How are Arsenal going to contrive to ruin another perfectly good weekend?

A little later, we took to parking in Drayton Park Road and visiting the burger van outside the Drayton Park pub. Well, when I say we, I mean me. Being the lad, I got the gig of running to the van in all weathers and ordering up three burgers, all laden with sweet, sticky onions. We'd then stink out the interior of Dad's Sierra and make predictions for the game. Grandad and I would predict a win but Dad, ever the realist, would predict a score draw at best.

Stuart Pierce: Quality Fish Bar in Finsbury Park for our usual saveloy, chips and can of Coke. I remember Bolton Wanderers fans invading the place for the FA Cup match (Feb 1994), all asking for chips, mushy peas and curry sauce.

Roberto Puzzi: It is not easy to support Arsenal living in Italy and it is difficult to have some pre-match rituals. But when I come over, usually two or three times a year, I always try to meet all my friends over there, including Les, Andrew, Leonard, Kevin, Ian, Ben, John and many others. A brief chat with them makes me feel like a season ticket holder who can enjoy pre-match every 15 days. Unfortunately, it is not the same feeling after the match when I head to the airport.

Michael Cherrington: Always get off the tube at Finsbury Park, buy a programme from the seller outside the shop and walk down St Thomas' Road towards Highbury.

Kayne Goddard-Knell: Always go to the pin badge stalls.

Ben Sharpe: Ever since I first started going to Highbury, I always went into The Workman's Café on Blackstock Road, Finsbury Park for breakfast. I remember going in there in my teenage years to have double of everything on my breakfast with a drink and it would cost £5.00 Bargain! It was such a ritual that, without fail, I would go into autopilot, park in Queen's Road (off Blackstock Road) and walk round to the café.

Tom Humphrey: Me and my dad (and sometimes my brother Liam too – yes, he's also named after an Arsenal legend) had a fairly routine pre-match ritual. We'd either drive to Cockfosters station and catch the tube from there or catch the train to Waterloo and connect to Arsenal/Finsbury Park by tube. When we arrived at Highbury, we'd always buy a couple of programmes, Dad would meet up with friends that he only ever saw at Arsenal and he would buy me a bag of sweets from the stalls outside the ground. We normally won during that era, so I guess it was fairly lucky!

Andrew Peters: Before evening games, Dad and I went to the Greasy Spoon, which is now situated very near the East Stand Bridge at The Ems. Not much in the way of pre-game rituals but we did enjoy a bagel from the great kiosk in the West upper concourse. My enduring memory will be the smell of cigar smoke that hit you when you reached the top of the stairs. To this day, when I smell cigar smoke, it takes me straight back to that Highbury concourse.

70

Match day pubs, past and present

The Arsenal Tavern: 175 Blackstock Road, Finsbury Park, N4 2JS.

Arsenal Football Supporters' Club: 154 St Thomas's Road, Finsbury Park, N4 2QP.

Bank of Friendship: 226 Blackstock Road, Highbury, N5 1EA.

Benwell Arms: 40 Benwell Road, Holloway, N7 7BA.

The BlackStock: 284 Seven Sisters Road, Finsbury Park, N4 2HY.#

The Drayton Park: 66 Drayton Park, N5 1ND.

The Highbury Brewery Tap: 54 Holloway Road, Islington, N7 (last changed its name to The Lamb in 2012)

The Gunners: 204 Blackstock Road, Highbury, N5 1EN.

The Highbury Barn Tavern: 26 Highbury Park, Highbury East, N5 2AB.

The Holloway Tavern:

Kings Head: 126 Blackstock Road, Finsbury Park, N4 2DR.

The Montague Arms: 40 Benwell Road, N7 7BE (closed in 2008 for residential use).

The Park Tavern: 164 Tollington Park, Finsbury Park, N4 3AD.

The Plimsoll Arms: 52 St Thomas Road, Finsbury Park, N4 (changed to The Auld Triangle, 2011)

The Silver Bullet: 4-5 Station Place, Finsbury Park, N4 2DH (closed in June 2016).

The Sir George Robey: 240 Seven Sisters Road, Finsbury Park (changed to The Powerhaus, then The Robey, before closing in 2004).

The Famous Cock Tavern: 259 Upper Street, Highbury, N1 1RU.

The Twelve Pins: 263 Seven Sisters Road, Finsbury Park, N4 2DE.

The Woodbine: 215 Blackstock Road, Highbury East, N5 2LL.

**Photos
MASAHIDE
TOMIKOSHI**

73

3 MEMORABLE MATCHES AND MOMENTS

O VER the years there have been many classic and memorable matches at Highbury, some involving triumphant victories for Arsenal, others notable for crushing defeats.

From the unforgettable European Fairs Cup Final victory over Anderlecht in 1970 and Ian Wright's hat-trick before the North Bank terrace was demolished in 1992, to the epic 4-0 Premier League championship-clinching mastery of Everton by *The Invincibles in 2004* and Cup victories over Liverpool and Manchester Utd, there have been innumerable special occasions to savour.

Sometimes, however, it's the finer details, quirky recollections and amusing anecdotes surrounding a match that stick in the memory as much as the football itself.

What about that afternoon in 1966, when little more than 4,500 hardy souls turned up to see Leeds United amid threats of a supporters' boycott, George Eastham hurrying from a local betting shop, the fan who got off a stretcher to see Gunners win their first European trophy, Sammy Nelson dropping his shorts in front of the North Bank, TV pundit Jimmy Hill taking over as linesman, a kick in the head from an Arsenal legend, crowd violence in the dark days of hooliganism, a chat with the manager on the way to the tube station, post-match kisses from Thierry Henry . . . our contributors have seen it all.

Q: What stands out as your most vivid memory from a game at Highbury? It could be an unusual incident, or something bizarre, amusing or controversial.

Tony Fisher: Funny incident. Aged 10, arriving for a Christmas game with rosette, scarf and rattle for an afternoon fixture, only to end up in tears outside as it had kicked-off at 11 o'clock! It must have been v Blackpool (28/12/1953), as I know I had wanted to see Stanley Matthews.

Richard Boyes: In the mid-1950s Joe Mercer was our captain in the twilight of his career. We had bought him from Everton when we were at our lowest ebb just after the war and were nearly relegated. He led us to the league title in 1948 and 1953 and the FA Cup in 1950.

We were playing at home v Liverpool (10/4/1954) and our left-back, a local lad named Joe Wade, went in for a tackle against a forward and accidentally kicked Joe, breaking his leg. This happened on the edge of the penalty area at the North Bank end and we heard the crack from the south bank.

As he waved to the crowd while being carried off on the stretcher, we all knew that, at the age of 39, it was the end of a great career.

I would rate Joe as equal to Tony Adams as the greatest of Arsenal captains.

Bernard Chaplin: v Blackpool (17/12/1955). After a poor run of results, younger players were brought in and the League leaders were beaten. With the score 4-0, a whistle blew for what many thought was the end of the match. An excited Dennis Evans, the Arsenal full-back, turned round and booted the ball past goalkeeper Con Sullivan and into the net. Next thing, the referee was pointing to the centre spot. He had not blown his whistle; someone in the crowd had!

Despite realising what had happened, he had no option but to award a goal to Blackpool.

Dennis Evans

The match officially finished seconds later. Thank goodness we were winning.

Manchester Utd played their last game on English soil (1/2/1958) before the Munich disaster and it is remembered as a classic. Up against the league champions, Gunners were outclassed in the first-half (0-3). But within a few minutes of the second-half the score was 3-3.

United, in all-white, again showed their class to go 5-3 ahead, before Arsenal struck back by scoring a fourth and then hit the post. A great match watched by 63,578. There was not the hostility between the teams that existed in the latter years at Highbury. We had to respect the Busby Babes for being a great team.

Arsenal: Jack Kelsey, Stan Charlton, Dennis Evans, Jim Fotheringham, Jimmy Bloomfield, Dave Bowen, Gerry Ward, David Herd, Derek Tapscott, Gordon Nutt, Vic Groves.

Scorers: Herd, Bloomfield (2), Tapscott.

Manchester Utd: Harry Gregg, Roger Byrne, Bill Foulkes, Mark Jones, Eddie Colman, Duncan Ed2wards, Kenny Morgans, Albert Scanlon, Bobby Charlton, Tommy Taylor, Dennis Viollet.

Scorers: Edwards, Charlton, Viollet, Taylor (2).

Five days after this game, Byrne, Jones, Colman, Taylor and Edwards were among the Manchester United party who tragically lost their lives as a result of the Munich air crash on February 6, 1958.

Bernard Kiernan: My most enduring memory is of goalkeeper Jack Kelsey. Between 1961and '65 I stood at the very front behind the goal at the Clock End. Kelsey always used to hoof the ball out of his hands to poor old Alan Skirton on the wing. As I recall, the jury was out about Skirton. He was the butt of some jokes and abuse but a lot of fans, including myself, liked him because he was a trier and always gave 100 per cent, although he was often in and out of the team.

Duncan Edwards' final game in England.

But Kelsey was in no doubt. Not only would Kelsey always mutter some profanities about Skirton after turning to face us on the way back to the goalline after a kick out, he would also sometimes join in with the crowd's anguish about one of poor Alan's errors during open play. Priceless.

Graham Lister: Arsenal hosted Liverpool in the FA Cup fifth round (15/2/1964). It was the second successive season in which Bill Shankly's resurgent Reds (they finished the campaign as League champions) had visited Highbury at that same stage of the competition. In the weather-disrupted 1962-63 season they had triumphed 2-1 to end Arsenal's cup hopes for another year.

Now they were back, and although Gunners' League form was frustratingly inconsistent (with 14 wins, seven draws and nine defeats going into the tie), there were hopes that Billy Wright's team might go far in the Cup. They'd disposed of first division rivals Wolves and West Brom in the earlier rounds, and lost just one of their last eight fixtures when Liverpool came to town.

Gunners were exhilarating going forward but wide open defensively, as a League goals tally by mid-February of 76-61 underlined; yet at Highbury they'd suffered only two defeats all season and were a stern test for any visiting team. Liverpool were third in the table at the time, two places and one point ahead of us, though they'd just lost the Merseyside derby 3-1 to defending champions Everton, whom they were destined to dethrone by the end of the season.

The stage was therefore set for a thrilling FA Cup tie, and so it proved, in some respects, on a cold, filthy afternoon on a quagmire of a Highbury pitch.

Ian St John beat Arsenal's former Liverpool goalkeeper Jim Furnell after 15 minutes to put the visitors ahead but Arsenal's attacking strengths – with the mercurial, inventive George Eastham creating chances for twin strikers Geoff Strong and irrepressible Joe Baker – meant the game remained very much in the balance.

The big talking-point occurred in the 38th minute, when Baker clashed with Ron

Joe Baker

Yeats. Liverpool's captain and centre-half was something of a *cause celebre* as far as Shankly was concerned. His towering, muscle-bound fellow Scot stood 6ft 2in tall, and when he'd signed him for Liverpool the manager had introduced him to the press by inviting journalists to: "Go on, walk around him. He's a colossus!"

Baker, in contrast, stood 5ft 7in and weighed 74 kilos (163 lbs) but was tough as well as quick, skilful and brave. So when Yeats dumped him in the mud with an agricultural challenge, Joe hauled himself to his feet clutching a soggy divot which he hurled at Yeats, giving him an earful of mud, before decking the big man with a perfectly timed uppercut and trudging towards the touchline without waiting for his orders.

It was a stunning moment, and not only for Yeats. The Highbury crowd of 61,295 gasped in amazement. Long before red cards became commonplace, dismissals were very rare and highly controversial when they did occur. Referee JK Taylor immediately ordered both men off, Yeats complaining: "I swear I never hit him. I asked the referee if I had hit myself to get my cut and bleeding eye but he would not listen."

Sadly, although Furnell saved a penalty from Roger Hunt in the 90th minute, Arsenal couldn't find an equaliser and were out of the Cup. But Baker's cult status among Highbury fans had been raised several more notches.

Keith Weedon: I was with the group of friends I used to go with – Alfie Jameson, Johnny Burgess and a few others from Hackney – and we were drinking outside the Bank of Friendship pub when George Eastham came rushing out of the nearby betting office. It must have been getting on for a quarter-to-three and he was in such a rush to get to the ground in time for kick-off that after he got in his car to drive it around the corner to the stadium, he wound up his window just as a young kid was putting his hand out to ask for his autograph. The fan's hand actually got stuck in the window and he was running alongside George's car for a few yards! It was such a funny thing to see.

I used to take photographs for the weekly *Soccer Star* magazine in the late 60s and it was great to sit on your camera case beside the goal in front of the North Bank, where all my mates were standing. It was a great experience just to walk out of the same tunnel as the players and to sit that close to the pitch.

One day – I can't remember the game, but I think it was an FA Cup tie – I was following the flight of a cross from the wing through the viewfinder when George Armstrong arrived at the far post, right on the by-line, and tried to meet the ball on the volley. Unfortunately, he missed the ball completely but kicked me in the back of the head!

I fell off my camera case, was knocked out for a few seconds and had to be carried away on a stretcher to the St. John's Ambulance room for treatment – how embarrassing! Thankfully, the only damage was a bruise to my head. Even so, the first aid people wrapped a bandage around my head and when I returned to my position on the edge of the pitch, the North Bank gave me a rapturous reception.

SNOW DAY! v WEDNESDAY

James Anthony: The league game v Sheffield Wednesday (9/12/1967) that had to be abandoned just after half-time due to heavy snowfall. For once the undersoil heating couldn't save the day and referee E.T. Jennings called a halt with Arsenal a goal to the good thanks to a Frank McLintock shot. It was the last time a game at Highbury had to be abandoned. But all's well that ends well: the match was re-staged (11/1/1968), resulting in a 2-0 Gunners win.

Peter Wilday: I was there for the Sheffield Wednesday game (9/12/1967) abandoned at 1-0 to The Arsenal. Bob Wilson was on the pitch for about five minutes before a copper told him both teams were in the dressing rooms!

Evocative images that capture the spirit of Highbury from different eras. The two (above right) taken in the 1970s also confirm that the Arsenal team didn't always have a perfectly manicured turf on which to perform. The photo (below) shows fans scurrying towards the South Bank for the FA Cup tie against Chelsea in January, 1930.

ARSENAL 3 ANDERLECHT 0

Inter-Cities' Fairs Cup Final, 2nd leg, Tuesday, April 28, 1970
Arsenal won 4-3 on aggregate
Att: 51,612

ARSENAL: Bob Wilson, Peter Storey, Bob McNab, Eddie Kelly, Frank McLintock (c), Peter Simpson, George Armstrong, Jon Sammels, John Radford, Charlie George, George Graham.
Unused subs: Sammy Nelson, John Roberts, Peter Marinello, Ray Kennedy, Geoff Barnett (gk).
Manager: Bertie Mee
Scorers: Kelly, Radford, Sammels
ANDERLECHT: Jean-Marie Trappeniers, Georges Heylens, Maurice Martens, Tomas Nordahl, Roland Velkeneers, Julien Kialunda, Gerard Desanghere, Johan Devrindt, Jan Mulder, Paul Van Himst (c), Wilfried Puis.
Unused subs: J Cornelis, A Peters, P Hanon, G Bergholtz, W Deraeve.
Manager: Pierre Sinibaldi

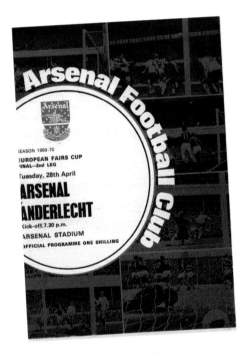

Steve Cooper: In 1970 I was 18-years-old and yet to taste glory as a Gooner. Our last piece of silverware had come 17 long years before, when we pipped Preston North End to the first division title on goal-average in 1953. I was only a year-old at the time, so I think I can be forgiven for allowing it to pass me by somewhat.

The 60s had not been a great time to be an Arsenal fan but things began to pick up as the decade came to a close and we made the League Cup Final in 1968 and 1969. I managed to get tickets to both finals and was absolutely heartbroken when we lost 3-1 to third division Swindon Town and 1-0 to Leeds Utd respectively. In my darkest moments, I began to wonder if I would ever experience the elation of watching the boys lift some silverware.

The following year, Arsenal qualified for the Fairs Cup and when we made it through to the two-legged final against 14-times Belgian champions Anderlecht, I approached the game with the trepidation of someone who'd been waiting for more than a decade to see us win something. I had learned the hard way that hope was a dangerous thing, yet as the match drew close, visions of what might be swamped my thoughts.

My trepidation proved well placed when Arsenal quickly raced into a three-goal deficit in the first leg six nights earlier, although a Ray Kennedy goal in the closing stages was just the lifeline we needed. If we could just win by two clear goals at Highbury the following week the club would win its first-ever European honour. But it would be a tall order. Anderlecht had knocked out a very strong Inter Milan side in the semi-finals and looked well worth their lead from the first leg.

One oft-forgotten fact is that after intense pressure from Arsenal, UEFA had accepted that if we won the second leg by 2-0, we would win the tie due to our away goal – a rule that didn't exist at the start of the competition. For six days, every single possibility ran through my mind.

At the time I was working in Spitalfields Market, in my family's West Indian import business (during my time there I also met David Dein who was a fellow importer before he joined the club) and on the day of the game my working hours were 3.30am to 2.00pm. Needless to say, I didn't get much sleep the night before.

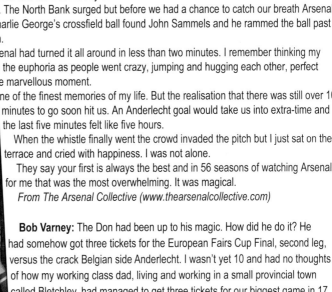

When I got to work, everyone was talking about the game. The market was full of Gooners and as soon as my shift was over I went home to my place in the West End, changed and got the tube to the stadium at about 5.00pm. You had to be early or you didn't get in back then – there were no advance tickets and I wasn't taking any chances.

Once on the North Bank, I soon found my mates (I always stood with the same group of lads in the middle of the terrace) and realised that, like myself, they were shitting themselves.

I had never seen the North Bank so tense – we all just sort of nodded at each other rather than actually speak – but as kick-off approached the atmosphere became electric. I spent several decades watching the boys from the North Bank but I can't remember an atmosphere to rival this night. All that anxiety, energy and hope was being transformed into a wall of noise which I'll never forget. I remember not being able speak for a couple of days afterwards.

Arsenal were clearly up for it and when Eddie Kelly blasted us in front from the edge of the area after half an hour, you could feel the stadium willing the boys forward. Belief had replaced hope.

One more goal . . .

The second-half was all Arsenal. Wave after wave of attack pounded against a resolute Anderlecht defence yet with 18 minutes left the moment arrived. A fine cross from Bob McNab was met by John Radford and his header found the corner of the net. The North Bank surged but before we had a chance to catch our breath Arsenal were on the attack again. Charlie George's crossfield ball found John Sammels and he rammed the ball past the Belgian keeper. Cue delirium.

After waiting for 17 years, Arsenal had turned it all around in less than two minutes. I remember thinking my heart was going to explode amid the euphoria as people went crazy, jumping and hugging each other, perfect strangers brought together in one marvellous moment.

I don't mind admitting it was one of the finest memories of my life. But the realisation that there was still over 10 minutes to go soon hit us. An Anderlecht goal would take us into extra-time and the last five minutes felt like five hours.

When the whistle finally went the crowd invaded the pitch but I just sat on the terrace and cried with happiness. I was not alone.

They say your first is always the best and in 56 seasons of watching Arsenal, for me that was the most overwhelming. It was magical.

From The Arsenal Collective (www.thearsenalcollective.com)

Bob Varney: The Don had been up to his magic. How did he do it? He had somehow got three tickets for the European Fairs Cup Final, second leg, versus the crack Belgian side Anderlecht. I wasn't yet 10 and had no thoughts of how my working class dad, living and working in a small provincial town called Bletchley, had managed to get three tickets for our biggest game in 17 years. The Don, Steve, my older and only sibling, and me. And 51,611 others. What a night. To be honest, my memories of the night are a little sketchy.

John Radford and Charlie George celebrate Raddy's goal.

I do remember we sat in the West lower. I do remember it was still light when Eddie Kelly hit a 'grass cutter' into the Clock End goal. I do remember it was pitch black when John Radford headed the second at the North Bank end. The unique Arsenal floodlights illuminating our giant centre-forward as he 'hung' so high in the air, his feet surely level with the crossbar, before he powered a header into the far corner of the net – 2-0 (3-3 on agg). We were ahead on away goals. The place went bonkers. Bonkers.

The Don had told me all about 'away goals' after the first leg. We had got one. It was important, The Don had said. Jon Sammels went on to make this important away goal irrelevant. We won 3-0 (4-3 on aggregate). Our first trophy for 17 years. And more importantly, 'our' first trophy of many.

I do remember we had had a fry-up at the Euston Grill on the way home. I have no idea if I went to school the next day.

The three of us would go on to share many wonderful adventures right through to the very last season at the grand old stadium that was Highbury. The Don never went to The Emirates. It wasn't for him. I think he was right. The Don was Arsenal through and through and Highbury was a special place for the three of us.

John Powell: Of all the very many wonderful memories, the 1969-70 Fairs Cup run was a clear stand out, and to have season tickets for this season was perfect timing.

Foreign clubs were intriguing and magical. We knew very little about most of them. This included the semi-final v Ajax. We thought it incredibly funny to be playing a club whose name was the same as a popular brand of bath cleaner. We lustily joined the chants of 'Vim-Vim-Vim' and thought this was the height of subtle British humour.

The final under the lights at Highbury is forever etched in my memory banks. One strange memory was seeing Bob Wilson during the friendly pitch invasion at the end, without his shirt and displaying the red marks and bruises from the encounter. A far more physical game in those days, particularly for the keeper.

We wouldn't have recognised it at the time but to watch The Arsenal win a trophy at Highbury was clearly unique. Although League championships/Premiership trophies were won and displayed at Highbury over the years, there was something very special about a major knockout cup.

John Blair: We were on the North Bank an hour before kick-off, when I developed chronic stomach pain and was taken on a stretcher to the St John's Ambulance bay at the Clock End, where a medic examined me and said: "Sonny, you've got appendicitis and you are going straight to hospital."

'Sod that' I thought, so I jumped off the stretcher and ran back to the North Bank. I was in agony watching our incredible 3-0 win.

Next day I had my appendix out!

Robert Thaine: Bob Wilson always says that the crowd that night was the loudest he'd ever heard it and I think he's absolutely right. The atmosphere that night was never matched.

Jeremy Doltis: My first massive night at Highbury. I was 14 and the scenes at the end were unreal – I went on the pitch with all my mates from Burnt Oak.

Lee Pritchett: My most vivid memory is the 1970 Fairs Cup Final. 50,000-odd crammed into Highbury that night, having to win 2-0 to win the trophy. The noise was deafening for a 12-year-old boy fit to burst. When Jon Sammels scored that third goal I have never heard a roar like it, and still haven't. It was so loud that the roof of the stand was vibrating. That is still my greatest night watching The Arsenal.

Lester Allen: Standing in the Clock End getting soaking wet, celebrating victory. There were a number of Anderlecht supporters around us and one had a type of fisherman's hat. My brother David took it off the man's head and a load of money fell to the ground. The Belgian just laughed and wished us good luck.

After the final whistle I ran onto the pitch and up to the North Bank. I was covered with mud all up my legs.

Peter Coombs: When the third, winning, goal went in, I remember the delirium in the North Bank, the experience of the concrete bouncing under our feet. Truly a night I will never forget.

Peter Lewis: I recall seeing grown men crying with joy at the end after 17 bleak years. It remains my favourite Arsenal moment/game of all time, even 50-plus years later. You'd have to be a Highbury veteran to appreciate how it felt. My kids (now in their 30s) are bored with me going on about that night. I've always said that my worst and best Arsenal experiences were Swindon '69 and Fairs Cup '70. Everything since has fallen in between.

Marc Beaumont: I was just seven. I knew of Arsenal only from the 1969-70 *Soccer Stars* sticker album. Some of the players on the Arsenal page had old-style haircuts and navy-and-white hooped socks.

The Anderlecht second leg was my first live match. We had seats in the East Stand lower tier. I recall very little, as I couldn't see much – the people in front kept standing up. The noise was deafening. I recall a flash of blond hair – Eddie Kelly – and the ball hitting the back of the net for our opening goal. Wild celebrations.

We needed another goal. I had a wobbly tooth. My mother saved all of my baby teeth. She had all of those I had so far lost. She sent us to the match with sandwiches and an apple. At 2-0, I bit into the apple. My wobbly tooth remained embedded in the apple and, in shock, I dropped both apple and embedded tooth.

As I rummaged on the ground searching for mother's latest memento, we scored the winner. I missed the goal and, in fact, didn't see it until Bob Wilson's 40th anniversary dinner.

But mother's tooth collection remained complete.

Joe O'Connor: Having been introduced to Arsenal by my dad Martin during the 1967-68 season, nothing prepared me for that night under the floodlights at Highbury. Just turned 11-years old, it was to be the game that cemented my love affair with the club.

The match is a blur but the noise and then running onto the pitch at the final whistle will always live with me. I ran around the pitch with hundreds of others as Frank McLintock held the Fairs Cup trophy high. When Dad joined me on the pitch, we stood in the centre circle looking towards the North Bank, with the floodlights gleaming. What a night!

Frank McLintock, followed by Bob Wilson, John Roberts and Peter Storey, parade the trophy.

Richard Jones (@Reg791): I was born and raised in the 60s in Chadwell Heath, not far from West Ham's training ground. Spurs had won trophies, Chelsea were the glamour club and West Ham had won cups and of course had Moore, Hurst and Peters.

Even our school colours were claret-and-blue. And it was only when I was responding to your questionnaire that my brother Steve told me how our mum (June) sewed the Arsenal badge over the top of his Warren School blazer badge in protest!

Arsenal had been in the doldrums and me and Steve, being the only Gunners fans in the town, took hell's abuse for years.

Mum actually took us to the Anderlecht game, because Dad (Les) had sadly died in 1967. He was a Highbury regular throughout the 1940s and 50s and regaled us with tales of the greats such as Mercer, Logie and Rooke.

Despite the late night I didn't need to be prised out of bed next morning – I couldn't wait to get to school to ram the years of insults down people's throats.

We'd lost to Leeds in '68 (League Cup Final) and then we had the Swindon debacle in '69, so that night against Anderlecht was all the more special. And a year later!

None of us at Highbury that night will ever forget it.

Mark Adams (@pommiegooner): I was nine-years-old and with my dad, Robert. Unfortunately, he passed away 25 years ago but that night we stood in the West Stand, down near the North Bank, while my brother Brian and sister Pauline stood on the North Bank. Dad used to bring a stool that I could stand on against the barrier or fence.

I have lived in Perth, Western Australia for the past 30 years but I always remember the great atmosphere that night and how Dad always believed in Arsenal. He used to go to all the home games and occasionally away.

Highbury goes wild as Mee's men crush Belgian

GLORY, GLORY GUNNERS!

HIGHBURY housed the greatest knees-up in the history of British football last night when Arsenal ended 17 barren years by storming from behind to win the Fairs Cup from Anderlecht of Belgium.

More than 5,000 joyous fans joined their team in a lap of honour, engulfing their heroes in such jubilation that it looked as if some of them would have to drink their champagne in hospital.

But that was only the start. They climbed goal posts, formed giant snake lines to dance the Conga and, inevitably, massed together in front

By
PETER BATT

Arsenal 3
Anderlecht . . 0

Arsenal win 4-3 on agg.

IT! Skipper McLintock holds aloft trophy as fans carry him off.

Arsenal heroes — Eddie Kelly (left) who scored the first goal congratulates John Radford after his header put Arsenal level.

The happy fac of victory

By PETER BLACKMAN

ARSENAL, having made a whopping five changes for the sixth time this season, turned on

In those days, photographers could go just about anywhere in the stadium. I was in the players' bar after the game when George Armstrong came in and apologised for having kicked me in the head.

Bernard Chaplin: A 3-0 friendly win v Glasgow Rangers (5/8/1967) is remembered for all the wrong reasons. After WW2 Arsenal resumed a tradition that dated back to the 1930s by playing Rangers on a regular basis, alternately home and away. This season we hosted them at home – and it was my most frightening moment at Highbury.

Rangers fans not adverse to a 'bevvy or two' arrived in a state with whisky and beer bottles in tow. They started throwing bottles at the roof of the stand and the crowd was showered with glass. They were not invited back to Highbury for almost another 30 years – until Nigel Winterburn's testimonial game (13/5/1997).

Keith Weedon: We used to regularly play Glasgow Rangers in a pre-season friendly. I was standing with friends on the North Bank in the days when there was no segregation. The Arsenal boys were towards the front half of the terracing with the Rangers lot behind us, towards the back. All of a sudden, you heard a "shhh", followed by the Rangers fans bombarding us with bottles. It all went off.

Paul Harris: Not long before England's glorious triumph in 1966, all was not so happy at Highbury, where supporters were campaigning to remove England and Wolves legend Billy Wright from (mis)managing Arsenal. Many had talked about a boycott and on this day (5/5/1966) fewer than 5,000 turned out for the game (official attendance was 4,554).

I arrived late and was astonished to see supporters lounging and, in some cases, sitting on the terraces with plenty of room. Our opponents were Leeds United who won 3-0. It was a low moment, indeed, and we were often reminded that the club had won nothing since 1953. Roll on 1970.

Jeremy Doltis: I sat next to then Prime Minister and Labour party leader Harold Wilson in the East Stand for the League Cup semi-final against his team, Huddersfield Town (17/1/1968).

On another occasion, my mates and I were at the back of the North Bank when Man City 'took' the back shelf. My grandma bought me a new bobble hat that the Mancs stole off the back of my head. Gutted.

Richard Boyes: On Boxing Day, 1968 I took my five-year-old son Richard to see his first game at Highbury, v Man Utd (26/12/1968). We got there about 90 minutes early to find that the ground was full and the roads around the stadium packed with disappointed fans, so I made my way to the main entrance and walked into the famous marble hall, where I was met by a very smart uniformed commissionaire who smiled and explained that they were full.

Just then, Arsenal manager Bertie Mee walked past and smiled at my son, who was dressed in an Arsenal kit that his mum Gwen had made – a one-off in those days. Bertie asked me if he could help. He spoke to the commissionaire, shook my hand and walked away.

The commissionaire asked us to follow him. We went down some stairs and then heard a clatter of boots made by the Arsenal team coming back from their warm-up – in those days they did it in an area behind the Clock End. The first player we saw was John Radford – what a thrill for my son.

We were escorted to seats, just behind where the squad and staff sat, near the halfway line. We had a perfect view and to cap it all we won 3-0 with goals from George Armstrong, David Court and Radford against one of the top sides, including the likes of Denis Law, Bobby Charlton, George Best and Nobby Stiles. A perfect end to a perfect day.

My son and I have never forgotten the kindness shown to a little boy by that very humble and great man, Bertie Mee.

Wayne Flatman: I was on my own, aged 10, in the schoolboys' enclosure for a game v Chelsea when I had my big red-and-white bobble hat pinched off my head.

Emilio Zorlakki: v Chelsea (3/4/1971). My father and I came out of Arsenal tube and I looked in horror as I saw the queue going way up Highbury Hill. Highbury was buzzing big-time, as we had just beaten Stoke City to reach the FA Cup Final. The excitement was tangible and the street sellers were doing a roaring trade.

We quickly took our place and waited patiently as the queue inched slowly towards the turnstiles. We were two or three persons away from the turnstile, when suddenly my father exclaimed: "Oh no! There are no more tickets! We can't get in!"

I asked why not? My father repeated: "No more tickets."

"That's OK, we'll go in the North Bank," I said as a matter of fact. "Are you joking, you're too small and you'll be crushed!" Somehow, I persuaded Dad to take me into the North Bank.

We positioned ourselves right at the back of the north-west corner and there was already a youth game in progress on the pitch as an aperitif to the main event. When the game began my father lifted me up onto his shoulders, so that I could see. I looked behind me and noticed these spiky railings and a very big drop as well. I almost strangled my father to make sure he wouldn't drop me backwards. I was eight at the time and a little chubby, so there were occasions when my father would put me back down, so that he could rest a little.

It was while he was lifting me up again that I managed to see Ray Kennedy scoring his and Arsenal's second goal, which my father unfortunately missed!

I remember looking at the people walking through the gangways below me. I noticed this large group of skinheads with blue and white scarves. They looked quite menacing and intimidating – and they were girls!

At the time, Chelsea were a 'bogey' side for us – we had beaten them only once in about eight or nine years. The official attendance was 62,087 but in those days many fans could 'bribe' the turnstile operator to allow an extra person in and, thus, there were often a few thousand more inside the ground than the official attendance.

A photo of Ray Kennedy's second goal appeared in the Newcastle Utd programme a fortnight later. It clearly shows two very tiny heads at the top of the crowd – it's me and another boy of similar age both sitting on their fathers' shoulders!

Derek Barclay: Part of the Arsenal experience in the 70s was the marching Met Police Band (with the impressive singing by the rotund PC Alex Morgan) – and the band leader Major W. Williams who would toss his huge (well, it seemed huge to me) baton up in the air

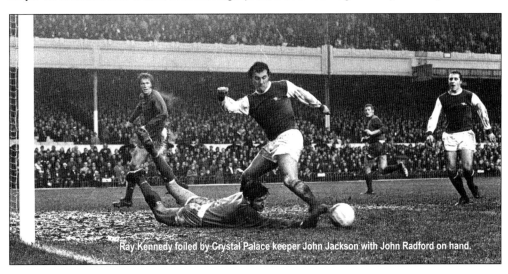
Ray Kennedy foiled by Crystal Palace keeper John Jackson with John Radford on hand.

and catch it. So when he did and the one legendary occasion he dropped it . . . well, that was a memorable moment.

I also remember a very wayward shot (not sure from whom) ended up on the roof of the North Bank and as the ball rolled back it went behind the crest at the centre of the front of the roof. I often wonder if it was still there when the North Bank was finally demolished all those years later.

Emilio Zorlakki: I hope you don't mind me adding the FA Cup quarter-final at Chelsea (17/3/1973). My father and I went to watch this match at the Rainbow Theatre, Finsbury Park. Tickets were hard to come by – one side of Stamford Bridge was not in use because the infamous triple-tier stand was in the process of being built. We arrived at the 'Rainbow' quite late – 2.30pm to be precise – and saw the queue extending all the way to where the Sobell Centre would be (I cannot remember whether it was built yet). As we walked past the main entrance, the doors opened and my father said: "Come on" and we bunked in the front of the queue, with a couple of shouts of "Oi! You can't push in!" But we did and found ourselves in the front row of the upper balcony. I was about to watch a big game in a bizarre venue.

Incredibly, the match was shown in black and white, without commentary but with the sounds of the crowd. When Peter Osgood scored the opening goal, you could have heard a pin drop in the theatre, except for a guy behind me saying: "F****** good goal"(In fact, it won *MOTD's* 1973 Goal of the Season). Bob Wilson would later boast about his spectacular dive!

Thankfully, we didn't have to wait long to hit back and we scored two goals in as many minutes. The scenes in the Rainbow Theatre were amazing and surreal. The whole building was shaking and the noise was deafening. I was frightened and exhilarated at the same time. I had recently seen a film with Victor Mature playing the role of Samson and, if you remember, in the climax of the film he managed to make a building collapse by pushing the pillars apart. I honestly thought the same was about to happen here. I also noticed our fans jump on the stage and thought they were about to rip the screens down!

The whole occasion was a 'one-off' and you had to be there to appreciate what it was like. The game finished 2-2 and at the replay the following Tuesday, we were at the front of the queue in Gillespie Road by 4.30pm. A police horse had left an unpleasant deposit on my shoes, which I didn't approve of, but an elderly guy said: "Don't worry, it's lucky!" The turnstiles opened at 6.00 and I promise you the stadium was full at 6.20.

Unlike the match in 1971, we were in the seats in the West Stand lower and were amazed at the scenes witnessed behind both goals.

At the Clock End there were Chelsea fans hanging off the back of the corrugated iron fencing and some were trying to climb the clock itself (in those days, Arsenal supporters mixed with away fans). While at the opposite end, there were quite a number of Arsenal fans sitting on the roof of the North Bank. Health and Safety nightmare! You could tell how packed the ground was, because all you could see on the terraces were heads and no bodies visible.

Thankfully, another great win over Chelsea, 2-1 this time, with goals from Alan Ball (pen) and Ray Kennedy, and an official attendance of 62,746.

Tony Fisher: Frank McLintock literally dragging the ref over to the linesman to get a penalty decision in the 1973 FA Cup quarter-final replay v Chelsea (20/3/1973). Bally duly obliged in our 2-1 victory.

John Morley: Being in the North Bank for an evening North London derby v Tottenham (10/4/1979). Spurs fans had got into the North Bank and a mighty fight erupted before kick-off a couple of feet away from where I was standing. Eventually, the police waded in and pushed the Spurs fans out of the North Bank onto the open terrace, resulting in me being totally surrounded by them for the whole game.

ARSENAL 0 LIVERPOOL 0
Football League Division One
Saturday, September 16, 1972

Arsenal were hosting champions-elect Liverpool, when linesman Dennis Drewitt pulled a muscle and was unable to continue. FA rules stated that the match could not be completed without a referee and two linesmen, so the game was in danger of being abandoned.

The match day announcer put a message over the loudspeaker asking if anyone was a qualified referee and would volunteer to run the line.

Out of the crowd emerged Hill, the former Fulham player, Coventry City manager and best known as TV presenter/pundit for ITV's The Big Match and BBC's Match of the Day. Hill had been at Highbury that day merely as a spectator but he was a qualified referee.

With the agreement of referee Pat Partridge and both managers, Bertie Mee and Bill Shankly, he quickly donned a tracksuit and stepped in for the injured Mr Drewitt.

The match ended in a 0-0 draw but will forever be remembered for the antics of Jimmy Hill.

Keith Wilsher: I think Jimmy wore a light blue tracksuit and red trainers.

Terry Robinson: I was about 19 and had just passed my referees' exam and my dad, Fred, gave my name to a steward. I reffed games in the Essex Sunday Combination, in Dagenham, Barking, Hainault Forest and Wanstead Flats. At the time I was really pleased that I didn't take over as linesman but now I think I'd like to have done it. Who knows, it might have changed my life.

Peter Nelson: They called for any qualified referees to come forward. I was in the West upper. I did think about volunteering but decided against it. While serving in the Army our CO made us take the referees' exam if we played for the unit's football team. But I don't really regret not putting myself forward – I would never have been able to live with myself if I'd flagged an Arsenal winner offside!

LINESMAN'S LIMP RUINS ARSENAL

JIMMY HILL returned to active football as the first £300-a-week linesman, volunteering for emergency duty in purple shirt and kipper tie. But the match he tried to save had already died in a quite unnecessary 10-minute standstill.

All the great football was played in the 14 minutes before Denis Drewitt, from Sussex, crumpled on his

Arsenal 0, Liverpool 0

By MIKE LANGLEY

will probably never again be

TV pundit Jimmy Hill answered an SOS call to take over from an injured linesman.

Another cheeky first for The Arsenal

By Andy Kelly (@Gooner_AK) and published on www.thearsenalhistory.com

THIS is an expanded version of the article we recently wrote for the History Lesson page for the Arsenal match day programme.

Throughout the club's history Arsenal have always had a reputation as pioneers and innovators. On March 23, 1974 the club was involved in one of football's more unusual firsts.

A new craze had taken the USA by storm the previous year and by 1974 it hit the headlines in the UK, even inspiring a number one hit single. Streaking was that year's big thing, with most major events being spiced up by someone who had stripped down to their socks and shoes.

Just before kick-off in the Arsenal v Manchester City game at Highbury towards the end of the 1973-74 season early arrivals witnessed football's first-ever streaker.

A somewhat hirsute middle-aged gentleman by the name of John Taylor divested himself of his clothes, climbed over the perimeter fence at the Clock End and ran around on the hallowed turf until he was apprehended by three policemen.

The *Islington Gazette* managed to capture him in full flight, while the *Daily Mirror* had colour photos of him being arrested just inside the penalty area at the North Bank end.

On the following Monday, 44-year-old Taylor, from Newbury, Berkshire, appeared before a magistrate at North London Court, where he was fined £10 and bound over for "using insulting behaviour whereby a breach of the peace was likely to be occasioned." The magistrate who heard the case, Mr Peter Goldstone, had actually been at Highbury and saw the events first hand.

Taylor said: "It just started off as a dare. When so many people got involved I couldn't get out of it. It was more of a sponsored streak." It was – he told the court that his streak had raised over £100 for Dr Barnado's Homes thanks to his workmates at Brentford fruit market.

I guess that today he would be banned from all football grounds and placed on the sex offenders' register.

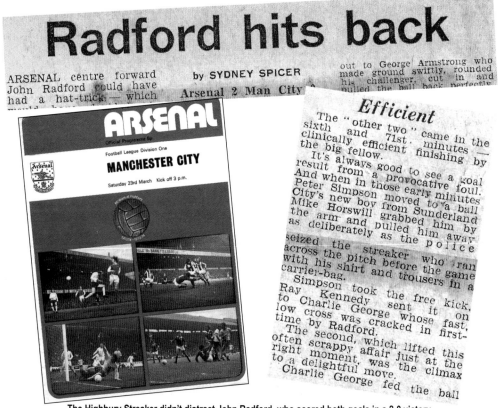

Radford hits back

ARSENAL centre forward John Radford could have had a hat-trick — which

by SYDNEY SPICER

Arsenal 2 Man City

out to George Armstrong who made ground swiftly, rounded his challenger, cut in and pulled the ball back perfectly

Efficient

The "other two" came in the sixth and 71st minutes — clinically efficient finishing by the big fellow.

It's always good to see a goal result from a provocative foul. And when in those early minutes Peter Simpson moved to a ball City's new boy from Sunderland Mike Horswill grabbed him by the arm and deliberately pulled him away as the police

seized the streaker who ran across the pitch before the game with his shirt and trousers in a carrier-bag.

Simpson took the free kick, Ray Kennedy sent it on to Charlie George whose low cross was cracked in first-time by Radford.

The second, which lifted this often scrappy affair just at the right moment, was the climax to a delightful move.

Charlie George fed the ball

Official Programme 5p

Football League Division One

MANCHESTER CITY

Saturday 23rd March   Kick off 3 p.m.

The Highbury Streaker didn't distract John Radford, who scored both goals in a 2-0 victory.

FA won't turn blind eye to Nelson

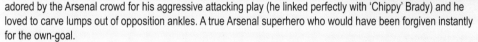

SAMMY Nelson, Arsenal's Northern Ireland international left-back, has been suspended for two weeks by his club and fined two weeks' wages for lowering his shorts in front of the crowd after equalising in the 1-1 draw against Coventry City at Highbury (3/4/1979). He also seems certain to be charged by the FA with bringing the game into disrepute.

Nelson's gesture came after he had been barracked by the crowd for putting the ball into his own goal in the first-half. The player is extremely contrite about his behaviour, and the only charitable thing that can be said is that it appeared to be entirely out of character.

The above headline and description of the Sammy Nelson mooning incident is taken from a contemporary newspaper. The following supporters' comments were posted on www.arseweb.com:

F. Greene: I was at the match in question and, at the time, it was the subject of much discussion. The facts of the matter are that, when questioned by schoolmates on the following day, I could recall no barracking of Sammy whatsoever during the match despite his initial aberration. Sammy was adored by the Arsenal crowd for his aggressive attacking play (he linked perfectly with 'Chippy' Brady) and he loved to carve lumps out of opposition ankles. A true Arsenal superhero who would have been forgiven instantly for the own-goal.

My reading of the incident then (and now) was that he mooned out of sheer delight at having got even with the opposition. I believe the story about him having been barracked was made up in haste (possibly by the press) who could think of no other reason for such a spontaneous display of jubilation. Their explanation has now become received wisdom but has never really been challenged.

My belief is strengthened by the fact that it was the North Bank which received the full brunt of Sammy's cheek. I suppose it's possible that there may have been some isolated whingeing in the upper East Stand, for example, but the notion of the North Bank giving Sammy stick is just unimaginable. We loved him.

Mike Winnett: My recollection is that it took place near the north-east corner, right in front of the North Bank, not very far from where I was standing. Likewise, I don't remember any barracking, Sammy was held in high esteem in the North Bank, and certainly the bum was definitely aimed in our direction. I'd agree with your explanation.

Bill Barber: Remember it well. It was a midweek game and the attendance was in the region of 48,000. The reason for that was that the club published the Cup Final application form in the programme on that night – no terrace season tickets in those days. The form had a space for each of your 24 vouchers from the home games (for those that don't know, they used to put one in each home programme).

Marvin Berglas: It further endeared Sammy Nelson to the fans and is an iconic Highbury moment. It's up there with the bizarre sight of the squirrel scuttling across Jens Lehmann's goal during that last European night at Highbury, the Champions League semi-final v Villarreal, in April 2006.

Bare-faced cheek of Sammy Nelson.

Liam Brady

I stood in silence, fearing for my safety, until I headed for the exit with a couple of minutes to go, to avoid any further trouble . . . only to miss Frank Stapleton score the winner in the last minute!

This was the sadder side of attending Highbury matches in the bad old days of hooliganism.

Bernard Chaplin: Leeds Utd had been a thorn in our side for many seasons. But we humiliated a full strength Leeds team, 7-0, in the League Cup second round, second leg (4/9/1979). Our scorers: Alan Sunderland (3), Liam Brady (2), Sammy Nelson, Frank Stapleton.

Gary Jones: My most vivid memory was Pat Jennings signing his autograph for me after we beat his former club Tottenham, 2-0 (30/8/1980). That day goalkeeper Pat was filming for the BBC's Jim'll Fix It. I still have the signature stuck in a book he released in 1983.

Another memory was walking to the tube station after a game with Terry Neill, Arsenal's manager at the time, early on in the 1981-82 season. He was talking about out next UEFA Cup opponents, Winterslag (since renamed KRC Genk) of Belgium. Something like that just wouldn't happen these days.

One final memory is the UEFA Cup, first round tie v Spartak Moscow (29/9/1982) – a night of pure football genius by the team from Russia. Arsenal played in emerald green that night and were blown away, 5-2, which earned the visitors a standing ovation at the end.

Robert Grainger: Last home game of the season (2/5/1980) and Aston Villa were going for the title. Arsenal beat them 2-0 (Willie Young and Brian McDermott) but Villa still won the league. My great memory was seeing Pele on the pitch at half-time and 67,000 fans roaring 'sign him up' as the Brazilian legend ran round the pitch applauding all the fans.

Stephen Simson: Seeing Pele do a lap of honour and getting a ball that was kicked into the crowd.

Sure it was the Villa game (2/5/1980) that we won 2-0 and they won the title.

Also, when I was a young teenager, Tony Woodcock once took a shot at the North Bank end that went so high, I caught it on the stairwell halfway up the terrace, in the middle of the singing section. It was an Adidas Tango. I booted it back onto the pitch, and I was like, 'Wow, I just touched the ball!' An amazing feeling.

A scary time for me was getting caught up in the infamous Arsenal v West Ham fight in the North Bank, where flares were going off. I managed to

Brian McDermott

get onto the pitch and stood by the goalpost. I think George Wood was our keeper. There was a picture in the paper next day and I was in it.

Alex Morrow: A bit of a weird one, but Aston Villa in the 1983 FA Cup quarter-final (12/3/1983). I remember seeing an old lady with one of those tartan shopping baskets, wearing an Aston Villa bobble hat and heading towards the Clock End. She must have been pushing 90. We won 2-0 (Tony Woodcock and Vladimir Petrovic) and I was convinced that I'd be making a trip to Wembley. But we drew Manchester Utd in the semi-final and that was the end of that.

John Hilditch: Mid-80s and we played Sp*rs. I think it was an 11.15 kick-off. It was definitely an all-ticket game and they had all of the Clock End. I was about 10 years of age and it was my first time on the Clock End. Yes, I was in with them. Lord knows why.

Anyway, it was the game when Graham Roberts booted Charlie Nicholas into the East Stand. I instinctively responded, as you'd expect any Arsenal fan to do, and then remembered I was surrounded by that lot. Luckily, because of my age, the people around me thought it was quite funny. This nutty little 10-year-old Gunner giving it his all in with their lot. Truth is, though, I kept quiet for the rest of the game despite my allegiances being revealed.

Ian Tredgett: Two events, both in Avenell Road, and neither actually from a game. Easter Monday, 1986, two days after losing the North London derby, and we are 2-0 down at home to Watford (31/3/1986) in front of a crowd of about 19,600. Manager Don Howe had left the week before and after another disappointing season there seemed little prospect of any hope on the horizon. The crowd began to chant "Outside Hill-Wood, Outside Hill-Wood", "Who on Earth is David Dein?" (or words to that effect) and "Don Howe and his Red and White Army". I stayed behind to watch the demonstrations, largely out of curiosity but also aware such protests were rare in our history and this would be looked back upon as a key turning point.

On a more personal level, and less than a year later, I travelled to the ground on the distinctly chilly afternoon of Tuesday, March 3, 1987 to queue up for a ticket for the League Cup semi-final replay at White Hart Lane the following night. Turning right from Gillespie Road into Avenell Road, I was horrified to see a huge queue trailing all the way up the hill from the Clock End turnstiles. I resigned myself for a long, bitterly cold and possibly fruitless wait.

Quite near the front of the queue, as I walked past towards my rightful place at the back, I was grabbed by the arm and the three guys who stood near me on the North Bank each week pulled me into the queue with them. (To those behind me in the queue I am truly sorry; to Jim, Neil and Larry from Guildford, if you're reading this, I am still eternally grateful!)

I managed to get a ticket and returned home to Reading feeling only slightly guilty. The next day, I got up to see snow everywhere and assumed the game was bound to be postponed. The sun must have shone on me in more ways than one, despite the brazen queue-jumping of the previous day. The snow had thawed by lunchtime, the game went ahead and the scenes after Rocky's goal remain one of the best celebrations I can EVER remember at a game.

Tony Bateman: Paul Davis* laying out Southampton's Glenn Cockerill with a left-hook in an off-the-ball incident unseen by the match officials (17/9/1988).

Although midfield playmaker Davis wasn't sent-off or even booked for his completely out of character actions, after viewing video evidence provided by ITV and BBC News cameras, the FA found him guilty of bringing the game into disrepute, issued him with an unprecedented nine-match ban and a then record £3,000 fine. Cockerill suffered a broken jaw.

Steve Martin: I have been going to Highbury since the early 1960s and have had many great times there. From my very first visit it was something magical. A stadium with Art Deco stands and huge terraces with one end open and the other partially under cover.

Paul Davis

95

There was obviously the Fairs Cup victory against Anderlecht in 1970, Leicester City in 2004, when we beat them to go a season undefeated, and of course beating Everton 4-0 to win the title in 1998. In fact, so many I'd need to write a book, not an article.

Having been to many games at Highbury, it's hard to think what the best were, so I have gone for a five-day period in late February 1988.

Season 1987-88 started poorly, yielding one win in the first five games. Then Arsenal went on a winning streak of 14 matches in all competitions that put us top of the league and going great guns.

Then, wallop! Arsenal hit a brick wall. During the next 13 games they won only three matches and slid to fifth in the table.

January 1988 saw Arsenal travel to Sheffield Wednesday and come away with a 1-0 League Cup quarter-final victory courtesy of a crazy goal from Nigel Winterburn (with the help of the Wednesday keeper), which meant Arsenal would play Everton in the semi-final.

A week later, in the FA Cup fourth round, Arsenal beat Brighton 2-1 at the Goldstone and were drawn to play Manchester Utd at home in the fifth round. We had already lost 2-1 at home to United in the league four weeks before this tie and they were third in the table.

My mates and I travelled to Goodison Park for the first leg and Arsenal came away with a 1-0 victory over Everton thanks to a goal from Perry Groves and in pole position to reach their second successive League Cup Final.

One more league match was played at Highbury, against Luton Town, which resulted in a 2-1 win for Gunners.

Now Arsenal went into two massive games at the Home of Football in the space of five days. 105,000 people were about to attend two massive matches in what I feel was the best week ever at Highbury in my lifetime.

First up was Manchester Utd in the FA Cup (20/2/1988). 54,000 packed into Highbury and on 20 minutes a cross from David Rocastle found Alan Smith, who headed in for 1-0. Then, with 40 minutes gone, an own-goal from United put us 2-0 in front. Early in the second-half United pulled one back through Brian McClair – 2-1. Kenny Sansom cleared one off the line. Viv Anderson could have made it 2-2 but shot across goal. Winterburn made a great tackle to stop United equalising. Michael Thomas was then through one-on-one but slipped at the vital moment trying to go round the keeper.

With only minutes left, Whiteside was brought down in the penalty area and the referee gave United a penalty. So it was McClair against Lukic to make it 2-2. 20,000 Arsenal supporters in the North Bank were screaming for McClair to miss. McClair stepped up and blasted his shot way over the bar – I'm told it re-entered Earth's atmosphere in June 1991. The Highbury crowd went mental and Nigel Winterburn had a few choice words for a distraught McClair as well. Arsenal were through to the sixth round.

Four days later and the lads and I were back, this time on the Clock End for the visit of Everton in the League Cup semi-final, second leg (24/2/88). Coke bottles half-filled with Coke, half with rum and packed in with 51,000 others. Great atmosphere, no 'Highbury the library' for these two matches.

Rocastle was through one-on-one with only Neville Southall to beat and, somehow, after rounding the keeper with the goal gaping at his mercy, he slid the ball wide. What a miss!

Martin Hayes went through for another one-on-one in this week of cup matches. Right on half-time, Hayes rounded Southall and was brought down. 'Penalty!' screamed the crowd and the referee agreed. Up stepped Hayes himself but blasted the ball wide. Arsenal were keeping Everton's hopes alive and giving the home crowd palpitations.

Early in the second-half Groves played the ball to Thomas, who finished coolly for 1-0 to Arsenal (2-0 on agg). Adrian Heath pulled one back for Everton. Groves, who played really well, beat two Everton players, then laid the ball square to Rocastle, who made no mistake this time for 2-1 on the night (3-1 on agg). No doubt who was going to Wembley now.

Rocastle to Winterburn, who drove into the area. Although his shot hit a defender, the ball fell kindly for Alan Smith. It's all over – 3-1 (4-1 on agg). "Wem-ber-ley! Wem-ber-ley! We're the famous Arsenal and we're going to Wem-ber-ley".

What a great few days at Highbury.

Neil Payne: This is a tricky but one that always sticks in my mind was the 2-1 FA Cup fifth round win over Manchester Utd (20/2/1988). More than 54,000 packed into Highbury – if you view the highlights on YouTube the footage shows stacks of fans watching on high level buildings behind the Clock End.

The game had pretty much everything: end-to-end, missed chances and of course that late and great penalty miss by Brian McClair which Nigel Winterburn, shall I say, seemed to enjoy more than most.

By that stage I had left school and was working, so my mate and I could afford the luxury of a season ticket in the East Stand upper tier. The atmosphere throughout the ground that day was simply amazing. In those days Arsenal gave over either all or three-quarters of the Clock End to visiting fans for Cup games and, as you would expect, United fans were out in force. After that McClair penalty miss three parts of the famous old ground literally erupted.

I also recall I had managed to get my dad a ticket in the West Stand lower and upon meeting him afterwards, he looked totally shattered.

"What's up with you?" I asked him.

"Bloody knackered, son. Had bundles of pissed-up Mancs sitting around me, so hardly sat down, been up and down like a yo-yo most of the game. Still, funny their reaction when the penalty hit the North Bank!"

Always remember getting home. He and Mum were due to be going out but, as in Dad's words: "I've had it." He kipped for most of the night! Some day that was.

Four days later, the League Cup semi-final v Everton (24/2/1988) very nearly matched it. Two amazing games.

Tom Eldridge: There are two Highbury moments for me that are so vivid. These are in addition to my first introduction to the East Stand upper in 1979. The first was nearly 10 years later, on that cold, clear night against Liverpool (9/11/1988) in the League Cup third round replay. Just over 54,000 packed into Highbury.

We were squeezed into the North Bank and could only find space to stand on the steps for the whole match. The game, against a Liverpool team that was arguably the best of the decade, was breathtaking. The noise and feeling in the North Bank was so strong and David Rocastle, Michael Thomas and Kevin Richardson matched this on the pitch. It was a sign of things to come in six months' time.

But what sticks out most from that night was that, coming into the ground, there was quite a crush and a few of the front garden walls on Gillespie Road actually fell in. It was such a squash, I remember actually being off my feet at one point. I was in the Clock End five months' later for the Newcastle Utd game on the day of the Hillsborough disaster (15/4/1989). I can't even begin to think what that was like. But I do think about the Gillespie Road experience quite a lot.

The second memory is a bit more random – and light-hearted. Arsenal v Birmingham City on another cold, but miserable Saturday in November (30/11/1985). I went with my school mate, Paul Newman, and his dad, and hardly any more than 16,500 others piled into Highbury. Nil-nil was the final score. The only thing that got the crowd on its feet for the whole 90 minutes was David O'Leary marshalling the ball-in-possession Birmingham centre-forward from about the centre circle right out to touch in front of the West Stand, without having to make a challenge. Paul Newman's dad didn't say much at the best of times but I remember him saying: "That 'Spider' can certainly defend." And he could.

Neil Davies: The most vivid memory is a strangely dark one. We played Liverpool in the League Cup, third round replay (9/11/1988) and there was trouble getting into the ground. I remember our drive taking ages and Dad fretting about getting in on time – this was a big game and missing it was unthinkable. As it was, we had to park up a good couple of miles from the ground and walk in.

We couldn't get in to our usual gate in the West Stand and the crowd was growing ever larger as more people made it to Highbury via road, rail and foot. People were pushing more and more but the gates had been shut. Before I knew it, police horses were among us and I saw some kids about my size being pulled out by the mounted police. I'd never seen Dad scared of anything until that moment, because I was beginning to lose myself under the weight of people and I'd even taken to rolling up my programme to use it as a makeshift breathing tube.

Dad grabbed my arm and fought his way through, yelling at me to keep pushing. I was trying not to panic but seeing him like that made it difficult. The gate was being pushed harder and harder by the sheer weight of people but it remained shut.

Dad somehow got us to enter the ground through the North Bank and from there, moving underneath the stands, we made it to the West Stand. People had spilled onto the slight running track which surrounded the pitch. Bill, the man who sat in front of us, a wise old-timer, turned to my dad and observed: "Can you imagine what would happen if we had those fences?"

The events which unfolded in South Yorkshire just a few months later sadly answered that terrible question. The fact that our ground didn't have metal fences surrounding the pitch, as they did to such tragic cost at Hillsborough, spoke a great deal of our fans and the outlook of Arsenal Football Club.

John Lawlor: The night I travelled from Dover, Kent to watch the League Cup tie v Liverpool (9/11/1988). I got to Highbury around six o'clock-ish, my regular ETA for an evening game, and the tube to Arsenal was packed more than usual for that time. On exiting the station, the streets were mobbed and there was absolutely loads already queuing, so I queued straight away. Not that the line was going very quickly and by about 7.15 I was still well away from the entrance to the gate on Gillespie Road. I think they closed the gate just before 7.45 and I was still about 30ft from it.

I couldn't believe I didn't get in, so I sulked all the way back to Dover even more annoyed that I hadn't bought a programme.

Craig Pottage: A steak pie flying around the North Bank, after Paul Merson had scored against Manchester City (14/10/1989), springs to mind. Also, my first North London derby, in 1980. The Old Man stood between the fence at the front of the North Bank and the advertising boards. So much trouble that day. Fighting in every stand.

George Lampshire: For the NLD v Spurs (20/1/1990) I'd come straight from work. When Tony Adams volleyed the winner, I lost a shoe in the celebrations. About 10 minutes later someone down the front held it up and it was passed back to me – too late to stop half the North Bank treading on my foot and giving me a black toenail!

George Stephanides: Only my second visit to Highbury, for the final home match of the 1989-90 season, v Southampton (2/5/1990). Arsenal won 2-1 after being 1-0 down. For the last 15 minutes of the match they were a joy to watch.

The second goal, scored by Dave Rocastle, was spectacular. He controlled the ball and attacked the Southampton defence from the wing, right side of the West Stand. He saw the goalkeeper covering his front post and with a stunning shot, he placed the ball in the far corner of the net. It was a Rocastle special.

I was very impressed when, after the match, all the fans gave the players and manager George Graham a standing ovation for their efforts throughout the season, despite the fact that Arsenal didn't win any silverware.

Guy Thompson: Three stand out but the first one has to be telling David Seaman to have a shot in the game v Derby County in 1990. It was blowing an absolute gale that day and I shouted "Have a shot, Dave!". He turned round and said to me in his deep Yorkshire accent: "Second-half." And we all know what happened next. I like to think I kind of helped with an assist on that one!

Lee Dixon knocking a policeman's helmet off with a ball during the warm-up was a funny moment. It was while the old brass band were playing. It was obviously followed by an almighty roar from us all behind the goal.

And 'Nutty Nigel' Winterburn having his infamous little word with McClair after his penalty miss in the FA Cup, fifth round tie v Man Utd (20/2/1988). Who could have guessed what THAT would lead to. I don't think I've ever enjoyed seeing a ball sail over a crossbar and over my head so much in my entire life.

Andrew Whitnall: Strangely, the 6-2 defeat to Manchester Utd in the League Cup, fourth round (28/11/1990). When they scored the fourth I decided to head for the tube but instead of leaving via Avenell Road, as I always did, I took my time and walked across the North Bank to the Gillespie Road exit, turning a number of times to get a perspective of the ground I wouldn't normally have. United scored their fifth as I did this and again as I reached the top of the stairway. That last view from the top of those steps is the image I always have in my mind of an evening game at Highbury, even though I exited the stadium by that route only once.

Kelvin Meadows: Maybe one from the 1990-91 season. About 15-20 of us had bought season tickets in the West upper, North Bank end. There was never any singing up there even though we tried for the bigger games. It was the game v Manchester Utd on the Bank Holiday Monday (6/5/1991). Liverpool had lost earlier in the day, so we'd already won the league.

The players did their warm-up in oversized baseball caps and enjoyed the carnival atmosphere. That was our best team. Lost one game, conceded just 18 goals, skipper locked up in Chelmsford nick and two points deducted after the brawl at Old Trafford.

We had the T-shirts on and put the word around that at a certain point we'd all start singing. The party mood must've spread to the other blocks, because – as one and on cue – we sang: "You can stick your f*****g two points up yer arse." Never heard the West upper sing as loud before or since.

David McConachie: I was lucky to get selected as a ball-boy as a Junior Gunner and even more fortunate to get Arsenal v Manchester Utd (22/3/1994). We twice came from behind to draw 2-2 (Pallister own-goal and Paul Merson) but what sticks out most is Eric Cantona's 88th minute red card. I was sat in front of the Clock End on my little stool, the goal away to my left. I momentarily lost my ball-boy 'professionalism' and was on my feet chanting "Off, off, off!" when a steward came up and reminded me that I needed to sit down, as I was "representing the club tonight". Was somewhat embarrassed and proud at the same time.

Yasir Matloub: New Year's Eve and The Arsenal were playing QPR (31/12/1994). Arsenal had a terrible season amid mounting pressure after manager George Graham was accused of accepting bungs. John Jensen had caught George's eye having scored for Denmark in their 1992 European Championship Final victory against Germany and was bought to add midfield steel and score goals.

But by this time his failure to score in 97 previous matches had become one of the

G. Graham *(Arsenal)*

most talked about subjects at Highbury. Every time he touched the ball in the opposition's half, fans would scream "Shoot!". Alas, John scored his only goal for the club (in 138 appearances) in front of the North Bank in a 3-1 defeat to Rangers.

My night was completed when I missed the last train from London Paddington to Cardiff and had to spend the night at the station until the first train out on New Year's Day.

Stuart Pierce: Watching the ball go beyond the flailing reach of QPR keeper Tony Roberts and into the top corner of the net from John Jensen's curling shot from outside the box (31/12/1994). I'm getting goose pimples just writing this!

Another vivid memory I have is the time I realised, as a nearly 10-year-old, that not everyone like me loved all of the players all of the time. The team line-up was read out before the match against Everton (12/4/1986), and went like this . . . "number nine, Niall Quinn" (crowd: "Yeaaaaay!"), "number 10, Charlie Nicholas ("yeaaaaay!"), number 11, Graham Rix ("boooooo!!") There was a weird thrill to it.

Ben Sharpe: One game that clearly stands out as a young kid was Dutch winger Glenn Helder's debut v Nottingham Forest (21/2/1995). It was the only time I sat in the Clock End and I thought how magnificent the North Bank looked under lights. We won the game 1-0 (Chris Kiwomya) and remember thinking that Helder – George Graham's last signing – was a world beater. Unfortunately, it never really worked out for him at Highbury.

Ian Mills: Dennis Bergkamp's first-ever Arsenal goal. He had gone just a paltry seven games in a Gunners shirt without scoring yet the English press were branding him a flop, partly due to his £7.5m price tag the previous summer. I could see Dennis was a player of genuine world class talent and had actually made a bet with a work colleague the Friday prior to this game v Southampton (23/9/1995) that he would score one or more goals in this game.

Just 17 minutes into this fixture, his fellow countryman Glenn Helder's deep cross to the back post was met with an emphatic volley into the bottom corner in front of the Clock End, where my mate Andrew and I celebrated wildly. We even made it onto that night's Match of the Day. Bergkamp scored again, while Ian Wright and Tony Adams completed a 4-2 win.

David Harman: Embarrassing incident. At the time my sister never really liked football but she had come along to a game with us anyway. If memory serves me correctly it was v Everton (20/1/1996).

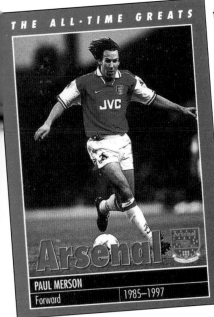

THE ALL-TIME GREATS

PAUL MERSON
Forward · 1985–1997

We were seated on the North Bank, front row and to the left of the goal. Before the game David Seaman was warming up with a coach. The ball was kicked towards us, hit the red metal barrier in front, went up in the air and I caught it as it came down.

Big Dave then turned around and walked towards us to retrieve the ball. As I chucked it back to him, my sister (behaving like a deranged fan at a Take That concert), much to my horror at the inappropriateness, screamed: "I love you, David Seaman!" Looking confused, Big Dave responded by saying something like: "Well, don't tell everyone, love."

Fellow fans who overheard this started laughing and making jokes at my expense. Along the lines of "I bet you're regretting bringing your 'little girlfriend' along to the football, aren't ya?" I tried to answer back with wit but in the end I just resorted to pretending I didn't know who she was. My credibility shot down, I was embarrassed.

To add insult to injury, we lost 2-1 (Wrighty scored a great goal, though, one of his best).

Barry Davison: 3-3 v Chelsea (4/9/1996). Goals by Frank Leboeuf (pen) and Gianluca Vialli left us two-nil down and my non-footballing dad seriously suggested we should leave at half-time. But Paul Merson got the first goal back, then Martin Keown's far-post header made it 2-2 before Wrighty put us in front from the edge of the box on 77 minutes . . . only for Dennis Wise to snatch a 90th-minute equaliser.

Mike Green: Beating Everton 4-0 (3/5/1998) to win the Premiership. The ball dropped to Tony Adams who had made his way forward and got onto the end of a brilliant Steve Bould pass. He lashed the ball into the net in front of the North Bank, where I was. He lifted his arms aloft and the whole place was going mental – pure theatre. A moment never, ever to be forgotten.

Nobby Ralfe: My two kids, Sammi and Jack, being guards of honour for the Junior Gunners' anniversary. Sammi stood in front of me with Arsène Wenger on the jumbotron behind her, while Jack stood next to a goalpost waving his flag with Jens Lehmann in goal.

I was lucky enough to be invited along to the first-ever training day at Highbury. Not only that but I was also chosen to win one of the players' training tops. Three of the five available – those worn by Thierry Henry, Gaël Clichy and Jérémie Aliadière – dropped from a bin-bag at my feet. I happened to grab Clichy's top but then I swapped it with someone for Aliadière's, as he was my daughter's beau.

All the shirts were signed by the players and mine reeked of French perfume.

The highlight of the day for me was seeing a young lad, dressed in Arsenal kit and wearing trainers, stood at the desk in the marble halls. I got him to sign the top I had on, which still hangs in my wardrobe. It turned out to be Cesc Fàbregas. He must have been 16.

George Pearson: One of the best games I've ever seen was the 3-1 Champions League second group stage win over Juventus (4/12/2001) and it will stay with me forever. Thierry Henry's 27th-minute curling freekick to beat Gianluigi Buffon, perhaps the best goalkeeper in the world at the time (who barely moved to his right as the ball floated in at his near-post) at the Clock End, and Dennis Bergkamp's pirouette on the edge of the box, to buy time for Freddie Ljungberg's run into space for his second goal on 88 minutes, are why we are all football fans. Magical.

Tom Humphrey: My most vivid memory of a game at Highbury was when we met Liverpool in the fourth round of the FA Cup (27/1/2002). Liverpool and Michael Owen broke my young heart when they somehow beat us in the 2001 FA Cup Final in Cardiff. It was time for revenge. I hated Liverpool for that. I still don't know how we lost it.

My memory of the '02 game was Jamie Carragher throwing a pound coin back to the crowd and getting sent-off. It nearly hit my dad! People were throwing everything at Carragher that day: money, burgers, hot dogs, they flew from the Arsenal end towards Carragher. Arsenal had two players sent off in all the chaos (Bergkamp and Keown if my memory serves me correctly) and the home fans started singing: "Nine men, we only had nine men!".

Revenge was definitely ever so sweet that day.

Dave Randall: A coin-throwing incident happened in front of where we sat for the FA Cup fourth round tie v Liverpool (27/1/2002) played in Sunday lunchtime drizzle. Dennis Bergkamp had given Arsenal a 1-0 lead by heading home Thierry Henry's first-time left-wing cross at the Clock End.

But Bergkamp, whose goal turned out to be the winner, became one of three sent-off by ref Mike Riley in the space of four minutes. Martin Keown was ordered off in the 67th minute for a 'last man' professional foul on Michael Owen and then Dennis was red-carded for going over the top on Jamie Carragher. It kicked off big-time on the pitch.

Then someone from five or six rows behind us in the East Stand threw a coin onto the pitch which landed at the feet of Carragher. He picked it up and threw it back – a gesture which earned him a sending-off too.

The atmosphere became as heated as I'd ever seen that close to where we sat. I believe the person that allegedly threw the coin was caught on camera and ejected at the next home game, although I'm possibly speculating here. There was definitely someone escorted away at that game.

Mark Aughterlony: This has to be Ipswich Town (21/4/2002). My uncle Jim (Westwood) called me up a couple of nights before with the offer of a spare ticket, so I attended this vitally important game in our Premiership challenge with him and his younger brother, my uncle Martin. Those who were there will recall that for an hour it was stalemate and it was looking increasingly as if we were going to drop two vital points at home. Then, up pops Freddie (and my uncle Martin).

It is fair to say that uncle Martin is not a small guy, and at the time was in his early-mid forties. Well, no sooner had Freddie Ljungberg scored the first of his double that afternoon in front of those of us sat in the North bank than up shoots Martin out of his seat, about seven rows back from the front, and proceeds to barge his way down the steps to join the mass of fellow Gooners at the foot of the stand in celebrating the goal.

It was at that moment that it genuinely hit home to me . . . The Arsenal meant equally as much to my uncles as they did to me. The look of sheer joy and elation on Martin's face

made me so proud to not only be a part of the Arsenal 'family', but also my own family as well.

Lorraine & Louise Haugh: We have so many happy memories at Highbury but without doubt the one that we cherish the most is when Thierry Henry came over to us in the crowd, kissed us on both cheeks and apologised.

It was a game against West Ham Utd (24/4/2002), when sometime in the first-half a decision went against Arsenal. Thierry got angry and kicked the ball full force into the crowd

Twin sisters Lorraine and Louise Haugh in the Highbury press room.

It headed straight towards us, narrowly avoiding our heads as we moved out of the way. We were sitting by the dug-out and looked over to see Arsène Wenger standing there looking our way and saying "sorry". Play continued as normal and we forgot about it.

At the final whistle we stood up to applaud the team. Then we looked over to see Dennis Bergkamp shouting over to Thierry – and pointing at us. The next minute, Thierry came over to us, said "sorry" and gave us both a kiss. I did ask for his shirt but he had already swapped it with a West Ham player.

All of this was shown live on Sky Sports, so we had friends phoning to ask if they had just seen us on TV with Thierry. That is definitely a story I'll tell my grandchildren one day.

James Smither: When I close my eyes and remember Highbury, my most vivid memory of quite how special it was comes from a game against West Ham from the run-in to the glorious league campaign in 2002. It was April 24 and a night game – which were always my favourites at Highbury. There was something about how the beautiful old place looked under its spotlights – the stands whiter, the pitch greener, the seats redder – and I generally found the atmosphere better for our midweek encounters as well: more focused, somehow.

Thierry Henry apologising to Lorraine and Louise Haugh.

It was a particularly intense affair, and West Ham set out to frustrate us – as most teams did in those days, given the attacking talent that filled our squad. Our committed opponents actually had a quite legitimate opener scored by Kanouté at the North Bank ruled out in the first-half for not having crossed the line (blown back into play by the Gooners behind the goal I liked to think, although in reality Ashley Cole managed to clear it while blocking the officials' view of how far it had travelled). Had the goal stood and we'd fallen behind, I am not sure anyone in the stadium that night could have taken the tension.

As it was, the necessity of winning to remain ahead of Manchester Utd in the title race and recapture the trophy they'd withheld from us in a variety of different manners over the preceding three seasons made the nerves around the stands unbearable. This seemingly transmitted itself to the players as well – our usually deadly pairing of Henry and Bergkamp up-front were frustratingly ineffective against a hardly world-class centre-back pairing of Repka and Dailly. The fear and desire escalated in tandem throughout the game – if you'd told anyone there that night "it's only a game" you'd have risked losing your front teeth – until the introduction of Kanu from the bench. As we poured forward seeking a winner, Kanu altered the equation and our patient build-up play finally yielded a breakthrough on 77 minutes. Dennis Bergkamp slipped in Ljungberg and Freddie finished expertly – as they both kept doing during that amazing purple patch – and Highbury absolutely erupted.

I've always said the loudest cheers you'll ever hear at football are for a second goal scored quickly following a first, and never was that more correct than when, with the North Bank upper still wobbling from the sheer explosion of joy and relief the Super Swede's goal had created, the languid Nigerian substitute deliciously slid home a second about 90 seconds later. Bedlam. It was genuinely the loudest cheer I think I ever heard at Highbury – or 'felt', would be more accurate: one of those totally lose-yourself, shred-your-throat-screaming, embrace-total-strangers, end-up-10-rows-from-your-seat-with-bruised-shins-the-next-morning occasions. A precise moment when 35,000-odd of us all simultaneously knew we were going to win the league, and that no-one could stop us.

Thinking and writing about it now still sends shivers running down my spine.

Barry Hughes: One of the most unusual memories from Highbury would be at the Liverpool home game (9/4/2004) during the Invincibles season. Being a ticket registration scheme member (later Silver member), my seat would never be the same from one game to the next. On this occasion I was in the North Bank lower, near the corner flag.

We had just been knocked out of the Champions League and FA Cup and there was a fear we could blow the league too despite being unbeaten up to this stage. Early on, Liverpool got a corner right in front of us and Harry Kewell came over to take it. He was delayed from taking it by the ref which gave some the chance to shout some friendly abuse at him about choosing Liverpool instead of The Arsenal when leaving Leeds in the previous summer. Kewell, to his credit, engaged in conversation and said something along the lines of being happy with his decision. He promptly took the corner and Liverpool scored.

As Kewell ran away he turned and winked at us. I can laugh at this now – Thierry turned on the style, scored a hat-trick and we won 4-2 – but at the time the goal was a huge worry. Even so, despite shouting abuse at Kewell, everyone around me had a begrudging respect for him. He had just done exactly what we would have done if we had been lucky enough to play for The Arsenal.

Graham Price: Too many to list. Bergkamp's goal to put us into the UEFA Cup; Pires/ Henry penalty miss; Reyes' goals v Chelsea in the FA Cup; Charlie Nicholas against Sp*rs; Henry from the halfway line v Sp*rs; Dixon's own-goal. Being in the North Bank as a 15-year-old: a goal is scored, and the crowd surging yards down the terrace. The Met Police band; the squirrel on the pitch; the terrible bands in the early days of Monday Night Football on Sky; Arsenal beating France; and Ian Wright's smile when he banged another goal in.

Mark White: I suppose the most vivid memories are those generated by the 'twelfth man' – the crowd. From leaving the tube station or walking with others; feeling it grow as you entered the ground . . . standing on the North Bank or sitting in the West Stand . . . watching it grow: the noise, the songs, the banter, the reactions, the sense of anticipation, the celebrations, the joy. Singing 'Liam Brady is magic' for what seemed like forever, coming from all around the ground, to the buzz that went around the ground when the crowd urged the team forward or danger threatened. The sense of urgency in a cup-tie, the crowd urging the players on. Sometimes the silence, the disappointment when the away team scored in an important game or against the run of play, or a player was seriously injured. The patience in a European tie. The emptiness of a defeat.

The sense of injustice felt by the crowd as one. And the anger, even the hostility. Malcolm Macdonald getting sent-off against Coventry City after five minutes following an horrendous tackle from behind by Terry Yorath. Supermac went down in a heap and as both players rose from the floor he hit Yorath with a right-hander that Frank Bruno would've been proud of. Yorath didn't see Macdonald get sent off – he was out cold for five minutes or so. However, he knew that Arsenal fans knew who the real victim was when he recovered. Although there were only around 30,000 fans in the ground, the atmosphere sounded like there was double that number as they booed the Coventry City hatchet man every time he got near the ball. The noise when Arsenal scored, what we all thought was the winner, right at the end of the game (only to be disallowed) was deafening.

The laughter: Sammy Nelson dropping his shorts. The Ruud Gullit lookalike warming up before one game, showing all his tricks and skills. The crowd thought we'd signed a new player. Turned out to be Mickey Thomas in a dreadlock wig.

The sheer size: official crowd of 57,960 for Arsenal v Manchester City in the League Cup (24/1/1978). Felt more like 70,000 were there as we won 1-0 (Liam Brady). Stood on the North Bank, the crowd swaying from side to side, back to front, as one.

The crowd triumphant, jubilant, beating Liverpool early in the season (8/9/1984). I'd just passed the Knowledge that week and it was a great way to celebrate with Brian Talbot scoring two great goals as Arsenal beat the League champions, 3-1, in style.

The night George Graham's team came of age in the League Cup semi-final, second leg (24/2/1988), when boys became men and Rocastle and Thomas overran the Everton midfield to clinch another final appearance.

Beating Manchester Utd (6/5/1991) to win the title emphatically after Liverpool had lost earlier in the day, with Alan Smith winning the Golden Boot.

Then there was David O'Leary's tempestuous record-breaking game in our 4-3 victory against Norwich City (4/11/1989).

Anders Limpar scoring from near the halfway line in our 4-0 thrashing of Liverpool (20/4/1992) in the sunshine.

Ian Wright joining Arsenal and scoring goals for fun. Scoring a hat-trick on the final day of the season, v Southampton (2/5/1992), to snatch the Golden Boot award from Tottenham's Gary Lineker and give the North Bank a rousing send-off before it was torn down at the end of the season.

Rob Macdonald: I loved what was designated as 'Dennis Bergkamp Day', when West Bromwich Albion visited (15/4/2006) towards the end of the final season. In celebration of the player's contribution to Arsenal, fans were given commemorative orange DB10 T-shirts – the colour of his national team, his initials and his squad number. Dennis himself came on as a second-half sub and set up the winning Robert Pires goal moments after Nigel Quashie had equalised. Fittingly, Bergkamp's 89th-minute goal – a trademark 35-yard screamer – proved to be his last for Gunners in competitive football. It couldn't have been better scripted.

Roberto Puzzi: The best – and probably worst – moment, as it was the last time I entered the Home of Football, was the last game v Wigan Athletic (7/5/2006). It was an emotional day and I was lucky enough to get a ticket along with my father. I enjoyed every moment of it. I was in the West Stand lower and the red shirt I wore that day is still one of my favourite pieces of memorabilia.

Arsenal players warming up before facing West Brom on Dennis Bergkamp Day.

ARSENAL 6 BENFICA 2

Pre-season friendly, August 4, 1971

BILLED as a pre-season friendly, this was anything but as things turned sour on the pitch after George Graham, looking suspiciously offside, scored Arsenal's fourth goal early in the second-half.

The Portuguese champions surrounded and jostled Cup Final referee Norman Burtenshaw to the extent that police came from behind the North Bank goal to restore order by the touchline.

John Roberts gave the newly-crowned First Division and FA Cup Double winners the lead. Graham (2), John Radford, George Armstrong and Peter Storey completed the home scoring. Benfica, who had won back-to-back European Cup finals in 1961 and '62 and were beaten finalists in '63, '65 and '68, pulled two goals back.

Many of the 44,244 crowd came to see the great Eusébio and were disappointed when the former European Footballer of the Year didn't reappear for the second-half.

Little known fact: this game in 1971 could have been Benfica's second visit to Highbury. Had the 1968 European Cup Final between the Lisbon giants and Manchester Utd at Wembley ended in a draw, the replay was scheduled for Highbury two nights later, on Friday, May 31. Arsenal even had to go to the trouble of producing what is a very rare and sought-after match day programme, in the same style as their standard pocked-sized 1967-68 design, but it turned out to be unnecessary – United beat them 4-1.

THE GUNNERS

WELCOME TO

THE
GUNNERS PUB

www.gunnerspubhighbury.co.uk

4 CHARACTERS

WHILE players have always been the main attraction, the entertainment has not been solely confined to the pitch. From the often cutting humour overheard on the old terraces and in the stands, to the unique individuals who enriched the match day experience, here our contributors recall some of the people who were part of the fabric of Highbury . . .

Q: Describe any 'characters' in the Highbury crowd and why they stood out?

Graham Lister: I watched games from most parts of Highbury over the years – most enjoyably when standing on the old North Bank; for a lengthy spell in the 1970s in the northernmost block of the lower West Stand, when it was important to be seated, as my young nephew was in tow at the time; and from 1989 onwards as a season ticket holder in the lower East.

There were characters to be encountered throughout the stadium, from the sellers of roasted peanuts weaving their way between crush barriers across the North Bank terracing, to the inventive wits in the middle and towards the back who could be relied upon to instigate new chants, to the bovver boys on the Clock End terraces forever looking to provoke a scrap with the opposition fans standing in close proximity.

Then there were the (mercifully few) moaners whose match day enjoyment centred around loudly complaining about the team and manager irrespective of what was happening on the pitch. And the guy in the lower East pathologically opposed to anything and everything Paul Merson did, however inspirational Merse's contribution might be. Or the bloke who could be relied upon to dash down the lower East steps five minutes after every game had started and cause major disruption for all those already in their places, who were obliged to stand and let him pass to reach his seat in the middle of the row.

Then there were the sardonic souls with a cruel line in put-downs of opposition players. I remember, for example, being stood near the front of the Clock End terrace on Boxing Day, 1968 as we beat Manchester Utd 3-0, and United's aesthetically-challenged Carlo Sartori coming towards us to retrieve the ball for a corner. Suddenly, a north London voice bellowed: "Ain't you ugly!" to a discomforted Sartori as the crowd in the vicinity howled with amusement.

On another occasion, in 1997, West Ham's Iain Dowie went to take a throw-in from the east touchline and was loudly and somewhat unhelpfully informed: "You're just a waste of skin, Dowie." Even the West Ham fans were yelling "Off! off! off!" when he was booked in the first-half, and subsequently demonstrated their understanding of irony by singing: "We all agree, Dowie is better than Bergkamp" when Dowie exhibited all the on-the-ball deftness of a lawnmower.

Chris Welstead: Two characters spring to mind. Back in the early 60s there was a guy who would appear from the Clock End terrace about 30 minutes before the game. He would run into the penalty area at the Clock End and proceed to juggle with an imaginary ball before placing it on the penalty spot and pretending to fire the ball into the top corner of the goal. This always brought a roar from the crowd. He would then disappear back into the crowd to watch the match.

Tony Fisher: The two guys who sat behind me for 30 years in the East Stand were like Waldorf & Statler from The Muppet Show. Such funny nonsense every game but there don't seem to be any wags in the crowd nowadays. Caroline Adams (Tony's mum) sitting near us for a couple of his early seasons and having a go at everyone and anyone who dared criticised him.

Bernard Chaplin: Many older fans will remember David Stacey, football programme dealer and in later years a good friend of mine. At important cup-ties or derby matches he would parade round the ground in a red and white dinner suit with tails and top hat. Although he passed away two or three years ago, he can still be seen on the pre-match montage that is shown before each match. A fitting memorial for an avid supporter of Arsenal and England.

Not in the crowd but during my early years walking from Drayton Park to the ground, we regularly passed a blind man selling matches from a tray. Whether he had any sales or what happened to him, I do not know.

Robert Thaine: Some old fella called 'Tom' who claimed to not have missed a game since he first started coming to Highbury in 1930. He always said win, lose or draw, he probably wouldn't come to the next game but always turned up.

Jeff Owens: In the early 60s, there was a short man who always seemed to wear a raincoat and a flat cap to every game. His only phrase seemed to be 'Come on, Arsenal – set 'em alight'. If we got to stand behind and above him on the terracing, we used to try and balance our empty peanut shells on the top of his cap.

Paul Harris: There is one particular character who stands out. He was an elderly man and still equipped with the 1930s gear of cloth cap and muffler. He was an Arsenal supporter but still extolled the 30s side and described the modern Arsenal (1980s) as poor by comparison. He loved to wind up those nearest to him on the terraces, and he seemed fearless and in deadly earnest. His best comment for me was when there was a narrow miss, he yelled out at the top of his voice: 'Third Division, North!' as if it was an unassailable insult.

Then there were those indefatigable peanut sellers who slipped through the crowd with the dexterity of eels and did not seem to stop moving even when conducting a sale.

David Roche: On the North Bank I remember a large Greek guy who used to ring a bell whenever we went forward.

Dave Randall: We had these two guys that sat in front of us – never knew their names but they were hugely comical. On DB10's debut against Boro in '95, he was flagged offside in the first 10 minutes, to which one of them exclaimed: "You can't do that, that's Dennis Bergkamp." You can watch endless football on Sky, or any other medium for that matter, but you can't match off the cuff moments like that.

On a romantic note, I sat behind my now partner Caroline for at least 15 years before, one day, we realised we were single. We've been a very happy couple ever since!

Lee Pritchett: There was this guy that used to stand behind us every game that was never happy – he used to drive my dad mad. "Sammels, you're useless. Court, you're crap. Brady, you're rubbish." There was just no pleasing him. Thank god there was no social media in those days.

Lester Allen: When we finally got season tickets for the 1979-80 season, they were in the lower tier West Stand. It was unreserved seating and the club made the centre block for season tickets. We sat the entire time with six others and still sit with four today at The Emirates, namely the family of the late Alan Ashby, Denise, Dave, Nicki, my two sons Lee and Jamie, as well as Shaun, Keith Wells and Nic Biggane. Plus three people who always sat behind us: Charlie, Biff and linesman Ken, who goes by the nickname 'Lino'.

Peter Coombs: The old school North Bank crowd of the late 1960s in their uniforms: white coats, the badges, scarves tied round their wrists or belt, the whole skinhead culture. DMs rule!

Tony Bateman: The bloke that used to yell out "Moosehead!" at random times in the North Bank.

Emilio Zorlakki: I was at the game v Everton (17/10/70) when I noticed this reasonably elderly man with this giant, elongated top hat with 'ARSENAL' plastered all over it. He was a bit of a joker and all of the people nearby were laughing and smiling with him. I would occasionally see him in the West Stand for the next couple of seasons, before he suddenly disappeared.

Nobby Ralfe: Tom Watt being interviewed back row of the North Bank before it was demolished. I have a 'I Was There' t-shirt still in its bag, unopened, from that day.

Andrew Whitnall: Comedian Rory McGrath often used to stand in front of me in the North Bank with his mates. I'm sure I remember Tony Robinson coming to a game with him.

John Hilditch: There are the obvious characters, such as Percy Dalton's peanut man, half-and-half man and Maria, but there was also a fella in the Clock End who had a cannon tattooed onto his cheek. I always thought that was dedication beyond my levels.

And then there was the fella in the last year at Highbury, who streaked across the pitch and did the same thing at Stamford Bridge in the next game, too.

Outside the ground, there was the bloke on the corner of Gillespie Road and Avenell Road who sold back issue programmes. A great place to get the programmes, or rather the vouchers you were missing as we got closer to Wembley.

Stephen Simson: I remember the 'Highbury Screamer', who sat in West upper and every time our opposition attacked, she would scream. Not sure of her name but what a character she was.

David Harman: The 'Highbury Screamer', although I never knew who she was. There was this miserable guy who would just complain the whole game. Funnily enough, the better Arsenal played, the more he moaned. I can't remember what game it was but I'm pretty sure Arsenal were two or three-nil up and playing well but this guy just sat there complaining and whining. My dad, fed up, eventually turned around and told him to shut up and enjoy it. To be fair, he did keep quiet after that.

Tom Humphrey: Everybody remembers the famous 'Highbury Screamer'. Whenever Arsenal conceded a goal at Highbury, you heard a woman screaming as soon as the ball hit the back of the net. Since the move to The Emirates, I haven't heard her.

Dad and me would often get a burger or hot dog before the game but none of the people that served us the food were quite as enthusiastic as one that we both remember to this day. He'd say things like: "Onions with that?", followed by his famous "lovely, lovely!". I used to hear him all the time in those days but he's another that I haven't heard from since the club switched grounds.

James Smither: By sitting all around the stadium during my Junior Gunners/Cannon Club days, I heard the 'North Bank Screamer' and Maria's unmistakeable "Come on, you Gunners!" countless times at close quarters.

The one encounter that stands out most is a clearly inebriated character wearing a tatty suit who sat nearby when I repaid a promise to a Liverpool-supporting university mate by bringing him to Highbury for a clash with his team in the autumn of 1997. A pretty dreary game, decided by a quality Steve McManaman goal, was most memorable for the incessant chatter of our neighbour, who, in loud and slurred speech, constantly berated Arsenal's defending with the singular expression I've never heard before or since: "What are they doing? They're SCRATCHING!"

Given little option but to respond, we soon adopted the phrase, helpfully pointing out additional instances of egregious 'scratching' for his approval for the remainder of the

'KNOWLEDGE' – Daniel Robert Feinstein

Private man who could recall details of every match

A MYSTERY Arsenal supporter best known by his nickname 'Knowledge' – in tribute to his astonishing encyclopaedic grasp of the club's history – has died suddenly.

Daniel Feinstein, 45, travelled across the country and Europe following Arsenal's first team, reserves and youth side.

He kept his own meticulous statistics of every match and player but was known to be fiercely private and would not let other fans see what was written in his notepads or give them his phone number. The notebooks were thought to contain minute details of how he spent his day and what he had seen.

Few fellow supporters were even aware of his real name – he preferred his terrace nickname, 'Knowledge' or 'Mr Knowledge'. He was an instantly recognisable figure, often weighed down with carrier bags filled with notepads and football programmes. A familiar face at every away trip, he even followed the second string and Arsenal's youth teams to seemingly meaningless games.

Without a car, Knowledge relied on public transport and lifts from other fans. When he was not seen at Arsenal's pre-season friendlies, supporters began to worry about his welfare, aware that he would not miss the annual match with lower-league Barnet without a good reason.

It is thought he died of kidney failure over the summer break (July 10, 2009). The first many fans knew of his death was an obituary in the match day magazine for the Arsenal-Portsmouth game two weeks ago. His relatives are understood to have contacted the club with the sad news.

"He was a virtual ever-present at reserve and academy fixtures for many years," the programme said. "His vast knowledge of the club at junior levels, in particular, had proved a great help to the club's publications over the years."

Mr Feinstein, who lived in south London, helped several footballer writers with statistics for their books, especially before the growth of the internet made detailed facts and figures about Arsenal easy to obtain.

He would often be seen waiting around the press entrance to the old Highbury ground, stopping journalists as they left matches and asking for team sheets and statistics given to sports reporters covering Gunners' matches.

He was described this week as "open and friendly" when talking about football but clammed up when asked about his own life.

Tribute in Islington Tribune by Richard Osley on September 4, 2009

WORD has got round since the beginning of this week that the supporter known best as 'Knowledge' passed away over the summer. There was concern among the away regulars that one of the usual characters was not at any of the pre-season matches. His sister apparently phoned Arsenal to relay news of his death over the summer and word has since spread.

He was something of a man of mystery but those that watched Arsenal away games regularly, as well as reserve and youth matches, knew him, although it seems that no-one really knew him that well away from Arsenal. I believe he got the name 'Knowledge' due to his encyclopedic knowledge of the club and liked to be referred to by this name. He was definitely an Arsenal character.

From a mixture of emails and forum posts, here is what others have said about him:

I bumped into Knowledge many times on European away trips and, as you say, he was a character all on his own. He was often scurrying around looking very hot and bothered trying to get programmes, team sheets or press passes so he could sit in the press area. I'm sure he wrote match reports for a 'zine or a blog and would use this as a way to get into games as a member of the press. Every time I met him he would always be laden down with carrier bags and a big heavy electronic typewriter. The reason for this was that he had had his laptop stolen on a train, travelling across some backend European country when he fell asleep. Therefore, the electronic typewriter travelled to Europe instead!

Used to see Knowledge at every home game and had many chats, as I am in the Family Enclosure with my son, and he also used to collect team sheets and hang around near the press. At the Rushden & Diamonds friendly last year, Knowledge was in the glass-fronted press box on his own and was very pleased with himself!

RIP, The Knowledge. He used to keep detailed notes of all the matches and god forbid if you ever tried to sneak a look at what he was writing. He could quote details from any match that he had attended – score, scorers, times of goals, and attendance, etc, off the top of his head.

He is clearly a man who goes back a long way. I used to attend a lot of the away games in the 70s and 80s – very infrequently now – but his picture kind of rings a bell. It's great that our club attracts people like that. Individuals who seek nothing for themselves but come rain or shine, come hell or high water, they are always there. It's their life and they give nothing less than everything they have and all they can to it. The sad thing is that they are often not seen until they are gone, if you follow me. But it's all part of our great club's noble tradition. And all the greater for enduring, through the seasons, out of the limelight. Let's hope we can do him proud by putting ourselves back at the top, where we belong, come next May.

An unusual character, indeed, but part of the Arsenal family nonetheless. Knowledge looked like that caricature of him that *The Gooner* did. It was spot on. (Ed's note – In the early 1990s the fanzine ran a quiz which I believe was partially inspired by the man himself, although it was before my time as editor.)

He used to carry around all these plastic bags full of paper and Rothmans yearbooks. He had not what you call any friends but plenty of acquaintances. Nobody had his phone number and he was most upset if you did not address him as Knowledge. I knew his real name but he hated people knowing it.

He went to EVERY first, reserve and youth team game. On Arsenal TV, you used to see him in the background in those youth games at the training ground. He used to write notes during games but nobody knew what for and he never used to let you see them.

Knowledge was well known but not liked at the club, as he used to apply for press passes for all games and was rude to the head of the press office, so she used to throw him off the European press lists – much to his annoyance.

I went to the Maidenhead game last week and Andrew Miller asked me if I had seen him at the game, because nobody had seen him all pre-season. Andrew said: "He must be dead, as he would never miss these games."

Unfortunately, he was proved right. Apparently, he died in July but nobody knows the exact causes. His sister just rang the club to let them know.

So he died in mystery, just the way he lived his life – a fitting ending. He was a nutter, sometimes rude but he was a character who loved Arsenal and I will miss bumping into him and chatting to him.

Tribute written for www.onlinegooner.com by editor Kevin Whitcher on August 5, 2009

gooner (Sarrie62): Anyone remember Danny 'The Knowledge'? Don't think he was anywhere near as old as he looked and he was like the encyclopaedia of Arsenal. Thick glasses, thinning dark Brylcreamed hair brushed back, he wore an overcoat.

Brian Kendal: I remember 'The Knowledge' on some away trips on The Arsenal Travel Club trains in the mid-80s. On one occasion I recall he was carrying a mini typewriter.

game. Despite its uncertain etymology, it remains a phrase used between us to describe particularly atrocious examples of the art of defending.

I never saw him at another game again. I wonder if he renounced coming to games in protest at our abject display, of if anyone else ever encountered this peculiar individual and his catchphrase? From what I recall, it was in either the East or West lower.

Alex Morrow: There was always one old bloke who sat behind me. He chain-smoked thin cigars and complained about everything that happened on the pitch. There was also a guy that was pretty full of himself and would make up a song that he would sing on his own at the top of his voice. And in our stand singing was rare. During the dire League form of the mid-90s he would sing: "It's entertaining, entertaining, in the West Stand on a Saturday afternoon."

We also had what we dubbed 'Celebrity Row' in front of us in the West upper. Frank Carson was a regular, as was Tony Hadley. Best of all was Mark Burdis, who years before I saw him at Arsenal had played Christopher 'Stewpot' Stewart in Grange Hill. He would often arrive five minutes late and shake hands with people on his way down to the front of the stand. We always used to say that he was late because he was being beaten up in the toilets by Gripper – but I cannot confirm that this was the case.

Tom Eldridge: During the 1988-89 season there was a girl selling the 'Make Money with Arsenal' scratch cards. She used to come round to the Clock End and I only ever bought those stupid cards when she was selling them. I didn't ever win a thing but spent a fortune on them. And I know I wasn't the only one trying to Make Money with Arsenal and steal a smile at the same time.

Neil Davies: The character who comes to mind most is one of the Greek family a couple of rows in front of us in the West Stand. Whenever a goal was scored either way, he would spend the next couple of minutes stood up waving two fingers to the away fans in the Clock End – he loved the abuse that would come back at him and it would just stiffen his resolve to keep flicking those fingers. He was a tall, broad man with a shock of grey hair who looked like he could certainly look after himself.

Ben Sharpe: In the early days I was mostly in the family enclosure but once I hit my teenage years, I was lucky enough to sit in the North Bank and this is where I stayed for the next eight years. While watching the game, I always remember, when the atmosphere quietened, a man in the East lower, maybe 15 rows back close to the North Bank, would stand up and start singing "We're the East Stand, we're the East Stand, we're the East Stand Highbury" which would then be the start of the 'stand chants', as I call them.

Ian Tredgett: During the last years at Highbury I had a season ticket in the North Bank lower and the guy next to me used to shout "Fix Bayonets" just before kick-off every game. It always amused me anyway.

MARIA

Chris Welstead: Maria, well known to many of the Highbury faithful. At every home game, she would wait for a lull in the action before shouting: "Come on, you Gunners" at the top of her voice. It never failed to bring a cheer from the crowd.

Peter Lewis: Aside from Maria "Come on, you Gunners" Petri, whom I met in 2006, I think of one man with no teeth standing at the Clock End singing and whistling at the same time!

Stuart Pierce: Maria and her "Come on, you Gunners!" shout. There was also a chap on the North Bank who nearly keeled over every time Andy Linighan was on the ball.

James Miller: Biggest one for me was our Pat, who worked behind the bar in the Arsenal Supporters' Club. She always gave me a bag of crisps, and then when I took my own son, she did the same with him. Pat, John, Peggy, they helped make memories. Nowadays, my favourite Arsenal fan is Maria, an amazing lady.

The Don, The Arsenal and the George Graham years

By Bob Varney

GEORGE Graham was a big part of our lives for many years. He was there for me at the very beginning, scoring the third goal in 'my' debut win at home to Everton in December 1968. And he was the 'star' in what was one of The Don's best stories.

George's playing career spanned the 1960s and 70s and he was part of our famous Double-winning team that triumphed in 1971. We had all seen him play many times. 'Stroller' Graham.

However, we got to know him personally when he became manager in 1986. His appointment coincided with the three of us becoming season ticket holders for the first time. East upper, Block D, Row C, Seats 109, 110 and 111. We sat in age order. We always sat in age order. It tickled me. The Don, elder brother Steve and me.

The Don's seat was adjacent to the directors' box and he soon became acquainted with Richard Carr, a director on the board and one of the largest shareholders. This relationship would eventually lead to us being invited to half a dozen or so away matches as guests of Arsenal FC seated with the Arsenal directors in the directors' box. On one occasion at Carrow Road, Norwich, it was David Dein who greeted us in reception. It was in this environment that we got to know George Graham.

George was a great manager and The Don was a big fan. Some years later we sponsored the match ball at Villa Park. It was New Year's Eve and The Don had decided we should take the train so we could have a drink. After the game, a 1-0-win courtesy of David Rocastle, if I recall correctly, Steve and I were having a drink, and quite probably a prawn sandwich or two, when The Don came over and asked if we knew the way to the M6? Steve replied: "Of course we do" but we were on the train. "Not anymore," replied The Don, "George is giving us a lift home!"

And so, he did. In his 7 series BMW, down the M6 and M1 on New Year's Eve. You couldn't make it up.

We went on to win the League that year. It was during this period that we became good friends with Bob Davies and Freddie Rollason. Freddie, the eldest, a City gent with dandruff an ever-present on his equally ever-present Harrods blazer. Old money. Bob was . . . Bob. A larger-than-life extrovert who always chose the wine – sometimes to the consternation of Freddie who was often heard to growl: "There's nothing wrong with a perfectly good Cote de Rhone." Bob was new money. I was the youngest and sat on the end. I always sat on the end.

We saw a lot of each other during the George Graham years. Virtually every away game. From Middlesbrough to Southampton, Wrexham to Norwich. We seldom saw each other at home games. Freddie sat among the Executive Club in the West Stand, where we ventured a couple of times. Bob had an Executive Box in the Clock End, where we were invited from time to time. It was from here we saw the great Tony Adams smash home that classic strike against Everton on the last day of the season to clinch yet another title.

George Graham had gone by then. And what was latterly dubbed 'The Gourmet Gooners' was coming to an end too. Freddie died. The Don stopped going to away matches and we lost contact with Bob.

It was many years later, while I was having lunch at The Swan in Salford, that I fortuitously bumped into Bob again. We were reunited and rekindled our friendship. Bob was now based at Woburn Sands, just a few hundred metres from The Don, who was living in The Burlington Care Home. The Don and Bob rekindled their friendship too. And Bob read the eulogy at The Don's funeral.

'BADGER'

Kelvin Meadows: John and Mary 'Badger', who stood on the North Bank, down the front just to the left of the goal. John covered in badges and Mary with her Union flag spread out in front of the fence.

In the mid-late 70s there was a bloke called Harry, who stood in the lower west paddock, had a loud voice and wanted to get things going other than on the North Bank.

And, of course, the legend that is Maria.

John Blair: Badger on the North Bank with his cowboy hat and leather coat covered in hundreds of Arsenal badges.

David Hillyard: I remember taking the day off school to watch Arsenal v Derby County on a Tuesday afternoon. Climbing over the fence at school after getting my mark, catching the bus to Finsbury Park, and then buying a small crusty loaf and bag of chips. I took all the dough out the middle and placed the chips inside it with loads of vinegar. "Mmm . . . that's dinner sorted." Into the ground I went while following a guy called Badger and admiring all the badges on his butcher's coat.

StevieBoy595cTMTR (@stevieboy591): We had a discussion about badger awhile back, about his real name. Him and his missus were John and Mary Crowe.

'SHIRTS'

Brian Dawes (@Gooner48): 'Shirts' (aka Michael Farmer), an Irishman who also worked on the old stadium demolition and new stadium build. Lovely guy. He also wore a red beret.

Alan W (@wildy_73): There was a bloke who sat at the front of the North Bank with a bag of shirts, and he'd change shirts each time we scored to that of the goalscorer! In the early 2000s,he had a (Francis) Jeffers shirt.

'BAZZO'

Gary Biggs: Barry Match, the half-and-half kit wearer. Still is to this day. Good bloke.

Graham Price: The man in the half-half kit and shorts, whatever the weather. *The Gooner* seller, whom I also saw selling the fanzine at my local club Harrow Borough, and 'Come on, you rip-roaring reds' man.

'RIP-ROAR'

Paul Manel: From about 1985 I graduated from the seats to the North Bank. There were a number of characters, including the world famous 'Rip -Roar'. The North Bank would sing: "Rip-Roar, Rip-Roar, give us a song." He would then bellow out: "Come on, you rip-roaring reds." This would be followed by a huge cheer of approval. Whatever happened to him? He disappeared after the North Bank was bulldozed in 1992.

There was also another 'shouter outer' who used to periodically scream "You red and white goal-scoring dream machine." I used to enjoy the North Bank banter between the topside and middle. I think the leader of topside was called 'Big Nose'. There would be a lot of "Big Nose, Big Nose give us a song."

Barry Hughes: The man in the North Bank that always shouted "Come on, you rip-roaring, goal-scoring Gunners" as the whistle went at the start of the game.

GOD IS A GOONER (@stevessr): Rip-Roar was a big character on the North Bank when I was a kid. I stood middle of the North Bank and although I never met him, the fans used to sing for him to give us a song. Great days.

Tick Tock @BlackScarfAFC): Rip-Roar who used to be near the front centre of the North Bank. "COME ON, YOU RIP-ROARING REDDDS!"

Simon MacMichael: Rip-Roar geezer. The "Rrrrrrrroasted Peanuts!" bloke. The person, front row of North Bank behind the goal in late 70s/80s, who used to wave a union flag whenever we hit the net.

FLORRIE 'FLO' BURGESS

Marvin Berglas: There was the old lady 'Flo' in a father Xmas suit, front of the North Bank, when I was a kid. She seemed ancient then. Also, I've seen pictures of David Stacey who was like the official fan welcoming the fans in the 40s and 50s.

JOHNNY HOY

65Gooner (@IncompleteUser1): Johnny Hoy in his white butcher's coat.

wozzle1959 (@gkv1959): Remember Johnny Hoy when I first started going away games on the Football Specials in around 1970-71. They used to say he was the leader of the North Bank. Didn't know what that meant – I was only 10. Someone told me he lived on Highbury Quadrant. Don't know if that's correct?

'PEANUTS'

Bernard Kiernan: I can't recall any characters among the fans but I do vividly remember the roasted peanut seller in the Clock End who had a remarkable endless drone of a voice which you could hear from miles away but, bizarrely, was never very loud as he approached. "Peanuts, roasted peanuts, peanuts . . ." An institution.

Neil Payne: The fella calling out "peanuts" in the North Bank pre all-seater days. What was weird is that no matter how big the crowd was, and the North Bank for the top games would always be rammed, he always got around with his big bag of peanuts, calling out and selling with reasonable ease. Never an issue. Think he was very well respected.

Derek Barclay: I used to go to the London speedway tracks in the 1970s, too – and you'd see the same peanut seller at White City on Wednesday, Hackney Speedway on Friday and at Highbury on the Saturday. All-seater grounds did for many things, including the familiar sight and sound of these peanut sellers.

OTHERS

Keith English: I had a season ticket in the lower tier East Stand for years. A lady, whose name I can't recall, used to sit in front of us and she always had hot coffee for half-time. Lovely lady. When we went to Belgium for the Cup Winners' Cup Final in 1980, there she was, sitting right in front of us.

Tim McCarthy (@The_DorfMeister): What about the old man whose wild white hair made him looked a bit like Catweazle? Saw him at games since the 80s.

Brian Kendal (@BKtheMaverick): During the 80s, in the North Bank middle upper section, stood a very loud Greek Guy called (I think) Alex. A bit of a character who used to say some amusing stuff. If memory serves, 'Timber Penis' was his nickname for Tony Woodcock. I'm sure he had other witticisms too but I can't recall them.

Vin (@afcvini): What about 'Big Nose' in the North Bank, mid-to-late 80s, who used to start most of the songs from the middle. "Big Nose give us a song."

Gary Jones: Peggy, who runs the Supporters' Club shop and used to organise the away travel. She's part of the fabric of the club, a real stalwart.

Nancy Wright: Fella up the Clock End, used to wear a khaki jacket and hat covered in badges. He was the one with the radio and we relied on him for updates at crucial times. Bit of a loner – never saw him speak to anyone apart from when he was asked for a score.

Chris Hudson: A man called Harry, who stood on the west side paddock. "Harry, Harry, give us a wave" sung from North Bank. He was a DJ from Harrow.

AdeAwayDayz (@AwayDaysAde): Ernest Crouch (right). Couldn't believe it when I found out he was actually a milkman. Last Away game with us was at Norwich, where a policeman walked with him and helped him back to the coach. Ernie walked very slowly. He always had people to walk alongside him and give him lifts. A friend called Claude really helped him out.

Faces in the crowd . . . two nostalgic views of fans standing at the Clock End. The photo (right) was taken during the FA Cup tie v Liverpool on March 9, 1963.

The green railings and goal stanchions were a Highbury 'thing' for years.

5 GREAT GOALS

WONDER goals by legends Ian Wright, Dennis Bergkamp and Thierry Henry are worthy of a chapter each and you will find plenty of their most memorable strikes here among our contributors' nominations.

But there have been many other great or memorable goals to savour from other strikers such as David Herd, Ray Kennedy, Frank Stapleton and Alan Sunderland. Thunderbolts from Charlie George and Patrick Vieira, Charlie Nicholas ripping Spurs to shreds, Anders Limpar's lob, Paul Davis' diving header, Brian Talbot's freekick, a piece of Merson magic, Rocky's rocket, class from Brady and some Pires panache.

Not forgetting a few unlikely goal-getters from the defensive department. Tony Adams sparking title celebrations against Everton before striking that iconic pose, a right-footed Winterburn rarity and that one and only John Jensen special.

Q: Greatest goals you've seen scored at Highbury by Arsenal players?

Graham Lister: The 1960-61 season was a gloomy one for Gooners. Bill Nicholson's Spurs were sweeping towards the Double while chronic inconsistency kept Arsenal becalmed in mid-table obscurity, nowhere near the honours. And although the skilful George Eastham finally arrived from Newcastle Utd in December, top scorer David Herd would break my heart, at least for a while, by leaving for Manchester Utd at the end of the season.

Herd made a major contribution in his final season, however, scoring 30 goals – including four hat-tricks – and this one against Manchester City (14/1/1961) that prompted the subsequent *Official Arsenal Handbook* to ask 'Was this the goal of the season?' long before awards for such things were ritually bestowed.

It came in a nine-goal thriller which Gunners won 5-4, and was the end-product of a swift counter-attack that relieved some intense City pressure on the Arsenal defence. A ball played up the middle of the pitch saw Herd race onto it and thunder a characteristically fierce effort beyond Bert Trautmann, only to see it cannon back off the bar. Herd's reactions were razor-sharp as he flung himself headlong above the Highbury mud to meet the rebound with a powerful diving header that gave Trautmann no chance on its way into the back of the Clock End net. I was in awe of his technique, although sadly Gunners would win only three more of their remaining 16 matches that season.

Tony Porter: So many great goals – 1958: three in five second-half minutes by Jimmy Bloomfield (2) and David Herd to draw level with the Busby Babes, who had been 3-0 up at half-time in what proved to be their last game in England. 1961: George Eastham cheekily sending Sheffield Wednesday's England keeper Ron Springett the wrong way from the penalty spot, feinting with his left but actually side-footing it with his right into the left-hand corner. 1984: Charlie Nicholas gets possession just outside the Spurs penalty area after a corner, beats one man, beats another – you begin to think, 'He could do this' and, lo and behold, he's beaten four defenders, rounded the keeper and tapped it in. Cue boundless joy on the North Bank.

Graham Lister: I was on the East terracing near the corner flag to get an even better view of another picture-book diving header. Johnny MacLeod whipped over a finely judged centre from just in front of us on the right-wing, so I was perfectly placed to see Geoff Strong bring together the elements of timing, athleticism, bravery and power as he launched himself horizontally a couple of feet off the ground and headed the ball unstoppably into the net for Arsenal's first goal in a 2-1 FA Cup third round victory over Wolverhampton Wanderers (4/1/1964).

Lester Allen: George Johnston v Leeds Utd (7/5/1968) in our 4-3 end of season victory. He dribbled past three or four players and placed the ball in the bottom corner.

Robert Thaine: A home game v Leeds Utd, when Liam 'Chippy' Brady scored with a beautiful curling shot past the helpless David Harvey. Jon Sammels' block-busting 40-yarder v Manchester Utd (20/9/1969).

Paul Harris: It is surprising how difficult it is to recall goals after seeing so many – and certainly my choice is not a great goal but a vital one. I choose Jon Sammels, who could hit the ball as hard as Peter Lorimer, scoring the third goal against Anderlecht in the Fairs Cup Final (30/4/1970). It meant we were ahead by a 'real' goal and not just on away goals. That was important.

I was thrown so high in the air, I caught a glimpse of goalkeeper Bob Wilson celebrating at the Clock End goal. I have never known such poignant elation since, despite our many successes. Of course, Ray Kennedy's goal that clinched the Double at the gates of the enemy at White Hart Lane was just as special. But to be honest, I did not see the header going in through the arms already raised in anticipation.

I recall the players' wild reaction on both occasions and realised how much it meant to them. At the Anderlecht game, after Sammels' goal, Frank McLintock gestured again and again to the North Bank to raise the volume. He even came out earlier than everyone else just before the start of the second-half to do the same.

Tony Fisher: For its huge significance, Jon Sammels smashing in the winning goal, right-hand corner of the box, v Anderlecht in the Fairs Cup Final.

Peter Coombs: Too many to remember . . . Wrighty, Bergkamp, Thierry . . . but, instead, I'll go for Charlie George's (right) 71st-minute winner against Newcastle Utd (17/4/1971) on the way to our first Double. He played a one-two off a Newcastle player before shooting powerfully into the North Bank goal.

Lee Pritchett: I've seen many great goals at Highbury. Henry's flick and shot v Man Utd, George Graham's volley v Wolves but I think the best was v Grasshoppers in the European Cup, second round, second leg (3/11/1971). Charlie George struck a shot (not a lob) from the halfway line and he hit it so hard that when it found the net, the goalkeeper hadn't moved – he hadn't seen it. That boy had power in his shooting boots.

Marvin Berglas: In a tightly-packed Highbury crowd of more than 60,000 for the FA Cup sixth round replay against Chelsea (20/3/1973), Alan Ball found overlapping full-back Bob McNab who cut inside and floated a glorious cross which Ray Kennedy rose emphatically to head home the winner in the top corner. It happened right in front of the North Bank faithful who, like me, exploded into a cacophony of noise. Probably my first feeling of light headedness at football caused from relief mixed with delirium.

Alan Thompsett: Frank Stapleton scoring from a seemingly impossible angle v Nottingham Forest (3/9/1977), my first game. Tony Adams v Everton (3/5/1998) and Alan Smith v Norwich City (1/5/1989), with an assist from John Lukic's massive goalkick.

Graham Lister: Leeds Utd, in the first game of Jock Stein's brief reign as manager, were the visitors on the opening day of the 1978-79 season (19/8/1978). On a lush, manicured playing surface bathed in sunlight, two artists were at work, one for either side. Arsenal's master craftsman Liam Brady and Leeds playmaker Tony Currie were determined to outdo each other in a compelling battle of creative wits.

Both figured memorably on the score-sheet in a 2-2 draw. Brady scored twice – a penalty,

then a truly breathtaking effort that he curled home unstoppably from 20 yards before celebrating in front of the ecstatic North Bank where I was standing – a scene captured in an iconic image made into a poster that hung on many a Gooner's bedroom wall. Sportingly, if unusually, when Currie took the ball almost to the goal-line, shaped to cross then lashed it into the net from the tightest angle, even that packed North Bank felt obliged to applaud him.

Emilio Zorlakki: I met Alan Sunderland at a 1979 reunion function a few years ago at The Emirates and people were saying to him that his 1979 FA Cup-winning goal was his best, when I interjected: "No, Alan, you scored a better one in the quarter-final replay against Southampton (21/3/1979). Receiving the ball back to goal about 40 yards out, you spun and did a sort of pirouette and unleashed a screamer from about 35 yards out, straight into the far corner of the goal at the North Bank end."

Alan walked towards me and said: "Nice one!" as we fist-pumped in 'high five' fashion. "It's my best goal ever and nobody remembers it! So thank you."

Gary Jones: Tony Woodcock v West Bromwich Albion (16/10/1982), a half-volley hit to perfection.

Tony Bateman: Vladimir Petrovic v Stoke City (15/1/1983). Having since consumed far too much beer since and never seen television footage of the goal, it's now just a vague memory.

Guy Thompson: Brian Talbot's freekick v Liverpool (8/9/1984). What a goal. Seeing it curl into the top corner was amazing. A truly wonderful goal from one of my favourite players. Total grafter was Talbot – 70 games in one season! And players complain nowadays about fixture congestion. On paper, we had an amazing team from 1983-86 but they never quite clicked. We were left with fleeting moments of magic and Talbot's freekick was certainly one of them. I was gutted when he left.

Brian Talbot

Paul Hemming: I'll give you a different one. Arsenal v Barnsley in the FA Cup fifth round (21/2/1987), Charlie Nicholas, a diamond in a pile of coal. He'd been dropped but he came on in the No.12 shirt and scored a worldie. He won possession 10 yards inside the Barnsley half and wriggled past two defenders before chipping the ball over the keeper and in off the far-post at the Clock End. 10,000 Charlie hair cuts on the North Bank and that's what they came for.

Mark Aughterlony: Too numerous to mention by Ian Wright, Dennis Bergkamp and Thierry Henry. Alan Smith's first goals for us at Highbury, a hat-trick in a 6-0 thumping of Portsmouth (29/8/1987), will live long in the memory (as will the look on my Pompey-supporting mate Steve's face as he walked back to meet me after being kept back at the final whistle – poor guy!).

Craig Pottage: Steve Williams v Oxford Utd (10/10/1987) springs to mind. Hit the ball from around 30 yards and it flew into the net. Also, Martin Hayes the year earlier at home to Leicester City (20/4/1987), just after Alan Smith had joined us and gone back on loan to them. Ran from the halfway line, I believe. Finally, Anders Limpar chipping the Liverpool keeper from the halfway line (20/4/1992).

Ian Tredgett: I always think great goals can be either spectacular (Bergkamp at Filbert Street, eg) or significant (Thomas at Anfield). The most spectacular was probably Henry's against Spurs in the 2002-03 season; you somehow sensed that he was going to do something special as he ran towards the rabbits in his headlights (or was that the Spurs defence?). I also recall Anders Limpar's chip from the halfway line against Liverpool in 1992. It was my last game on the North Bank (I couldn't attend the Southampton game a couple of weeks later), so to see a goal like that on my last time on the North Bank terrace was very special.

In terms of significance, I guess you could argue in hindsight every goal in the 1988-89 season was hugely significant. In those days we didn't score as many spectacular ones but the late David Rocastle scored a wonderful goal against Middlesbrough (19/11/1988) in the last minute. It didn't change the result (we were 2-0 up before he scored) but if he hadn't, the title wouldn't have been 'up for grabs' in the way it was six months later. It also doesn't feel right to be sharing my Highbury memories here without mentioning Rocky.

Paul Davis

Alex Morrow: Loads to pick from, so I'll go for one that I bet nobody else mentions. It was our title season of 1988-89, and we were playing Charlton Athletic in an evening game (21/3/1989). Paul Davis picked up the ball on the edge of our box and sprayed it out to the left-hand side. I can't actually remember who had it next, because I was too busy watching Davis sprinting down the middle of the pitch towards the Clock End. He kept going and going, getting faster and faster, until he arrived in their box just in time to meet the cross with a diving header that must have topped 100 mph. Fantastic!

I saw him in a restaurant years later, told him how clearly I remember that goal and he thanked me for mentioning it.

Stuart Pierce: Paul Davis' diving header from a Kevin Richardson right-wing cross in our 2-2 draw v Charlton Athletic (21/3/1989) after starting the move in his own half. Also, Davis v Aston Villa (3/4/1991), a half-volley bicycle kick from the edge of the box that capped a 5-0 win.

Paul Manel: David Rocastle v Middlesbrough (19/11/1988). We were attacking the Clock End and he went on one of his mazy runs. He slalomed past three or four Boro defenders and hit a shot in off the underside of the bar. A magnificent goal from an Arsenal legend.

Neil Davies: David Rocastle v Middlesbrough (19/11/1988). Rocky was well known for his ability to glide past people, bamboozling them with his pace and skill, but on this day he scored a goal which just oozed the world class that all Gooners knew he had. It was one of the few goals that I didn't greet with my usual tsunami of waving arms and legs and screaming. I simply stood up and held my arms open, as if welcoming a god into my house. Watching him weave through the Middlesbrough players in such a way was majestic. I'd seen Barnes weaving at Liverpool and I'd seen clips of Jairzinho slalom past hapless defenders for Brazil. But here was Rocky, one of us, doing it on *our* pitch. When he finally let fly, we all knew where it was headed – into the top corner via the inside of the post. An absolutely magic moment.

Tom Eldridge: First, Paul Davis' diving header v Charlton Athletic (21/3/1989). He rarely scored and certainly didn't score headline goals. If you ignore the result (2-2), this was awesome. How did he get to the ball? He looked miles away from it. What a header.

Second, Rocky v Middlesbrough in the same season (19/11/1988). There weren't enough Boro players on the pitch for him to beat, so he beat some of them more than once! Power and precision from the genius. Even Dennis would have wanted one of those goals in his locker.

Third and final, Brian Talbot's freekick v Liverpool (8/9/1984). 'Noddy' picks his spot. I reckon it is still the best freekick I have ever seen live. And the scene behind the goal in the Clock End when you watch it on TV is phenomenal.

Stephen Simson: Nigel Winterburn's screamer against his former club Wimbledon (17/5/1989) in 2-2 draw. A long ball from Tony Adams was headed out towards Arsenal's left-wing, where left-back Winterburn latched onto it and, amazingly, with his weaker right foot from around 25 yards, hit a screamer into the far top corner of the net at the Clock End. You knew it was in as soon as he hit it. Beautiful goal.

Guy Thompson: Alan Smith's diving header in our 6-1 victory v Austria Vienna (then known as Austria Memphis) in the European Cup first round, first leg (18/9/1991) is another that stands out. From where I was positioned, it came straight at us. Seeing Smudger flying through the air and connecting at full stretch with his head and watching the ball arrow into the net. Wow!

George Lampshire: I still maintain the back end of the 1991-92 season was the best I'd seen from any Arsenal side in terms of excitement. Four goals v Crystal Palace and Liverpool, seven v Sheffield Wednesday and five v Southampton on the last day of the terraced North Bank. We were just blowing teams away with fast-flowing football and devastating finishing.

Of course, the goal from the Super Swede Limpar v Liverpool was a worldie but my favourite goal I witnessed was Paul Merson's chip v Sheff Wed in the 7-1 (15/2/1992). We were all over them and had just scored three in about five minutes. The ball got played to Merse and we were all willing him to have a run into the box but he dug out a chip from the corner of the area that sailed over Chris Woods. Given the timing and the pure impudence in attempting a chip from there, we went wild.

Michael Thomas

I think also Michael Thomas' goal in the League Cup semi-final, second leg v Everton (24/2/1988) stands out. Nothing special but the tension, anxiety and anticipation in a packed North Bank that night was special. We'd missed a penalty by Martin Hayes, Rocky had missed an open goal and we were just waiting for it to happen. When Thomas lifted it over Southall down at the Clock End, the stadium erupted. It laid the foundation for two more goals and a cruise through to the final against Luton Town. The less said about that the better.

Stuart Pierce: Kevin Campbell scored a belting half-volley v Crystal Palace

(11/4/1992) at the Clock End. Ian Wright flying through the Southampton team (2/5/1992) in pursuit of the Golden Boot on the final day of 1991-92 (and North Bank). David Seaman just about kept the ball in play, threw it to Wright on the left-hand touchline, and he surged past three Southampton players, including a handing-off of Terry Hurlock, and smashed his shot past Tim Flowers. Weirdly, the goal was later featured on an episode of the Australian TV soap series Neighbours.

Guy Thompson: Ian Wright's second goal of his hat-trick v Southampton (2/5/1992). Everything about it was class. David Seaman scooping the ball out of the air, bowling it out to Wright, and then just watching him run like a gazelle on amphetamines towards the Southampton goal. And the way he breezed past Terry Hurlock. Not many forwards did that without getting lumps kicked out of them. We all knew where the ball was gonna end up. The North Bank went absolutely mental. And we were banging in some quality goals at that time.

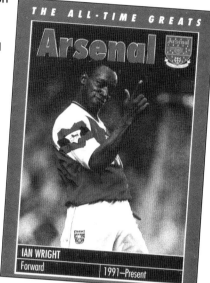

THE ALL-TIME GREATS

Arsenal

IAN WRIGHT
Forward   1991–Present

Plus a mention for Alan Smith's goal v Liverpool (2/12/1990). The skilful back-heel by Paul Merson to set it up and the clinical finish under Grobbelaar. "What a super goal" (Jimmy Greaves). Indeed!

Neil Davies: Ian Wright v Nottingham Forest, FA Cup fifth round (13/2/1993). Games against Forest were always tough – they had some top players and a legendary manager in Brian Clough, and so the fifth round tie was far from an expected win. I remember Wrighty picking the ball up about 40 yards from goal. I expected him to just burst clear with his pace and slide it past the keeper but he was clearly intent on letting fly early. I began to yell 'no!' because I obviously know better than Wrighty. He hit the ball on the half-volley and it went like a rocket into the top corner, past a despairing Steve Sutton, who was a very good goalkeeper at the time. The goal would have been remembered better if the actual North Bank was behind it, rather than that ridiculous mural.

Bryan Austin: Ian Wright v Everton (28/8/1993). Controlling David Seaman's long pass, he juggled the ball past Everton defender Matt Jackson, then lobbed Neville Southall, rated by many as the best keeper in the world at the time, at the North Bank end. Wrighty made a mug of him.

John Blair: Wrighty juggling the ball from one boot to the other, over Everton defenders, before lobbing Southall was utter genius.

Barry Hughes: John Jensen's solitary goal, in his 98th appearance. Miserable game v QPR (31/12/1994), which we lost 3-1, It was on a cold, damp New Year's eve. We had been singing for what felt like seasons 'We'll be there when Jensen scores'. Then, out of the blue, he tried his luck . . . again. This time it went in and the place went berserk. For the rest of the game everyone was singing 'We were there when Jensen scored' in complete disbelief. The score was forgotten and outside after the game t-shirt sellers had the song emblazoned on the shirts. How long they had them printed up for, god only knows.

James Smither: Goals generally acclaimed among Arsenal's finest ever that I was fortunate enough to witness live and in person at Highbury included Ian Wright playing keepy-uppy with himself before volleying into the corner past Neville Southall of Everton in 1993; Thierry Henry's "whazzuuuuuurp" flick-turn-and-volley screamer against Barthez to beat Manchester Utd 1-0 in 2000; his slaloming 60-yard run and finish against Spurs (and

Graham Lister: Between 1997 and 2004, the biggest rivalry in English football was that between Arsenal and Manchester Utd, so when defending champions United visited Highbury early in the 2000-01 season (1/10/2000) it was a genuine clash of the titans. The game was decided by a moment of sheer brilliance, a piece of invention conjured instinctively and executed indelibly by the man destined to become Arsenal's all-time leading scorer.

When Gilles Grimandi played the ball forward into the feet of his compatriot Thierry Henry, the striker was a good 20 yards out with his back to goal, Denis Irwin crowding him from behind and Paul Scholes closing in fast. It was the sort of challenge Henry relished. Holding Irwin at bay, he flicked the ball up and spun round to volley home a shot that rose, then dipped unerringly into the top corner of the Clock End net beyond Henry's France and former Monaco team-mate Fabien Barthez.

Neil Payne: Just one of many memorable Henry moments. Simply stunning the way in which he deliberately ensured the ball left the floor at an angle to enable a first-time volley. Watching from the North Bank upper tier that day, it was like time stood still, as we all watched in awe and waited for the net to bulge. We simply just shook our heads in disbelief at watching something very special. For Sir Alex to question the utter brilliance of the skill and strike afterwards was laughable.

John Morley: The type of goal only someone like Thierry would think of scoring.

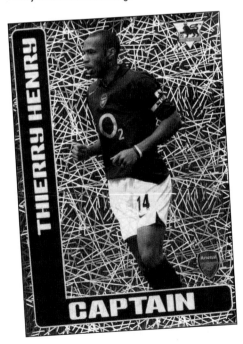

THIERRY HENRY

CAPTAIN

even longer run to celebrate in front of their unimpressed fans in the Clock End) in the North London derby in November 2002; Dennis Bergkamp's outrageous lob to seal a 4-1 Champions League drubbing of Bayer Leverkusen in February of that year; and the same player's ridiculously intricate and brilliant assist for Freddie Ljungberg's late goal to conclude a home win v Juventus earlier on in the competition.

However, more esoteric personal favourites of mine include a Vieira screamer against Newcastle as we marched towards Wenger's first league title in 1998 – it may still be the hardest-hit shot I've yet seen hit the net from an Arsenal player's boot; Dennis Bergkamp capping his first season in London by arrowing a similarly perfect strike into the top corner to beat Bolton Wanderers and seal a European spot at Tottenham's expense (sound familiar?) on the last day of the 1996 season; and – perhaps most obscurely of all – a John Hartson half-volley v Manchester City, also in 1996, during an otherwise barren spell of matches I attended in the late George Graham/Stewart Houston/Bruce Rioch 'wilderness' period when it felt like I personally hadn't seen us score more than one goal, or win a game, at home for an absolute lifetime.

David Harman: Ian Wright v Everton (20/1/1996). Receiving a pass from John Jensen, he showed great ball control, skipped around three defenders and from the 18-yard line drilled it left-footed past Neville Southall and into the bottom corner at the Clock End. Not having the best view, I didn't realise how good it was until I saw it again on Match of the Day.

John Skinner: Dennis Bergkamp's 20-yarder against Bolton Wanderers (5/5/1996). Receiving a pass from David Platt on the edge of the box, he turned and let fly a thunderous shot that went in the top corner at the Clock End. It put us back into Europe and a legend was born.

John Morley: Dennis Bergkamp's stoppage-time goal against Spurs (24/11/1996). Brought down a deep right-wing cross from Ian Wright with a majestic first touch with his left foot, which took him inside the sliding defender, before placing the ball, right-footed, past Ian Walker into the corner of the North Bank net. Pure class. It clinched a 3-1 Sunday afternoon victory – Arsène Wenger's first derby success.

Barry Hughes: Ian Wright's record-breaker against Bolton Wanderers (13/9/1997). Everyone had been wishing for it to happen for some time. I was in the East Stand lower. Wasn't the prettiest goal ever – a simple tap-in from two yards – and he couldn't really miss it. But he was such a darling of Highbury, everyone was so ecstatic for him.

Graham Lister: All three of Gunners' goals in this showdown with defending champions Manchester Utd (9/11/1997) were exceptional but the second, from Patrick Vieira, was the pick of the bunch. Coming in the 27th minute at the Clock End, it gave Arsenal a 2-0 lead following Nicolas Anelka's opener in a crucial contest that finished 3-2 in our favour.

A Ray Parlour corner was headed out by Henning Berg, under pressure from Tony Adams at the near-post, but it got no further than Vieira, racing to meet it on the edge of the penalty area. The midfielder did not even break his stride as he lashed an unstoppable effort back over Peter Schmeichel in United's goal and in off the underside of the bar.

The noise from the Arsenal fans was deafening, drowning out Vieira's own whoop of joy as he raced away and slid across the turf on his knees in celebration. Ironically, in doing so he sustained an injury that kept him out of the second-half. But David Platt's brilliant late header ensured Gunners claimed all three points.

John Hilditch: There are so many. However, Kanu's against Deportivo La Coruna in the 5-1 UEFA Cup fourth round (2/3/2000). It summed up that period for me. Majestic. Comical too. Typical Kanu, took two players out, including putting the keeper on his arse without touching the ball, and then tapped it in from a yard. The simplicity was beautiful. All in the body movement.

David McConachie: Saw many great and important goals, but the one that sticks out most is Ray Parlour v Valencia in the Champions League quarter-final, first leg (4/4/2001). We had gone 1-0 down to an Ayala goal, got it back to 1-1 through Thierry Henry in the 58th-minute and then a couple of minutes later Ray picked up possession on the edge of the centre circle. He drove forward and drilled in a 20-yarder, top corner, in front of the North Bank. I was sat right behind his shot and remember it veering into the top corner, the keeper's left, and I have never felt a stand move as much as at that moment. Crowd went wild and the North Bank seemed to shake. Incredible.

Neil Payne: A proper European night at Highbury (4/12/2001). Two quality sides and a Champions League group game played with real flair and panache. Juventus were a decent outfit but Arsenal threatened to blow them away, racing into a two-goal lead. The Italians pulled a goal back and the old ground was suddenly full of tension.

Step forward Dennis Berkgamp to stamp his class. As Juventus pressed, Arsenal pressed and Bergkamp was presented with the ball, with an apparent intent to play keep-ball. Suddenly, with three Juve defenders surrounding him, he dazzled them all with a neat drag-back, clever turn on a sixpence and then had the audacity to notice Freddie Ljungberg charging into the penalty area as support. The deftest of chips allowed Freddie to run on, without breaking stride, and lift the ball over the advancing Buffon to settle the tie. To Freddie, the glory of seeing his name up in lights as goalscorer but all made possible by the genius of Bergkamp.

Ben Sharpe: One of my favourite goals came at home to Aston Villa (9/12/2001) in the Double-winning season. We were 2-0 down at half-time (Paul Merson scored Villa's opener) but, in the best way possible, we came back to win 3-2. Our first two goals came from a Sylvain Wiltord volley from a deflected Ray Parlour cross and a curling left-wing cross from Patrick Vieira that Thierry Henry controlled before tucking away from close range.

But Thierry's second, in the last minute, was something I'll never forget. Villa keeper Peter Enckelman kicked the ball high but not as far as the halfway line, where Robert Pires won possession and slid the ball through to Thierry, who in turn slotted it low into the North Bank net.

Up until that point I'd never heard an atmosphere like it at Highbury before. It was incredible.

Dave Randall: Robert Pires v Southampton (7/5/2003) which put the seal on an easy 6-1 victory on the night Jermaine Pennant scored a first-half hat-trick on his Premier League debut. Saints defender Telfer made a pathetic attempt to clear. Pires, without a second thought, looked up, saw keeper Jones off his line and, with a first-time curling right-foot chip, found the North Bank net from 25 yards to complete his hat-trick in style.

Roberto Puzzi: Difficult to say but probably the best goal I've seen was the one v Man City (1/2/2004) by Thierry Henry. What an outstanding shot it was. He received a pass from Robert Pires just outside the left edge of City's penalty area. In an instant he drilled a rising right-foot shot that flew past keeper David James into the far top corner of the net before celebrating with a knee-slide in front of the adoring North Bank. His stunning 83rd-minute strike clinched a 2-1 win (Ed: former Gunner Nicolas Anelka pulled one back for City in the last minute and was sent off by ref Alan Wiley in the ensuing melee with Ashley Cole) and put us back on top of the league.

Dan Hill: I was only able to attend two Highbury games, so my favourite goals both came v Crystal Palace (14/2/2005). Henry's first was a one-two with Dennis Bergkamp before hitting the ball just inside the box and hitting a shot into the top corner of the Clock End goal. His second involved a great bit of play by Bergkamp before passing to Henry, who dribbled by two players inside the box and hit that into the top corner as well but in front of us in the North Bank.

Henry was my favourite because of how world class he was and always scored great and important goals for us. At times he was just incredible to watch. Bergkamp was a great player who scored just as many as he set up and was a perfect partner for Henry and for me there was no better strike partnership in Premier League history.

David Harman: Thierry Henry's 77th-minute second goal in our 5-1 victory v Crystal Palace (14/2/2005). Bergkamp had the ball by the corner flag, wriggled away from a defender and passed to Henry on the edge of the penalty area. He shifted it left, as if to shoot, then cut onto his right and blasted it past Kiraly and high into the corner of the North Bank net from outside the area. I was right behind the goal, so got a good view.

Ben Sharpe: One of the most special goals I saw at Highbury came on Dennis Bergkamp Day – the stadium awash with orange – against West Bromwich Albion (15/4/2006) in the last season at Highbury. I remember Dennis – a 72nd-minute substitute for Robin van Persie – receiving the ball just outside the area at the Clock End and in typical Bergkamp style, he just opened up his body and bent it round keeper Kuszczak. It was so special because it was his last goal for the club, on the occasion dedicated to him.

Robert Pires

FIVE CLASSIC GOALS

ANDERS LIMPAR

v Liverpool, Football League Division One, April 20, 1992

Graham Lister: Arsenal completed the final season of the First Division – which was also the last in front of the old North Bank – with a flurry of goals: 18 in their last six matches, 13 of them at Highbury. But Anders Limpar claimed the most spectacular, Arsenal's third in an emphatic 4-0 thrashing of Liverpool, the dominant club of the previous 15 years.

Limpar won the ball off Ian Rush inside his own half and dribbled to his right of the centre circle, although there appeared to be no immediate danger for a well-placed Liverpool defence, especially as the only Gunner ahead of Limpar, Kevin Campbell, was in danger of being caught offside with opponents fast converging on the quicksilver winger.

Instantly sizing up his options, Limpar executed a precisely-judged lob from fully 40 yards. Its glorious parabola took it over stranded Reds keeper Mike Hooper and under the crossbar into the net as delighted team-mates raced to congratulate the little Swede, lifting him off his feet in celebration.

Neil Davies: Limpar from the half-way line. OK, it wasn't quite the halfway line but it may as well have been. This was a day when we truly destroyed Liverpool. We began their downfall in 1989 but this finalised their collapse. It was a complete demolition.

When Anders picked up the ball, there was an instant buzz, as there often was when this genial Swede took possession, but we'd all noticed Mike Hooper off his line . . . and so had Anders. He struck the ball with so little effort, so little back-lift that it seemed impossible for him to cover the distance. But as the ball flew, the ground seemed to lift off with excitement. Hooper was hopeless and his shoulders dropped as the ball sailed into the North Bank net. Cries of "He's gonna cry in a minute!" rained down on John Barnes and it summed up a rare moment of true superiority. We had the best team and the best players and that goal proved it.

Neil Payne: Arsenal were finishing the season like a train but too late to have a say in the title battle between Leeds Utd and Manchester Utd. It was always a pleasure to beat Liverpool, given the hatred I had of them in those days. This particular day Arsenal simply destroyed a club fast falling into decline and Limpar's goal in a 4-0 win always lives in my memory.

Nobby Ralfe: I had the pleasure of meeting the Swede and have a card signed by the great man. It's inscribed: 'I was there when he scored from the halfway line'.

DENNIS BERGKAMP

v Southampton, Premier League, September 23, 1995

Graham Lister: Early in his first season with Arsenal, Dennis Bergkamp scored twice in a 4-2 victory over Southampton at Highbury, and both goals are among the greatest I saw at the old stadium. Not necessarily because of their technical qualities, although both were superbly struck, but because of their emotional significance, which was evident in the reaction of every Arsenal fan among the 38,136 crowd.

132

Anders Limpar

After seven games we'd seen enough of his sublime passes and deft touches to know Bergkamp was a special player. What we hadn't seen yet was a goal from the Dutchman – and predictably, the tabloid press was going to town about it, trying to heap pressure on both the player and manager Bruce Rioch's judgement in bringing him to north London for what was then a club record fee.

Then, 17 minutes into the game, Glenn Helder crossed from the left-wing and there was Bergkamp, bringing all his technique to bear, as he leant back and volleyed the ball into the far corner. Highbury erupted in a heady mixture of joy, relief, admiration – and empathy with a player who had just cemented his bond with the fans in such emphatic style.

Remarkably, Saints pulled back a two-goal deficit, equalising on the stroke of half-time and threatening to spoil the party. But Bergkamp then restored Arsenal's lead, this time with an even better goal. Receiving the ball just inside the opposition half, he made the most of the space in front of him before shaking off his marker with a couple of subtle body-swerves and unleashing a spectacular shot that flew 30 yards into the roof of the net to spark another ecstatic eruption.

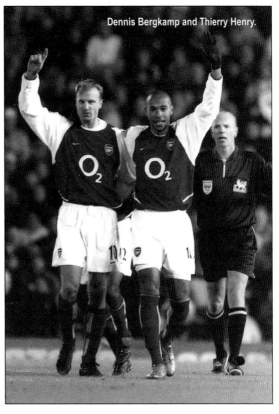
Dennis Bergkamp and Thierry Henry.

Mike Green: Bergkamp's first goal for Arsenal, when he volleyed a cross from Helder into the net. His technique was brilliant and this was a time when everyone was calling him a waste of money (a then club record £7.5m). He must have been under a lot of pressure but showed his true class.

Andrew Whitnall: Bergkamp's brace against Southampton (23/9/1995). I sat in the North Bank upper tier and it would rock up and down when a really big goal was celebrated. It rocked big-time that day.

Stuart Pierce: The emotion was accelerated by the arrival of *his* day after so much laughable criticism in the tabloid press.

TONY ADAMS

v Everton, Premier League, May 3, 1998

Graham Lister: There could not have been a more popular scorer of the goal that put the tin lid on Arsenal's Premier League title triumph in 1998 than captain Tony Adams. Unbeaten in the League since December 13, Gunners had come from behind, overhauling Manchester Utd's seemingly unassailable lead with an awesome run of nine straight wins, and needed only to beat Everton at Highbury to be crowned champions in Arsène Wenger's first full season at the helm.

They were already 3-0 up when Steve Bould replaced Christopher Wreh in the 80th minute. And with just one minute to go Highbury was getting ready to party. That's when Bould, in midfield, took possession of the ball with his long-time defensive partner Adams ahead of him in an even more advanced position.

In a passage of play that seemed to encapsulate the emancipated thinking Wenger had instilled in his players, Bould chipped a perfectly weighted pass over Everton's back four and into the path of his skipper. Adams was suddenly through on goal in a classic one-on-one and, controlling the ball with aplomb, he hit it on the half-volley into the North Bank net. We hadn't realised until it happened, but it was exactly what the occasion demanded.

And Tony's iconic celebration is now immortalised in bronze outside Emirates Stadium.

John Morley: After scoring, Tony Adams stood motionless in the sunshine, arms outstretched. Doesn't get much better than that.

Paul Manel: How fitting that two members of our legendary 'back five' were involved. TA stood with his arms outstretched savouring the adulation and the moment. Pure unbridled joy.

Derek Barclay: I always remember an amazing flying header by John Roberts against West Bromwich Albion (18/12/1971) in a match in which he scored both Arsenal goals in a 2-0 win. But nothing can beat the goal scored by another Arsenal No.6. Tony Adams receiving a silky pass from his old pal Steve Bould, delivered like a midfield maestro. Tony controlling the ball and smashing it home, then celebrating in a Christ-like pose. The fourth goal, of course, as we clinched the title in 1998.

THIERRY HENRY

v Tottenham Hotspur, Premier League, November 16, 2002

Graham Lister: Henry scored the goal voted the best of 2002-03 when Gunners met Tottenham at Highbury in the first north London derby of the season. It was the opening goal in a 3-0 win and came on 13 minutes, when Henry collected the ball from Patrick Vieira's headed clearance a little way outside the Arsenal penalty area.

Epitomising the art of switching defence into attack in a heartbeat, Henry turned and raced forward on a mesmerising 70-yard run that saw him beat Matthew Etherington, Ledley King, Stephen Carr and finally keeper Kasey Keller with a dummy before firing into the net.

Cue delirium among the assembled Gooners as Henry raced away in manic celebration, concluding with an iconic knee-slide that has been immortalised in

Marvin Berglas, Highbury's former resident magician, performs a card trick with Tony Adams and Thierry Henry, who produced magical goals to delight the fans.

135

bronze outside Emirates Stadium.

Tony Fisher: After waltzing so arrogantly through their team from our own area, thinking, 'is he really doing this? . . . no, surely not . . . oh, you're joking . . . did you see that?'

Marvin Berglas: Like a footballing superhero, it was a masterclass. The celebration was just as good, sprinting the full length of the pitch and sliding on his knees in front of the distraught opposition fans. Different class. It deserved a statue. Oh yeah!

Neil Payne: This goal probably epitomises everything that was Thierry Henry. Picking up the ball in Arsenal's half, he brushed aside Etherington before embarking on a solo run. I can recall screaming at him to pick out Bergkamp, who was to his left as he approached the penalty area. Silly me. A quick adjustment of his balance, he side-stepped the bemused Spurs defenders, before burying a left-foot shot past Keller. 'A long distance goal followed by a long distance celebration' was how commentator Clive Tyldesley called it – one of the few times he called anything spot on!

Paul Manel: The goal and the celebration. Thierry beat about five Spurs players with pure pace. He scored in front of the North Bank. He then sprinted to the Clock End and slid in front of the Spurs fans who vented their anger. Thierry, that is why we love you!

James Miller: I was an Arsenal steward since 1988-89 and for many years the supervisor for the South Track, so after every goal all the track stewards would stand and face the crowd. I used to walk the track in case any steward needed assistance to calm any over the top celebrations.

So when Henry scored that solo goal and slid on his knees in front of the Tottenham fans, I was facing them. They then turned very abusive and angry. I turned to see why and, in front of me and still on his knees, was the man himself. I shouted at him to 'move it', as it was getting a bit hostile.

The next day, the celebratory picture appeared in the national papers, and since then it's been widely shared on Facebook and Twitter. People have even had tattoos of it. Signed, framed photos can still be bought online.

In an interview, Thierry spoke about that picture as his favourite. It was placed above his locker at Barcelona and he has it in his house. Now the image has been preserved in the form of his statue at The Emirates.

I realised I'm now part of the club's history. My grandkids love showing that picture off to their friends and whoever else will listen to them!

Iain Murray: Henry's knee-slide. Chapter over!

THIERRY HENRY

v Liverpool, Premier League, April 9, 2004

Graham Lister: As a pure life-affirming tonic whose ingredients included impeccable timing, momentous significance and sheer footballing genius, this gem from Thierry Henry takes some beating.

Context was critical. On the morning of April 3, Arsenal looked well-placed to storm to the Treble. But a narrow defeat to Manchester Utd in the FA Cup semi-final at Villa Park had been followed three days later by cruel elimination from the Champions League by Chelsea at the quarter-final stage. Now only the Premier League title remained as a target. Gunners were top, and still unbeaten, but at half-time on Good Friday found themselves 2-1 down to Liverpool. Momentum can be everything in football, and Arsenal's seemed suddenly to have gone into reverse.

But Robert Pires grabbed an equaliser, and in the next minute Gilberto Silva slipped the ball to Henry, who had dropped deep to gain possession and make a difference. Nevertheless, the situation looked unpromising with virtually the whole Liverpool team ranged defensively ahead of him.

Henry's response was to run at them with menacing intent, dribbling past the first opponent and causing others to back off nervously as he approached and entered their area. He beat Jamie Carragher, who collided with a team-mate, creating space for Henry to beat Jerzy Dudek low to the keeper's left. Henry went on to complete his hat-trick; Gunners were back on course and duly finished the season as invincible champions.

Jeff Owens: Greatest goal I've ever seen at Highbury has to be Henry's second against Liverpool, where he twisted Jamie Carragher and the entire Liverpool defence in knots before calmly side-footing into the net. A close runner up is Ray Parlour's long range rocket against Valencia in the Champions League.

Neil Payne: Dreams of a treble destroyed and now the unbeaten thus-far league season seriously under threat. Step forward Henry. Already he had equalised and assisted in the second leveller before taking centre stage. From memory, watching the goal it was almost mesmerising, as if he had waltzed around half the Liverpool defence before the trademark side-foot finish. The reality was some joke Liverpool defending had contributed but at that time the fear factor that Henry provided was in the main too much for most opposition defences. This day was one of those but the importance of the goal cannot be overestimated.

Barry Hughes: After Thierry scored his second, all the tension and worries of the last 10 days evaporated.

Silk (or satin if your prefer) scarves were very much in vogue in the early 70s, whether worn around the neck or tied to the wrist or waist band. This immaculate gem from more than 50 years ago was sent in by Ian Castle.

These home and away scarves were sent in by Eileen Clark. They were worn by her late husband Steve to both Double-winning matches, at White Hart Lane and Wembley, in May, 1971. Eileen said: "He was a true Gooner until his very sad, far too early death in 2006, aged just 54." The two woolen scarves on this page belong to John Hilditch.

HOME-MADE

Nothing epitomised the 60s and 70s for football fans quite like a woollen scarf lovingly knitted at home by Mum or another relative.

Here's Sheila Rainsford, who knitted this beauty (which also appears on our back cover). It features the names of the 13 squad players who made club history by winning the European Fairs Cup in 1970, plus manager Bertie Mee and coach Don Howe. The photo was taken in 2021, shortly before this book was first published, so her creative work of art has stood the test of time for more than 50 years!

Her son Pat explained: "Mum has been a big Arsenal fan since coming over from Ballyhea, County Cork, Ireland in 1956. She lived in Holloway – we were raised off Essex Road in Islington – and began going to Highbury probably in 1960 or 1961. She is 83 now.

"Mum was at the Fairs Cup Final, second leg in 1970 with my dad Patsy and older brother Tom. I was only five-years-old at the time, so I missed that one. Mum started knitting the scarf in celebration of that victory. It was then worn by Tom at Wembley the following year, when we clinched the Double in 1971 (a Scouser offered to buy the scarf from Dad and Tom on the way home but, obviously, they would never part with it).

"Dad passed away in March, 2018 and loved The Arsenal. He took me to my first game in 1972 and we had season tickets in the East lower for many years."

Right: This scarf, knitted by Rita Lewis in Gunners' then away change colours of yellow and blue, was sent in by her son Peter. The name of Alan Ball, a club record £220,000 signing from Everton in December, 1971, was added to those of the club's first Double winners.

Left: Another home-made product popular back in the day was the good, ol' wooden rattle. This one belongs to and was sent in by Lee Hisscott.

139

ARSENAL FOOTBALL
CLUB LTD.
Nº 9174

To be retained

ARSENAL STADIUM
HIGHBURY, N.5

Semi-Final Football League Cup, First Leg

ARSENAL
v
TOTTENHAM HOTSPUR

WEDNESDAY, 20th NOVEMBER, 1968
Kick off 7.30 p.m.

GILLESPIE ROAD
ENCLOSURE (Standing)

TURNSTILE E

ADMISSION 7/6

This Ticket must be intact when presented at Turnstile

Nº 9650 **A**

ARSENAL FOOTBALL CLUB LTD.
Arsenal Stadium, Highbury, London N5

CANON LEAGUE DIVISION ONE

ARSENAL
v
TOTTENHAM HOTSPUR

TUESDAY, 1st JANUARY 1985
K.O. — 11.30 a.m.

THIS PORTION TO
BE RETAINED
£2.50
INC. VAT

Nº 37

ARSENAL v.
TOTTENHAM HOTSP
MONDAY, APRIL 11th 1977

LOWER TIER SEATING £1.2
WEST STAND
Including

This voucher should be retained throughout the
and must be produced for inspection on dem
If today's Match is not played, this voucher m
returned to the Box Office by post together
addressed envelope, and the appropriate refun
be made.

No refunds will be made after May 31st next, fol

ARSENAL FOOTBALL
CLUB
C
0052

Barclays LEAGUE DIVISION ONE

ARSENAL
v
TOTTENHAM HOTSPUR

SATURDAY 30th NOVEMBER 1991
KICK-OFF 3.00 p.m.

YOU ARE ADVISED TO BE IN POSITION BY 2.15p.m.

STANDING TICKET
NORTH BANK GILLESPIE ROAD
(See Map on Reverse)

THIS PORTION TO BE RETAINED

$3.00
INC VAT

CONCESSION TICKET,
JUNIOR GUNNERS MEMBER

CLUB
1621

BARCLAYS LEAGUE DIVISION ONE

ARSENAL
v
TOTTENHAM HOTSPUR

SATURDAY 30th NOVEMBER 1991
KICK-OFF 3.00p.m.

YOU ARE ADVISED TO BE IN POSITION BY 2.15p.m.

STANDING TICKET
VISITORS SECTION SOUTH TERRACE HIGHBURY HILL
(See Map on Reverse)

THIS PORTION TO BE RETAINED
£8
INC VAT

ARSENAL FOOTBALL CLUB P.L.C.

THE F.A. CARLING PREMIERSHIP
V TOTTENHAM HOTSPUR

18 MAR 2000 03:00 AFTERNOON
BOND HOLDERS SE
NORTH BANK UPPER TIER

ROW   SEAT   PRICE

B   **62** * **28.00**

MILLARD
23653

Dreamcast

SEGA   TO BE RETAINED   SEGA

Arsenal

Barclaycard Premiership

Arsenal v Tottenham Hotspur

08 Nov, 2003 Kick Off 15:00
TH BANK LOWER TIER

Block   Row   Seat

2   **M**   **34**   £31.00

Redwood
3648

O2

6 NORTH LONDON DERBIES

WHETHER challenging strongly for the league championship, pursuing domestic cup glory, battling for European qualification, or wallowing in mid-table obscurity, victories against your local rivals are always cause for celebration.

Weekends are made or ruined by north London derby results, the issue of gleeful bragging rights in the school playground and workplace on Monday mornings determined by the players of Arsenal in N5 and 'that lot' from four miles away, Tottenham Hotspur, in N17.

There have been countless classic battles between the teams since they first met in November 1887, so let's rewind as our contributors recall their standout derby clashes at Highbury.

Q: Favourite all-time north London derby (home game) memory from the Highbury era?

Richard Boyes: My favourite player Jimmy Logie (right) was 5ft 3ins and had all the skills required of what is now called a playmaker. He was wonderful, wore number 8, played just behind the forwards and scored when we beat Spurs 4-0 (7/2/53). We beat them home and away that season after a few years of being second best.

Kenny Rolfe: Without doubt, the best plot in the old Highbury ground if you were a youngster in a 60,000-plus crowd was above the exit at the Clock End, just beneath the clock. To get this position you had to be in the ground when the gates opened.

I was 10-years-old at the time and remember dragging my seven-year-old cousin across the Clock End terraces to get to my favourite vantage point. It was over the Christmas holidays (23/12/1961) and we were playing the great Tottenham Double side. And no doubt about it, they were one of the best teams in the history of The Football League.

Tottenham, kicking towards the Clock End, went in front after about 20 minutes from a corner that was only partially cleared and rolled outside the box to Dave Mackay, who hit an unstoppable shot from 25 yards. Jack Kelsey went full length but was unable to prevent it going in.

However, Arsenal were a different team in the second-half. Roared on by a 63,440 crowd and going all-out attack, a cross from Johnny Macleod found Mel Charles, who rose like a salmon to head a brilliant equaliser.

Then, with just minutes to go, Alan Skirton (right) picked the ball up on the right-wing, cut inside and as he reached the edge of the box, let one of his thunderbolts go that flew past Bill Brown into the roof of the net.

Graham Lister: With Spurs second and Arsenal – unusually for us at that time – only one point below them, the winners of this derby clash (15/10/1963) would go top. Moreover, the two teams boasted the First Division's most prolific forwards; the season was only a dozen games old but Joe Baker and Jimmy Greaves both had 15 goals to their names in all competitions, while Geoff Strong had 13. So the febrile derby atmosphere was even more intense than usual. No fewer than 67,857 crammed into Highbury, whose gates were shut 45 minutes before kick-off, with thousands still outside in the drizzle and several of those inside needing treatment in the crush.

The Tuesday evening game was a passionate, totally committed affair in which the high-flying visitors (fielding the same team that had won the Double in 1961 apart from Greaves, in for Les Allen) at times threatened to sweep Arsenal away but hadn't bargained for Gunners' fighting spirit and refusal to bow down.

The home fans feared the worst when Greaves applied a deft flick to Danny Blanchflower's freekick to put Spurs ahead after just three minutes. Then Bobby Smith blasted a Ron Henry cross past Ian McKechnie on 20 minutes. But Terry Dyson fouled George Armstrong in the box 10 minutes later, and George Eastham reduced the arrears by subtly stroking home the penalty. However, straight from the restart Dave Mackay powered forward to meet John White's pass and thump the ball beyond McKechnie. And it very nearly became 4-1 soon afterwards when Spurs had the ball in the net following a flowing move, only for referee Denis Howell (a future Labour Minister for Sport) to disallow it with Smith fractionally offside.

Arsenal took full advantage of the reprieve by scoring themselves just a minute later. The outstanding Eastham pounced on an ineffective clearance by Tottenham's under-pressure defence and arrowed the ball into the top corner of Bill Brown's net.

Yet Spurs reasserted their dominance before half-time when another slick attack involving White and Cliff Jones was finished off by Smith heading in White's centre.

Unbelievable day, with all goals being scored at the Clock End. An unforgettable experience.

Jeremy Doltis: My first NLD was a very memorable 5-4 defeat (15/10/63). We stood in the West Stand lower, because dad gave up his season ticket in the East Stand as a protest to out manager Billy Wright.

David Roche: I've seen many NLDs but the 4-0 win (16/9/1967) stands out. That morning George Graham got married to Marie Zia and Terry Venables was his Best Man. Later on that afternoon they were on opposing sides. Graham completed a happy day by scoring.

Lee Pritchett: I hate NLDs, especially at Highbury. In fact, all of my favourite NLDs have been at WHL: 1968, 1971, 1987 and 2004.

But two at Highbury stick in my mind. A 4-0 drubbing of a very good Spurs side in 1967 (there actually wasn't much between us then), with goals from Addison, Graham, Neill (pen) and Radford, with a few of the Double squad starting to emerge.

The other is our 3-0 win in 2002, Thierry's solo goal and subsequent

A 2nd TY-PHOO SERIES

CUT ALONG HERE

No. 17 TERRY NEILL

Despite relentless Arsenal pressure in the second-half, with Armstrong and Johnny MacLeod supplied and prompted by Eastham to make inroads down the flanks and target the agile Strong with repeated centres, it was still 4-2 with five minutes to go.

Then Joe Baker shrugged off Maurice Norman's attempted tackle and flashed a low shot into the net. Highbury was now at boiling point, and amid a raucous cacophony, Arsenal won two corners in quick succession in the final minute. From the second of them, by MacLeod, Strong rose high to head the ball home off the underside of the bar. There was just seconds left for Spurs to kick-off before Howell blew time on a momentous 4-4 draw.

Segregation of rival fans was still a long way off, and at the final whistle in the lower West Stand a strapping giant of a Spurs-supporting coalman embraced my dad in the next seat in a bear-hug, telling him: "Well done, mate. You deserved that!"

Chris Welstead: My favourite north London derby was not actually a victory. It occurred in October, 1963. The game was played in front of the largest crowd I had ever experienced (around 69,000 – the biggest in all my years at Highbury). At that time, Arsenal had a very lively attack but were just as likely to concede three or four and often did.

Arsenal fought back from being 4-2 down to score twice in the last five minutes and force a 4-4 draw. It was memorable for the sheer size of the crowd and the fantastic atmosphere. Also, scoring twice so late in the game, it felt like a victory. I was buzzing for a few days, until we lost our next game away to Aston Villa.

Bernard Kiernan: Probably the game that really hooked me as a 14-year-old kid and enabled me to put up with the misery of the lack of Arsenal success for the rest of the barren 1960s, until we won the Double in 1971 and emulated The Lilywhites.

iconic celebration slide towards their supporters. Magic.

Jeff Stevens: Not sure it's my favourite but I have fond memories of my first team 'debut' game against them at Highbury (I'd previously seen our reserves against them), when Terry Neill put us one up from the spot at the North Bank end (16/9/1967). I was up the Clock End, where I saw the other three goals we scored!

Paul Harris: The one that remains foremost in my memory was the League Cup Semi-final, first leg (20/11/1968), when John Radford scored the only goal in a tight game, an all-ticket affair and it cost me 25 pence (five shillings) to get in. Spurs seemed to be content for the draw but Radford seized on a defensive error in the second-half to score the only goal at the North Bank end. He also netted in the 1-1 second leg draw at Tottenham. Then there was Swindon in the final, and we have still not lived that one down.

Robert Thaine: Seeing Geordie Armstrong emerge as our unlikely hero by scoring both goals in a 2-0 win (5/9/1970) in our first Double-winning season.

Pete Mountford: Here's a less obvious one for you. The first home NLD I went to was near the end of the 1972-73 season (14/4/1973), a week after we'd had the shame of losing an FA Cup semi-final to second division Sunderland at Hillsborough. Due to a bizarre situation with fixtures, it was actually our last home game of the season.

Pat Jennings, then playing for Spurs, had just been voted Footballer of the Year and such was the sportsmanship towards opposition goalkeepers in those days (and him in particular), he got a standing ovation from all four sides. I still remember him coming for a cross during the first-half and actually catching it with one hand tucked under his armpit.

Emilio Zorlakki: Every north London derby victory is precious to me. I remember Malcolm Macdonald's winner (11/4/1977) and sitting quite close to the Spurs fans in the Clock End (there were also loads in the North Bank that day). It was a fairly late goal and it helped relegate Tottenham a few weeks later.

Also, for an evening match (10/4/1979), I found myself walking through the back streets near Seven Sisters Road in Finsbury Park, when suddenly I was

Bill McCullough challenges Cliff Jones in September, 1960.

in the middle of an ambush. There were about 10 of us and two or three times that number of Spurs fans. I recognised a very well known Arsenal supporter, Dainton Connell (aka 'The Bear', sadly no longer with us) and he shouted to us: "Anyone run, I'll find you!" I decided that it would be better to get beaten up there and then, rather than live in fear looking over my shoulder. The whole episode lasted about a minute, although it felt like ages, and I sort of managed to avoid the main scrap by standing in someone's front garden. But every so often a Spurs fan had a go at me and, I suppose, I fought back. I couldn't remember clearly, what with all that adrenalin rush.

Eventually, the cavalry (police) arrived and most of the fans ran off. Dainton walked up to me – with a little blood trickling from my nose I feared the worst – and said: "Nice one!". I hadn't really done anything but on the back of that incident I had acquired an undeserved reputation, which I helped to exaggerate by claiming that me and Dainton were "good mates"!

Towards the end of the same game a friend and I had agreed to leave just before the final whistle to avoid meeting up with Spurs fans in Wood Green, where we lived. We were standing by the exit on the steps of one of the blocks in the West Stand lower and my friend kept nagging away at me to go. "Just one more attack," I said optimistically, as the game entered injury-time. "Come on!" he moaned. "Hold on!". Then out of the blue, Frank Stapleton headed a last-gasp winner and during the celebrations there was a pile of bodies on the steps, with me underneath them all screaming with joy and in considerable pain, too. Who cares! We eventually got back to our feet and were screaming loudly as we ran out of the stand and the stadium. Quite an eventful evening.

Barry Hughes: First NLD was a 2-0 victory (27/12/1982) thanks to goals by Alan Sunderland and Tony Woodcock. Tried to get in the Clock End first. It was full but I did get on the North Bank with my dad and brother-in-law (Nick). It was so crammed, my feet never touched the floor. Which as a 12-year-old was very exciting. Only after Hillsborough did I realise how inherently dangerous this was.

Neil Davies: Maybe not a happy memory but the League Cup Semi-final in '87 (8/2/1987). I was nine. We lost 1-0. It was only my second Highbury game. I was gutted and yes, I may have cried. A guy in front of me in the West lower was a Spud. He offered me a Polo Mint and said: "You'll probably do us at our place." He knew! (Ed: Goals by Viv Anderson and Niall Quinn in a 2-1 second leg win at White Hart Lane saw Gunners through to Wembley,

144

Graham Lister: Charlie Nicholas had been Arsenal's big signing in the close season as the Scot opted for Highbury ahead of Anfield and Old Trafford. But his debut season had been somewhat frustrating, and his failure to fire on a regular basis had contributed to manager Terry Neill's dismissal shortly before Christmas. Yet the hugely popular, if inconsistent, Nicholas fully grasped the importance to fans of the north London derby, and showed impeccable timing by scoring his first goal since August in November's League Cup tie at White Hart Lane, where Arsenal won 2-1. Then on Boxing Day he'd grabbed his first League goals for four months – two of them – in a 4-2 victory at The Lane. Now Spurs were at Highbury (21/4/1984) in front of a crowd of 48,831; I was the one, standing on the North Bank.

Caretaker manager Don Howe was pitching for a permanent appointment on the back of just one defeat in eight games, while his Spurs counterpart Keith Burkinshaw had announced his intention to resign at the end of the season, disenchanted with Tottenham's owners.

The game – the 100th NLD – mirrored the prospects of the two managers, with Arsenal dominating the play and frequently outclassing their neighbours. This was not fully reflected in the 3-2 scoreline, which owed more to a couple of lapses in Arsenal's concentration than to Tottenham pressure. In fact Gunners should have been at least three-up by half-time but Tony Woodcock had a goal disallowed, Brian Talbot would normally have converted two good chances that fell his way and Tony Parks produced a string of fine saves. So the home fans had to settle for a 1-0 interval lead, courtesy of Stewart Robson's shot from the edge of the penalty area that took a deflection off Gary Mabbutt.

The second-half was lit up by a burst of four goals in eight minutes, sparked by a shimmering gem from Nicholas. In front of the adoring North Bank, he beat one Spurs defender after another on his mesmerising way from the edge of the area towards goal, then took the ball round Parks and slotted it gently between two Spurs men stationed on the goal-line. As it slowly but surely crossed the line, the massed terrace heaved and seethed in an explosion of the rarefied joy unique to derby matches.

Two long-serving derby day combatants, David O'Leary and Steve Perryman..

But the celebrations seemed to distract the players, because half-a-minute after the restart Spurs scored, Steve Archibald capitalising on a Garth Crooks pass as David O'Leary and Tommy Caton stood ball-watching.

No matter, Paul Mariner soon flicked the ball into Woodcock's path on the left. Tony sprinted onto it, leaving Paul Miller floundering in his wake, and beat Parks all ends up with a fierce low shot. Annoyingly, Arsenal again let Spurs reply almost immediately, Archibald making the most of another moment of distracted defending. But there was no doubt about it, Arsenal were emphatic winners.

Derek Barclay: The most memorable wins against Tottenham have always been away from home – too many to list! And also to this day, the north London derby remains the best game on the football calendar – there have been some simply amazing results/matches over the years. One earlier example of this was in 1983-84, when that Arsenal team Don Howe built, including established England internationals like Tony Woodcock, Paul Mariner, Brian Talbot, Viv Anderson and Kenny Sansom, beat the old enemy 3-2.

The star who never quite lived up to that billing was the crowd's darling, Charlie Nicholas – and Charlie maintained his popularity by always playing exceptionally well and scoring amazing goals against Tottenham. His goal in this one seems almost Bergkampesque, although a fortunate ricochet helped. No matter. It was a highlight of the season and (besides the 1987 League Cup Final) of Nicholas' Arsenal career.

Alex Morrow: All the wins but especially my first NLD, in April 1984. I had never experienced an atmosphere like that, nor seen the Clock End filled with away fans. Dad said we would leave early because he didn't want to get caught up in any crowd trouble (and there was some). When we left, with not more than about five minutes to go, we were winning 2-0. It was only when we were driving home that we heard the final score was 3-2 to Arsenal. Missing three goals was quite a feat, although thanks to Youtube, I have now seen them.

Gary Jones: Charlie Nicholas dancing through the Spurs defence in the Highbury sunshine. Magical.

George Lampshire: I went with a group of mates from school – we had tickets in the East Stand. Charlie Nicholas was my idol, so watching him waltz round Roberts and co. and dance in front of the North Bank . . . magic.

Tony Bateman: From what my alcohol-affected brain can remember, this was Charlie Nicholas' finest game, and a real brick-mover. Twice going two goals clear, with Archibald netting straight after.

Colin Whitehouse: The first one I went to, in 1984, and Charlie's goal in front of the North Bank.

Chris Bolister: Charlie Nicholas walking the ball through the entire Tottenham defence and rolling it across the line in what looked like slow motion. I was stood on the corner of the North Bank.

Tony Daisley: The 3-2 win in April, 1984, with Charlie Nicholas and Tony Woodcock excelling. It came near the end of the season when, under new manager Don Howe, we hit a purple patch by scoring 24 goals in the last 10 games.

Charlie Nicholas enjoyed himself against Tottenham, none more so than in April, 1984. Paul Davis seems impressed, too. It was a measure of Charlie's hero status and a man of his time that he adorned the front page of *New Musical Express* on November 24, 1984.

NME

CHARLIE NICHOLAS
HOW SOCCER'S BLOOD GUNNER GETS HIS KICKS
BY ADRIAN THRILLS

Graham Lister: Arsène Wenger's first derby match (24/11/1996) was played in apocalyptic conditions as the heavens opened over Highbury, a spiteful wind giving an added lash to the relentless downpour. But the weather was an incidental sideshow as Arsenal showed their recently-installed French boss just how important it is to win the north London derby. It was a victory built on team spirit and never-say-die persistence that brought its spectacular reward in the last three minutes of the match.

Having lost only their second League match of the season a week earlier – 1-0 at Old Trafford to champions Manchester United – Arsenal needed a win to keep in touch at the top of the table, quite apart from the question of local pride. But they hadn't beaten Spurs at Highbury for five years. Fortunately they had Dennis Bergkamp at No.10.

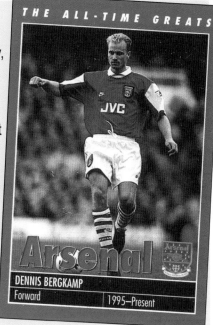

THE ALL-TIME GREATS

DENNIS BERGKAMP
Forward   1995–Present

The Dutchman's threat earned Gunners a penalty midway through the first half, when Clive Wilson impeded him in the area as they both chased a loose ball. Ian Wright gleefully converted the spot-kick and promptly revealed a T-shirt with the slogan: 'I love the lads'. The striker later explained: "It is an appreciation of the team here and what they all mean to me."

Teddy Sheringham had already squandered a good opportunity by then, and after the penalty Wright was denied a second when future Gunner Sol Campbell thwarted him with a timely tackle.

After the break John Lukic, deputising for injured David Seaman, saved well from Darren Anderton and Chris Armstrong, twice. But the keeper was unlucky just before the hour mark when Allan Neilsen's long throw was converted by Andy Sinton thanks to the considerable assistance of the post and the hapless Lukic's back.

With three minutes remaining, Bergkamp chipped the ball in to Tony Adams, whose enterprise had prompted him to take up an advanced position, and the captain volleyed the ball emphatically into the net. Two minutes later Wright turned his marker this way and that out on the wing before lofting a deep cross towards the far-post. Bergkamp controlled it instantly, turned deftly inside his defender and fired the ball into the opposite corner to put the issue beyond any doubt at 3-1. Being sopping wet and cold had never felt so good.

Marvin Berglas: The game looked to be heading for a 1-1 draw after Spurs cancelled out Ian Wright's penalty. But with two minutes remaining our Captain

Fantastic Tony Adams showed his shooting prowess with a great strike. Spurs' misery was compounded in injury-time, when Wright skinned the Spurs full-back and sent over a cross which Dutch master Dennis Bergkamp controlled beautifully before a trademark curler into the back of the net, to totally rub Spurs' noses in it. A mixture of grit and flair combining beautifully.

Neil Payne: This was a tough choice and my immediate thought was a 3-2 win in 1984, when Charlie Nicholas and Tony Woodcock scored two sublime goals between them. But the one that just seals it is the 3-1 win in the pouring rain in 1996. Dennis Bergkamp had oozed class throughout but with the scores level he produced two moments of impish brilliance to settle the derby. Firstly with a deft flick for Tony Adams to rifle home, and then the coup-de-grace with time running out. A stunning piece of ball control from Ian Wright's long, hopeful cross before a rasping drive beat Walker to conclusively settle the game in our favour.

It also came just days after Mr Amstrad had embarrassed himself with comments directed at the Dutch master along the lines of "he is just another Carlos Kick-a-ball here for the money" Oh, that was so sweet from DB10, Sugar!

Alex Morrow: My other favourite NLD after '84 was Arsène Wenger's first, in '96. Pouring rain, two minutes to go. Spurs (as usual) had cheated in order to equalise. Tony Adams volleying into the roof of the Spurs net at the North Bank end. Cue absolute bedlam. A perfect day was then rounded off by Bergkamp in injury-time. The Bergkamp goal was just icing on the cake. It was the Adams volley that brought the explosion of joy. We beat the scum 3-1.

John Lawlor: It was a horrible wet night. Gerry Francis was their manager and he hadn't lost against Arsenal whenever a team of his had played them. DB10 should have had an early penalty but it was waved away. When he was fouled again a little while later, the pen was given and up stepped Ian Wright to slot it home in front of the Clock End. We had a few chances before half-time but it wasn't to be. A game in which Wrighty uncharacteristically missed a few decent chances.

Peter Lewis: This was the first time I took my then eight-year-old daughter Rachel to a game. We sat in the North Bank – she loved it. She asked my why we hated Tottenham. I told her: "We just do, dear, we just do!" I referred to that moment in my father of the bride speech at her wedding.

John Hilditch: It might have been Arsène Wenger's first NLD. I think they were, er, unsporting by not throwing the ball back to us after an injury and scored an equaliser. They were very pleased with themselves. But the game ended with Tony Adams belting one in, in front of the North Bank, and us winning 3-1. Take that, you horrible lot.

Graham Price: In the pouring rain, when Bergkamp took the ball down at the far-post and shot in the next motion.

Keith English: We were simply outstanding that day.

where they beat Liverpool by the same score with a Charlie Nicholas brace.)

James Smither: As a rule, I actually hate the north London derby. I just find it too unbearably tense, and the consequences of not winning too horrible to contemplate, to be able to enjoy the games at all until the final whistle has blown and we have hopefully emerged victorious. That being said, I actually (touch wood) have a pretty good personal record in such fixtures and never saw us lose one at Highbury.

An obvious choice would be the game known for Lauren's amazingly (crazily) cool penalty dispatched to ensure a critical three points on our way to the league title in April 2002. But I don't have any particular memories related to that game, other than how tremendously relieved we all were when the final whistle went.

My first NLD (6/3/1988) was pretty memorable. I remember being so nervous during the preceding week that I bit every fingernail I had and could barely concentrate on schoolwork. Being a superstitious child, I decided to "cross my fingers for good luck". . . on about the Tuesday before the game (a Sunday kick-off live on TV)! I was actually taken to the match by a Stoke City-supporting colleague of my dad's, curious to witness the tribal enmity of the Seven Sisters Road rivals. My normal match day guardian, my grandfather, being away on holiday at the time.

In a noisier and fuller Highbury than I had seen for any previous game I'd attended, we took a first-half lead through Alan Smith, and then proceeded to miss a succession of chances to buttress our advantage before Clive Allen equalised, heartbreakingly, in the second period. The venomous pandemonium among the visiting supporters in the Clock End, relatively close to our seats in the West Upper, was possibly the most gut-wrenching sight and sound I had heard thus far in my life.

My 10-year-old heart was on the edge of breaking but, fortunately, Perry Groves – who, in a rare starting role up front, was one of the most guilty parties for squandering earlier opportunities – managed to turn in a shot at the North Bank to send me home happy and help build his own legend in the process.

When I attempted to uncross my fingers at the final whistle, they had almost moulded together. For a little while I feared my left hand might be permanently disfigured in that position but since I felt sure I had contributed to our success through this small sacrifice on my part, at that precise time I doubt I really minded.

Ian Tredgett: Our best memories from NLDs are probably not those played at Highbury (the League Cup semi in 1987, clinching the titles in 1971 and 2004, Wembley 1993 and Old Trafford 2001, for example). However, at home I did really enjoy a 2-0 New Year's win (2/1/1989).

It was also the day the clock was unveiled at the top of the then new South Stand. When you remember EVERY goal that season was crucial, it carries even greater significance in retrospect.

Merse put us into a first-half lead and although we did have the legendary back four playing, it was still tense as Spurs pushed for an equaliser. In the last minute, Mickey Thomas charged through the midfield and scored the second past Bobby Mimms to give us a bit of breathing space. I seem to remember he got another important last minute goal to seal a 2-0 win later that season . . .

Tom Eldridge: Best moment was in 1984 but that was really about Charlie Nicholas. So I'll go, instead, for the 2-0 win through Merse and Thomas (2/1/1989). It was at that point I really thought we could do it and go on and win the league.

James Murphy: My first NLD. Michael Thomas with an injury-time goal, clipping home Paul Merson's through ball, that was identical to his league winner later that season at Anfield.

Andrew Whitnall: The 2-0 win (2/1/1989) on the way to the title. My dad and I got attacked by a group of Spurs fans in Highbury Quadrant after the game. In between trying to throw punches, they were demanding from us an explanation as to why Michael Thomas celebrated his goal in front of the Tottenham supporters. I remember thinking of them on the coach coming back from Anfield, just after we had won the title, just how sick they must be that Mickey did it!

Robert Grainger: Tony Adams received dog's abuse from the away fans (20/1/1990), enduring 'Donkey' chants the entire game. Who popped up with the only goal? Captain Tony.

Paul Hemming: Queen's We Are The Champions was blasting out of the tannoy before kick-off (I don't even like the song), the North Bank was booming and vermin had those 'Adams is a Donkey' T-shirts on. But our riposte 'Donkey Wins the Derby' T-shirts were out for the next home game.

James Smither: Certainly the most emotional NLD I remember at Highbury was on March 31, 2001, when the players took to the field against the devastating backdrop of news, confirmed just that morning, that home crowd favourite David Rocastle had lost his fight with cancer at the tragically young age of 33, leaving behind his young family.

I took the news particularly badly. Rocky, a Lewisham boy like me, had been my favourite player growing up and my father had also suffered from (but in his case mercifully survived) a similar form of Lymphoma. I know for a fact that I wasn't the only person in the stadium with tears in their eyes looking at the famous picture of David giving a thumbs-up which was shown on the Jumbotrons during a minute's silence before kick-off, which the Spurs fans (to their credit) observed impeccably. Tottenham were actually playing their first game under Glenn Hoddle's management, so they also had plenty to play for.

But it was a strangely aimless game for the most part – perhaps because of the desperately sad news from earlier in the day. We got our act together in the final quarter and Robert Pires – signed at the start of that season and still in many fans' minds a luxury player without a stomach for the fight needed in English football – produced what would become a trademark finish throughout a glorious subsequent career at the club, curling a shot effortlessly past keeper Neil Sullivan on 70 minutes.

He later set up a clincher for Thierry Henry, and the resonance of our inspiration to beat our fiercest rivals having come from a player wearing Rocastle's No.7 shirt was lost on no-one inside the stadium that day. Pires would again be decisive as we beat the same opposition again eight days later in the FA Cup semi-final at Old Trafford, echoing Rocastle's starring role at the same stage of the League Cup run back in 1987. He would go on to torment our rivals seemingly every time we played them – perhaps inspired to do so by noted Spurs antagonist David's memory.

The 2-0 win wasn't exactly catharsis after such a traumatic loss for everyone involved with Arsenal that day but I feel sure it was the send-off fervent Gooner Rocky would have wanted.

Dave Randall: Has to be the 2-0 victory the day after Rocky died (31/3/2001). Robert Pires, wearing the No.7 shirt, curled an absolute beauty past Neil Sullivan to make it 1-0. The most fitting tribute to David Rocastle, who is truly without question an Arsenal legend.

John Skinner: The last-ever NLD at Highbury, a 1-1 draw (22/4/2006). Spurs played on and Robbie Keane scored in the 66th-minute when we had a man down – Eboue lay injured in the centre circle having collided with Gilberto. It was therefore so sweet when Thierry Henry – who came on as a sub for Robin Van Persie just after the hour mark – got the equaliser seven minutes from the end.

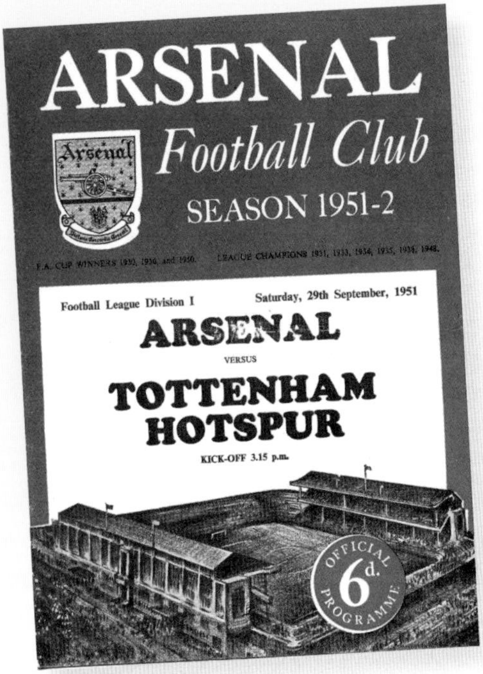

1951-52

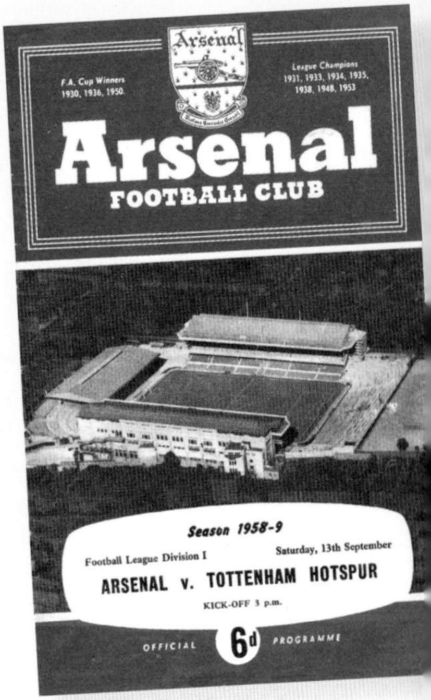

1958-59

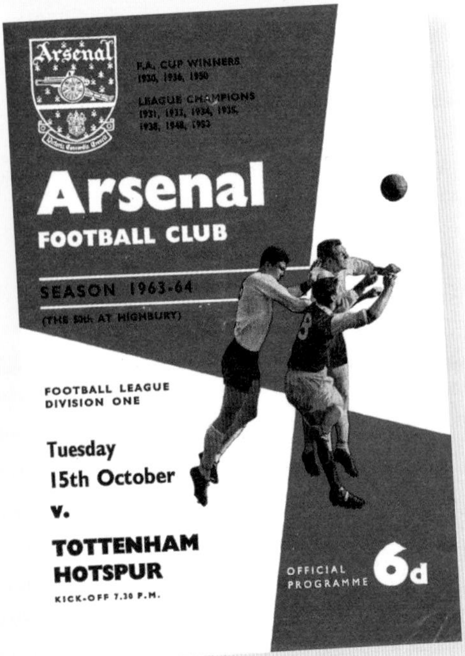

1963-64

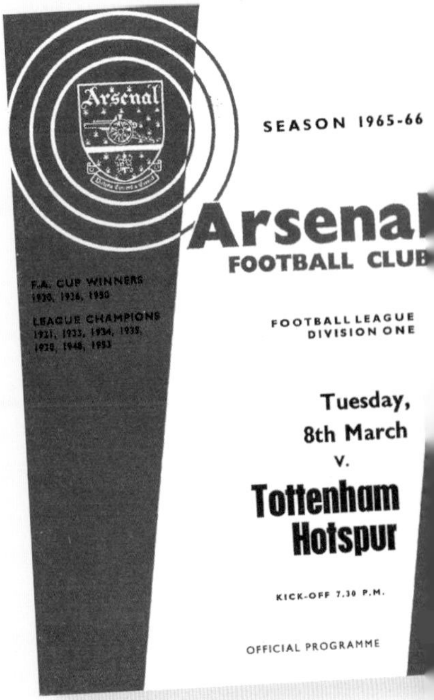

1965-66

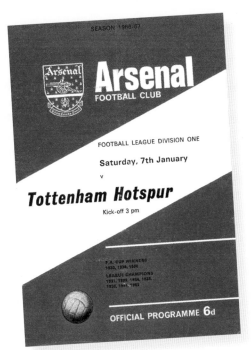

1966-67

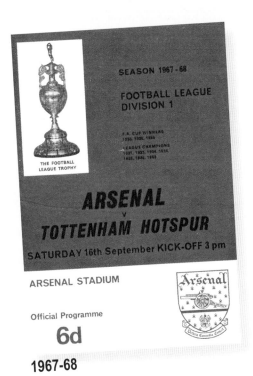

1967-68

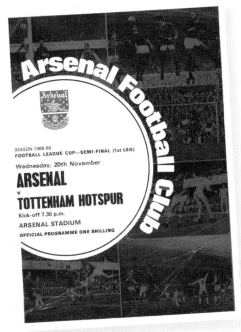

1968-69

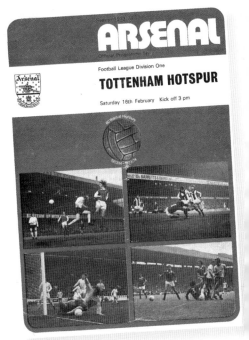

1973-74

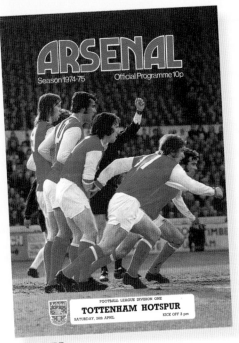

1974-75

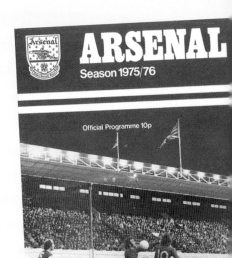

1975-76

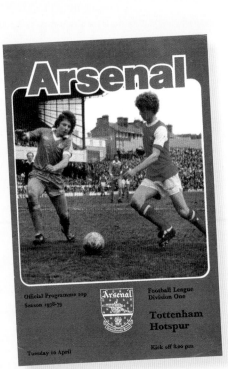

1978-79

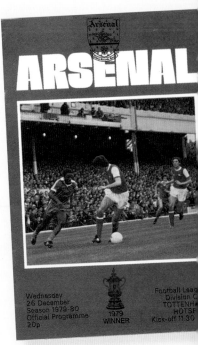

1979-80

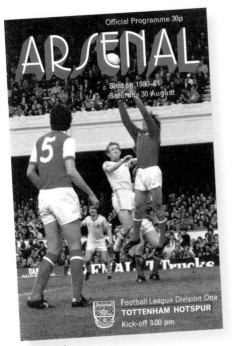

1980-81

1981-82

1982-83

1983-84

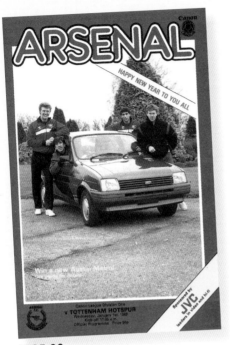

1985-86

1989-90

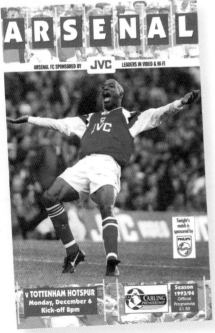

1993-94

1994-95

1997-98

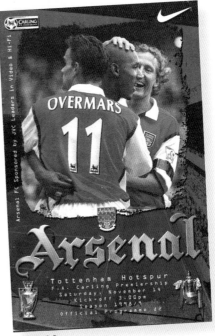

1998-99

1999-2000

2000-2001

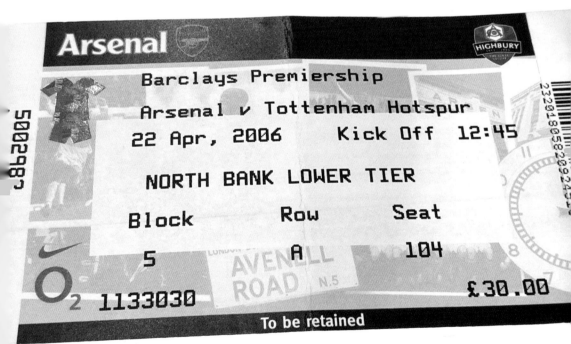

OFFICIAL PROGRAMME £3

Arsenal

v TOTTENHAM HOTSPUR

SATURDAY, APRIL 22, 2006   KICK-OFF: 12.45PM   SEASON 2005/2006

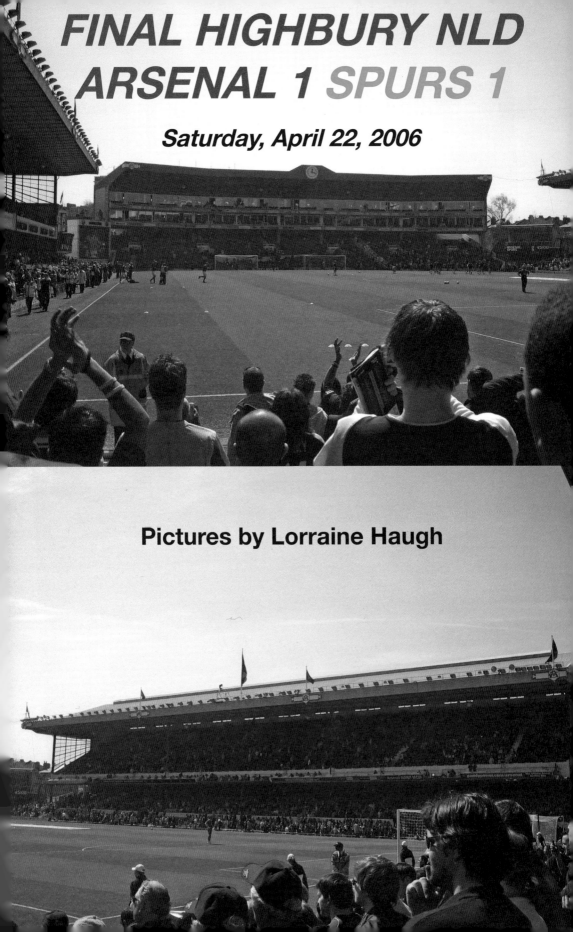

FINAL HIGHBURY NLD
ARSENAL 1 SPURS 1

Saturday, April 22, 2006

Pictures by Lorraine Haugh

93 YEARS OF MEMORIES

ICTORY THROUGH HARMONY

Inset: Thierry Henry celebrates his late equaliser in the last-ever NLD at Highbury, in April, 2006.

Alan Smith's hat-trick put a magical sheen on a 3-1 victory against Manchester Utd.

7 HIGHS & LOWS

SUPPORT any big club over a lengthy period and you are bound to experience unforgettable victories and heart-breaking defeats. But few fans get to see their team lift its first European trophy (1970), complete the first leg of an amazing double (1998) or seal a history-making season of league invincibility (2004) at home in front of its own ecstatic supporters.

On the flip side of that coin, the agony of Champions League defeat to London rivals Chelsea left a bitter taste, while some humiliating losses in the domestic cups to the likes of Tranmere Rovers and Walsall were also hard to swallow.

Q: The happiest and lowest you felt after watching Arsenal at Highbury – and why?

HIGHS

Richard Boyes: We had lost 3-1 to Anderlecht in the first leg of the European Fairs Cup Final – Ray Kennedy scored a late goal in Belgium to keep us competitive – so we had to win by three clear goals at home (28/4/1970). I drove to the game with my father-in-law Frank Brinkmen, a lifelong Arsenal supporter, and my six-year-old eldest son Richard. We had tickets in the West Stand lower tier, the first time we had ever sat down to watch a game. It was a misty night with a slight drizzle; the atmosphere was electric with plenty of noise and chanting.

Midway through the first-half Eddie Kelly scored our first, and John Radford added a second. We had a few frights and they hit the woodwork. And then with about 20 minutes to go Jon Sammels hit a screamer in the net, the team went into a scrum and the crowd went crazy – the noise was unbelievable.

We managed to hold on to win the game 3-0, our first trophy for 17 long years. The crowd ran onto the pitch at the final whistle.

In 80 years as a supporter I have watched Arsenal win titles at Tottenham, Manchester and Liverpool but I can actually relive that Anderlecht game and still feel the excitement.

Chris Welstead: We had come back from two goals down in the first leg in Anderlecht to win the trophy. The atmosphere was electric and it was the first trophy that I had seen Gunners win in my first 17 years of support. I will never forget the scenes at the end when the crowd invaded the pitch and chaired Frank McLintock around the ground.

Tony Fisher: There was an unbelievable atmosphere at Highbury that night, with the crowd behind the team non-stop. I remember arguing with the bloke next to me after the first goal went in, as he was complaining that it was only one! A bit like in *Fever Pitch*, you can't score two until you score one! Then the elation of Jon Sammels smashing in

Jon Sammels
INSIDE RIGHT

the winning goal from the right-hand corner of the box. The realisation that we had won our first trophy after so long and the joy of celebrating on the pitch with the players afterwards. Unless you were there it is impossible to describe that feeling of joy after watching many years of dross.

This is why I get upset at the modern fan who constantly criticises The Arsenal without ever having had to suffer countless years of awful football and failure. You can't appreciate the good until you've suffered the bad. Football, as in life.

Jeff Owens: Up until then I had no memory of Arsenal winning anything (I was not two-years-old when they won the league championship in 1953). I literally saw grown men cry with happiness that night – a really emotional occasion.

Keith Wilsher: My aunt worked for The Arsenal and had two tickets in the West Stand. As we were down 3-1 from the first leg, my cousin did not want to go (o ye of little faith), so my uncle Sid took me. After the game he left me, to go to the team's celebration party, which left this 11-year-old to make his own way back to Finchley. You couldn't let an 11-year-old do that today!

Bernard Chaplin: 4-4 draw v Spurs (15/10/1963). A rush to get to this midweek match after work and join nearly 68,000 – a record Highbury crowd for me. Crushed on the terraces, no season ticket for me until a few years later. Arsenal, 4-2 down with five minutes left and attacking. Joe Baker and Geoff Strong scored to bring the scores level.

Tom Eldridge: Happiest was watching Charlie Nicholas score twice against Spurs on Boxing Day, 1983. I loved Nicholas at the time. I didn't really appreciate the pressure he and the team were under then but the red and white colours of Highbury and him dancing through the Spurs defence was amazing. Topped only by Tony Adams running through the Everton defence and leathering that ball in the top corner to seal the Championship crown in 1998. What an end!

Ian Tredgett: The most obvious fondest memories are the titles wins in 1991, 1998, 2002 and completing the unbeaten season in 2004, all of which I was lucky enough to attend. One other favourite was the 3-1 defeat of Liverpool near the start of the 1984-85 season. A beautiful sunny day and the North Bank was packed as we comprehensively beat the defending English and European champions. I remember leaving the ground and the tannoy announcing that we had gone top of the league (for the first time in more than 10 years) "Arsenal are back" the crowd chanted in celebration. After only five games of the season it seemed a bit premature, and indeed it was, but it was nice while it lasted.

Andrew Whitnall: I'll go back to childhood for the happiest, which would be the FA Cup quarter-final v Aston Villa (12/3/1983). We'd been sent West Stand tickets by mistake (Dad had applied for a league game) but he managed to get the day off work to take me to my first cup-tie. To see Petrovic score in our 2-0 win was a bonus.

Mark Aughterlony: I was there (27/12/1987) when our club celebrated its centenary, Southampton being the opponents. I stood on the North Bank with my late father David and my uncle Chris watching true legends such as Ted Drake, Jack Kelsey and Joe Baker being (re-) introduced to the crowd that day. I had only read about most of these players, and it was clear that the club meant as much to them as it did us, the supporters.

John Hilditch: It might have been the League Cup semi-final win over Everton (24/2/1988). It's easy to say any of the championship wins, especially '91 and the Invincibles of 2004, and they were immensely proud moments. But for sheer joy, qualifying for Wembley

Today we celebrate 100 years of Arsenal... 1886-1986

with that win made me very, very happy. Three goals, floodlights and a pitch invasion. A marvellous night.

Guy Thompson: Happiest has gotta be the first time I ever went. Just being there was enough for me. More specifically, the league game v Liverpool (18/4/1990) was a special one. I know we'd beaten them at home in the League Cup six months before but this was the first time we'd played them in the League at Highbury since that incredible night at Anfield. We'd never been champions since I'd been a supporter, so just being able to sing "We won the League on Merseyside" and "Who put the ball in the Liverpool net . . . " at their fans in the Clock End was an amazing feeling. It's probably the loudest I've ever sung at a game and, up to that point, it was the loudest I'd ever heard the North Bank. I've worked in the rock 'n' roll business for many years and have been to some real ear-bending gigs but that night was something else. We were SO loud!

Another happy time was the game against Coventry City on the last day of the 1990-91 season (11/5/1991). It was a real carnival atmosphere and we absolutely ripped them apart, 6-1. I'd been to every home game that season and spent a lot of it standing on the crush barrier at the back of the North Bank, while hammering on the corrugated iron behind me. Suffering just one league defeat all season, we were the best in the land and we let everyone know. What a brilliant day that was.

Graham Lister: Possibly the most euphoric I've felt at Highbury was on 6/5/1991. Two days earlier Liverpool's unexpected 4-2 defeat at Chelsea made standing on a windblown terrace at Roker Park a lot more bearable. Arsenal's goalless draw against Sunderland meant Gunners could clinch the title on this Bank Holiday Monday if Liverpool lost at Nottingham Forest. Our visitors, though, were Manchester Utd – the only team to have beaten Arsenal at Highbury in over a year. It had also been against United – at Old Trafford in October – that a mass altercation broke out between the teams during the course of Arsenal's 1-0 win, behaviour the FA had punished by fining both clubs, imposing a two-point deduction on Gunners and stripping one point from United.

Now facing the same opponents in their penultimate fixture of the 1990-91 season, Arsenal could win the League. The game was due to kick off at 8.00pm but Liverpool's earlier 2-1 loss to Forest confirmed Arsenal as champions even before a ball had been kicked at Highbury – whose turnstiles were opened as soon as the news came through from Nottingham.

So what might have been a tense and anxious evening was suddenly a celebratory party, and fans flocked to the stadium early to join it. I drove across London from south of the river, and the carnival atmosphere was evident in the cacophony of blaring car horns long before I reached the ground.

Inside, the mood was ecstatic as the players and the fans shared their success in mutual appreciation. But there was still a match to play, and George Graham's team were determined to ensure there was no anti-climax. So they tore into United, Alan Smith's hat-trick in a 3-1 victory putting a magical sheen on an unforgettable night as the stadium rocked to the sound of Gooners telling the FA exactly what they could do with their two points.

Gary Jones: The atmosphere in the pubs and outside the ground was something else that day.

George Lampshire: Not just the game, but partying beforehand after watching Forest beat Liverpool in the Finsbury Park Tavern. We then romped United, before a street party in Avenell Road as the players hung out the dressing room window.

Robert Grainger: Arrived to enjoy a party atmosphere at the ground and watch the less than magnanimous Man U players applauding our team onto the pitch. Then beating them. Great day.

Mark White: The whole evening was a celebration under the floodlights. A few days later, Arsenal did it all again in the sunshine as they beat Coventry City 6-2 before receiving the First Division trophy.

John Lawlor: I got to Highbury fairly early. There was such a buzz outside the ground and I remember seeing the players hanging out of the changing room windows way before kick-off and I'm sure some of them came out wearing curly wigs for the pre-match warm-up.

We tore United apart for the whole game and 'Smudger' scoring a hat-trick – after we were awarded a penalty and usual spot-kick taker Lee Dixon gave him the ball – sparked a party on all four sides of the ground.

Stuart Pierce: Paul Davis' testimonial, v Celtic (30/7/1991), when my first hero, Charlie Nicholas not only played again at Highbury (and scored in a 2-2 draw) but threw his shirt into the North Bank. I was entranced in a glow of happiness for days after. I was so delighted that he had the chance to say goodbye like that. The Everton game in '98 should perhaps be the answer but I was so sure we'd win, I was free of all anxiety.

Alex Morrow: An FA Cup tie v Leeds Utd (25/1/1993) that we didn't even win! I was desperate to see us win the cup. We went 2-0 down and a couple of Leeds fans, who had somehow got into the West Upper, were standing up and telling us that we may as well go home, as Arsenal were finished. Ray Parlour pulled one back and I think Paul Merson ended up scoring a 25-yard equaliser near the end. Funnily enough, the Leeds fans shut up after that. We won the replay and the cup (thank you, Andy Linighan).

Neil Davies: After watching Arsenal beat Everton 4-3 in the final game of the 2001-02 season (11/5/2002). We were the champions, having won the title in Fergie's backyard, and we'd also wrapped up the FA Cup thanks to the Romford Pele and Super Freddie Ljungberg and Highbury was ready to party. I, along with many others, proudly wore a red stripe in my hair and there was a great sense of triumph in the air: a real sense that we, not United, were now the true power.

I was lucky enough to get my ticket through someone at work and was sat high in the East Stand. Before the game, I bumped into Jermaine Pennant outside the marble halls and stopped to have a quick word and have my picture taken with him.

I travelled to the game with my mates, Kris and Dave Cayless, who were bond holders in the North Bank and we had planned to meet up after the game. But due to the police shutting some roads, and the general chaos caused by 39,000 celebrating Gooners, we failed to meet up. However, as I stood on Gillespie Road, soaking up the atmosphere, I was tapped on the shoulder and was greeted by another mate, Allan Stoddon. He and his friends had visited the off licence and grabbed a couple of crates of Belgian lager. The next couple of hours went by in a haze of beer and dancing and singing and I eventually headed home sufficiently watered, minus a voice.

Gary Biggs: My happiest feeling was taking my sister Elaine Fowler and nephew Lewis Fowler to their first game, v Southampton (2/12/2000). It ended 1-0, with Patrick Vieira getting the late winner (or was it a Claus Lundekvam own-goal?). The emotion on their faces will always be with me. Very special.

James Smither: With those double cup exit disasters at the hands of hated opponents, Manchester Utd (in the FA Cup semi-final) and Chelsea (Champions League quarter-final) leading everyone in the media, and on the street, to forecast Arsenal's imminent total annihilation in the title race as well, an unwelcome clash with Liverpool just three days after the European debacle – on Easter Friday (9/4/2004) – seemed an unlikely candidate for my happiest-ever feeling at Highbury.

This was reinforced when our physically and emotionally drained looking players quickly fell behind to a Sami Hyypia header from a poorly defended corner after only five minutes. We battled gamely to refute the mounting sense that the wheels were well and truly coming

ARSENAL 4 EVERTON 0
Premier League, May 3, 1998

Neil Payne: Happiest – beating Everton 4-0 (3/5/1998) to win the Premier League in our own backyard for a change. There was so much expectation and nervousness around at the same time that day. The team just blew away an admittedly shocking Everton side that were woeful.

Of course the day is remembered more for the Tony Adams goal but it's Marc Overmars' strike that I remember more. He destroyed the Everton defence for pace before perfectly placing a left-footed shot for the third goal, which effectively decided the title was ours.

Dave Randall: The feeling of joy that day was like nothing else. We were back and good times were ahead.

Mike Slaughter: I recall my friend Mike next to me at one stage during the game saying: "At what point do we start chanting 'champions'?" Just at that moment, Tony Adams scored and we turned to each other in unison and said: "Now!".

Marvin Berglas: Happiest was that magnificent afternoon when our win against Everton secured us the league title in 1997-98 – the first leg of our historic double. As it was a very comfortable win, we could enjoy and savour every moment. The mouth-watering finish was our centre-backs combining to produce a Brazilian-style fiesta. Steve Bould chipped it forward like a seasoned midfield player to Tony Adams, who found himself surging forward in the manner of a top striker. After chesting it in his path, the ball sat up beautifully for him to unleash a left-footed half-volley that rifled

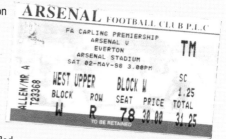

into the net. His iconic satisfied celebration summed up a glorious season for us all. The magical party that night, which I was lucky enough to be invited to at Dover Street, added to the happiest memories and a sore head.

Tony Porter: Our first championship under Arsène Wenger, in 1998. Everton were the visitors on a lovely spring afternoon. Tony Adams scoring the fourth . . . so many happy faces.

Craig Pottage: Adams' goal was supreme. I still thought we would blow it at two-nil up!

Alan Thompsett: Everything went right, couldn't be better, and my twin boys were due a couple of days later. Lee and Michael (named after Michael Thomas) were born on May 12, 1998.

Derek Barclay: I was there with my son Michael and daughter Rosie. On the way in they asked me to buy an inflatable Premier League trophy and were pestering me to inflate it. "No," I said, "it would be bad luck to do so." Even at 2-0 up at half-time I wasn't prepared to tempt fate. But when it got to 3-0 I, of course, relented, blew it up and tied a scarf to each handle.

We were in the front row of the North Bank upper tier (very close, in fact, to where I'd stood on the old terrace all those years before). Right in front of us was the camera well where the Sky TV cameraman was located. With a minute or so to go (after Tony's iconic fourth), the cameraman turned to me and said: "At the final whistle I want to get a shot of the kids holding the trophy" – they were aged eight and six respectively, so looked very cute.

So, the picture was staged really but it was broadcast to the world and by the time we got home all the family had been phoning my wife to say they'd seen the kids on TV. Sky used it in their opening credits sequence for the whole of the next season too.

Andrew Peters: Standing there at the end of the Everton game in 1998, when we clinched the league, and thinking, 'this is it, this is what it is all about. It won't get better than this feeling right here'. I was right.

Jeremy Doltis: After winning the league against Everton, with Wrighty hanging out the changing room window.

John Blair: I sobbed when Arsène Wenger lifted the trophy at Highbury in 1998. Gutted when Wayne Bridge scored Chelsea's winner in the Champions League quarter-final (6/4/2004), when the Invincibles should have won the trophy.

off our season and hauled ourselves level through Thierry Henry after half an hour. But Liverpool – with nothing else to play for and sensing an opportunity to really kick a team while we were down – drew ahead again through our old nemesis Michael Owen just before what became one of the most haunted and depressed half-time intervals I can recall. What followed was quite simply the most exhilarating and inspiring turnaround.

It wasn't really about Liverpool or how good they were or weren't that year. It was about a team of brilliant Arsenal players deciding they were winners, not losers, and through a perfect mixture of amazing talent, sheer bravery and determination, and ignoring the signals their battered bodies (and psyches) must have been sending them, reasserting control of our destiny.

We roared out of the interval, with first Robert Pires on 49 minutes and then Henry straight afterwards on 50 putting us in front, before Thierry completed perhaps his most important hat-trick for the club towards the game's conclusion.

Because of what had gone before and all it could have signified, I've never been prouder of a group of Arsenal players and never been happier leaving a home game. Never has a team been applauded off the pitch in a more heartfelt manner that I've witnessed, or the appreciation returned in a more meaningful way by the weary protagonists on the field.

Three games, five points and just over a fortnight later we were champions. Soon after that the 'impossible' unbeaten league season was completed and the Invincibles' special legacy – never more physically tangible than it was on that Good Friday lunchtime – secure.

James Miller: The final whistle after the 2-1 win v Leicester City (15/5/2004) that clinched the invincibles record.

Roberto Puzzi: Sitting in the North Bank lower when we beat Middlesbrough 5-3 (22/8/2004) during the 49-match unbeaten run. A great comeback from 3-1 down thanks to goals from Thierry Henry (2), José Antonio Reyes, Robert Pires and Dennis Bergkamp. The atmosphere in the sunshine after Reyes scored the fourth, driven high into the net at the Clock End from about 12 yards following a Bergkamp assist, was absolutely brilliant.

Dan Hill: A Monday night game v Crystal Palace (14/2/2005). This game was memorable for many reasons. Firstly, for the first time in Arsenal's history our 16-man squad didn't feature any British players (regulars Sol Campbell and Ashley Cole were both injured). And for a Palace fan who somehow got into the North Bank and occasionally shouted 'Eagles' as loud as she could.

We ran out 5-1 winners – a St Valentine's Day massacre – and I couldn't have had a better game to watch. Thierry Henry was my idol and Dennis Bergkamp ran him close for my favourite player (my other favourites at the time were Cesc Fabregas and Patrick Vieira) and both had a brilliant game.

Bergkamp put us 1-0 up from a low Reyes cross, quickly followed by a Reyes strike drilled into the bottom corner, and then Henry lashed home our third inside the far post at the Clock End to put us 3-0 up at half-time.

Vieira scored easily by rounding Palace keeper Kiraly and walking the ball into the net from a diagonal Henry pass. Andy Johnson scored a penalty but Henry rounded the game off with a second beauty, following classy work near the corner flag by Bergkamp.

Sadly, this was my second and last game I went to at Highbury (so had a 100 per cent record there!).

LOWS

Chris Welstead: My lowest point came in our penultimate home game of the season against Leeds Utd (5/5/1966). It was played on a Thursday night and clashed with the televising of one of the European cup finals. In those days, live matches were quite rare and thousands had obviously stayed away to watch this game on TV.

The Arsenal game was played in front of a crowd of only 4,554 and we lost 3-0. As the final goal hit the net, a wag at the Clock End played *The Last Post* on a trumpet. Why he had brought a trumpet into the ground, I'll never know but it certainly seemed appropriate at the time.

Tony Fisher: Standing in the rain in a crowd of little more than 4,500. Leeds were the dirtiest team ever and I remember poor George Eastham getting kicked to bits by Johnny Giles, Bobby Collins and Billy Bremner until he had to be carried off. We lost 3-0 to end a really awful season of poor football and very low gates, resulting in manager Billy Wright being sacked.

Graham Lister: I've experienced some lows at Highbury. There was the 3-1 defeat against a distinctly average Newcastle Utd side in the unhappy latter stages of Billy Wright's tenure (March, 1966), when winning was a distant memory and Avenell

George Eastham

Road was thronged after the game with angry fans baying for the manager and board to go, and bemoaning the sale of our star striker by singing 'Bring back Joe Baker to us' to the tune of *My Bonnie Lies Over the Ocean*.

There was the rain-sodden day in March, 1975, when West Ham Utd knocked us out of the FA Cup (2-0), the competition that had provided the only comfort in a season of grim decline in the league.

And there was a chastening defeat by Manchester Utd in the first leg of a League Cup semi-final in February, 1983, when the visitors, predictably inspired by ex-Gunner Frank Stapleton, scored four and might easily have had more before easing up with the game won. The 4-2 scoreline scarcely reflected the gulf in class that had been cruelly exposed to a hitherto hopeful Highbury.

But probably the lowest I felt after watching Arsenal at Highbury was (17/5/1989) when Wimbledon appeared to have put not so much a spoke in the wheel but a knife through the heart of our title aspirations. Despite a wobble of only one win in six from mid-February to mid-March, which had enabled resurgent Liverpool to gobble up most of our 19-point lead over them, Arsenal were still in pole position for the championship. We just needed to do the business in our remaining two home games – routine-looking fixtures against Derby County and Dons – to ensure that a draw at Anfield in the last match of the season would be enough to clinch the title, even if Liverpool won all their matches prior to hosting Gunners.

Then we imploded. It was excruciating to watch on the Saturday as Derby left Highbury with a 2-1 win. The team had been over-anxious, while Peter Shilton played a blinder for Rams. Liverpool were back on top. Our penultimate match was on the Wednesday, against a team we'd thrashed 5-1 at Plough Lane on the first day of the campaign.

But Wimbledon were the ultimate party-poopers. They had become specialists at bursting the balloons of more celebrated clubs. My nerves as I again stood on the North Bank were seriously fraying. And although Nigel Winterburn scored a screamer against his former club, and Paul Merson swivelled sharply in the area to volley Arsenal's second, debutant Paul McGee grabbed a late equaliser for Dons.

The 2-2 draw meant one point out of six had surely extinguished our remaining hopes of the title. All FA Cup winners Liverpool had to do now was avoid defeat by two goals against Arsenal in the season's final fixture and they would be crowned Double champions.

As the players who had seemingly thrown it all away by failing to win their last two home games trooped round the Highbury pitch in an almost embarrassed lap of appreciation of those fans still present, most of us were sunk in a trough of despondency. What we didn't know was that something extraordinary, if not miraculous, would unfold at Anfield nine days later.

Neil Davies: Wimbledon, 1989. The fact that we were poised to win the title a couple of weeks before made the draw seem more like a crushing defeat. Wimbledon were in the lower reaches of the First Division at the time and a fair distance from their new-found legendary status as FA Cup holders. We had already fallen to a shock defeat to Derby in the previous game, and what seemed to be a simple procession to the title was now becoming a living nightmare as we began the game one point behind Liverpool.

I felt like the footballing gods were on our sides as we witnessed something akin to a miracle – a Nigel Winterburn right-foot rocket! The thought that I could be about to see my team take a step towards becoming champions was almost too much to bear and the place seemed to be feeling just like I did – it never settled down and we surely all felt that we were about to falter again.

Of course, Alan Cork equalised before Merse hammered in a second but that did nothing to quell the nerves and feelings of imminent doom.

Hearing the final whistle, after Paul McGee's late equaliser, ripped the fight from the fans, as we knew that we now needed to go and beat Liverpool at Anfield in the final match to become champions. I genuinely felt that the game was up and that I would have to wait to see my team win the title. Liverpool's result the following night would only make the task more gargantuan.

Gary Jones: After the Wimbledon game (17/5/1989).The trip back to Cheltenham was a very quiet affair. The title had been thrown away. Or so we thought.

George Lampshire: Remember walking to Highbury & Islington station with my mate Phil, trying to work out what it would take to win it, as Liverpool had a game in hand v West Ham.

Dave Randall: Leaving the ground after we'd drawn with Wimbledon on that Wednesday night. A whole season (bar one game) which had promised us a first title in 18 years and we'd blown it. We'd had two chances to pick up three points from two relatively straightforward games, against Derby County and then Wimbledon, and we managed just one out of six. The walk up Highbury Hill was like climbing Everest, which after 23/05/89 appeared what we had to do after Liverpool beat West Ham 5-1. The rest, as we all know, is history.

Bernard Chaplin: Lows include humiliating defeats in the League Cup: 1-0 v Tranmere Rovers (2/10/1973) and 2-1 to Walsall (29/11/1983). Manager Terry Neill was sacked after this. Another that was hard to swallow was the 3-1 FA Cup quarter-final loss to Birmingham City (3/3/1956). A large near-68,000 crowd, myself included, really felt that we had an opportunity to reach a semi-final for the first time since 1950.

David Roche: The lowest I've felt was a 4-1 defeat by Ipswich Town (5/3/1977), which remains the worst Arsenal performance at Highbury I can recall.

Mark White: After the game v Aston Villa (4/2/1978), I queued up for a ticket to see the League Cup semi-final, second leg against Liverpool scheduled for 10 days later – and got beaten up at Finsbury Park station by a gang of about 15 youths who tried to steal my ticket. I didn't see the Liverpool game (0-0, lost 2-1 on aggregate), as my dad barred me from going to football. However, I was back to see Pat Rice lift the FA Cup at Wembley after Alan Sunderland's last-gasp winner against United in 1979.

Tom Eldridge: Two lowest points. Firstly, a horrible game v West Ham Utd (2/10/1982) which we lost 3-2. ICF head cases all over the ground, including the East Stand upper tier. A group of them sitting in front of us kept standing up and talking to their mates a few rows back. So my dad asked them to sit down because I couldn't see (I was 11). Cue the swearing, spitting, threats from all sides – no fists thrown but plenty of death threats throughout the game. Scared the living daylights out of me. And we weren't even on the terraces. Football in the 80s, eh?

Secondly, the midweek 2-2 draw with Wimbledon (17/5/1989). It felt like the world fell in that night.

Ian Tredgett: Not really a low but definitely lots of frustration. I rarely did the football pools but this particular weekend (26/4/1986) I did and a quirk of the fixture list meant there were 10 'easy' home wins to predict (ha!), one of which was the visit of already relegated West Bromwich Albion to Highbury. We took a 2-0 lead through Stewart Robson and Ian Allinson (pen), only to squander it and give the Baggies a rare away point. Giving away a two-goal lead is frustrating, to do it at home against the bottom side even more so, but it wasn't until the next day I realised I'd got nine home wins in the other games! I doubt it would have been life-changing but it was pretty annoying at the time.

That West Brom game is also notable for being watched by one of the lowest crowds – 14,843 – at Highbury for many years.

Tony Bateman: Highs and lows in one day. Beating Aston Villa 4-3 (27/3/1982). A cracking game in beautiful, warm spring sunshine. But I got home to the news that my first pet dog had died, aged 17.

Tony Porter: It has to be said that following Arsenal teaches you to be a good loser. But the lowest point of all for me was being 4-0 down in the League Cup semi-final, first leg to Manchester Utd (15/2/1983) after 60 minutes. I walked out of the ground in despair and never parked at Blackhorse Road again. I really wondered if I could go on supporting them. Even the news that we'd got two back didn't really improve my mood.

Marvin Berglas: Back in 1983-84, when a Gunners team containing stars such as Charlie Nicholas, Tony Woodcock, Kenny Sansom, Alan Sunderland and David O'Leary succumbed to lose 2-1 to Third Division Walsall in the League Cup fourth round (29/11/83). History repeating itself after mighty Arsenal were defeated by lowly Walsall 50 years previously.

Mukhtar Khan: Losing the NLD, 2-1, on New Year's Day, 1985. Atrocious all game.

Mark Aughterlony: The 3-1 FA Cup quarter-final defeat at home to Watford (14/3/1987). Although Ian Allinson had put us ahead on 12 minutes, at 2-1 down we were so bad I decided to cut my losses and beat the queues by leaving early to get the tube. As I was walking away from the ground (many others doing the same), I heard a loud roar – it didn't even enter my mind that we'd equalised, and I was right. When I got home I read on Ceefax that we'd let in a controversial third goal at the death (and I think Stevie Williams even managed to get himself sent-off at the death too, but I might be wrong on that one?).

Stuart Pierce: After David Seaman punched the ball in his own net v Wimbledon (15/12/1990) in the seventh minute of injury-time, to throw a 2-0 lead away and lose damaging points in the title race.

Andrew Whitnall: The 3-1 European Cup defeat by Benfica (6/11/1991). Optimistically, I thought we were more than good enough to win the European Cup that year.

John Lawlor: Last game of the 1991-92 season v Southampton (2/5/1992). Despite a great 5-1 win which saw Ian Wright score a hat-trick to collect the Golden Boot award, the occasion will always be remembered as the last standing game on the North Bank.

ARSENAL FOOTBALL CLUB PLC

BARCLAYS LEAGUE DIVISION ONE

ARSENAL
V
SOUTHAMPTON

SATURDAY 2nd MAY 1992
KICK-OFF 3.00p.m.

YOU ARE ADVISED TO BE IN POSITION BY 2.15p.m.

STANDING TICKET   **B**   **4740**

NORTH BANK AVENELL ROAD
(See Map on Reverse)

£8

THIS PORTION TO BE RETAINED   INC VAT

The terraces at that end seemed a lot fuller than at any other game for which I had stood there since '82. After the match finished and players did their lap of honour, fans were slowly making their way up the bank and to the sides, leaving the ground while saying their farewells to friends and even strangers, knowing it was the end of an era.

A few thousand of us refused to leave and started chanting that we wanted to see (vice-chairman) David Dein. After about half an hour he came down pitch-side with (managing director/secretary) Ken Friar, said what he had to say and left us to it.

It must have been at least another half an hour before we eventually started to move away. Grown men, including me, were crying. I had only stood on the North Bank for 10 years but some of them had been there for 30-40 years. We all felt the same sadness.

Guy Thompson: It's got to be the last day on the old North Bank. Even after the incredible result and Wrighty beating Lineker to the Golden Boot, it still didn't hide the gnawing realisation that this would be the very last time I'd ever stand underneath the famous North Bank roof. A 5-1 victory was a great way to see the old girl off but the elation was definitely tinged with real sadness.

I was one of the last ones to leave. It really did feel like we were being evicted from our home. It was uncertain times for a lot of us regulars, what with the dreaded Bond coming in. Because of the money being mentioned, I wasn't sure if I'd be able to sit or stand there ever again. I, like thousands of others, could afford to pay once or twice a week. But to be asked to come up with a lump sum, was something I know a lot of fans, myself included, just couldn't do. It felt like all those years of cheering the team on through thick or thin, counted for absolutely nothing. We were being priced out and now other people were gonna' be the beneficiaries of our solid support, just because they had more money.

There were a few occasions during the late 80's and early 90's when I happily joined in with the other regulars in singing "Where the f*** were you on Wednesday night?". I'd been there when it was heaving and we were squashed in like sardines. I'd been there when it was half-empty and you'd recognise most of the people individually. So to now be told I could only sit in the new stand if I came up with an extortionate amount of money for me at the time, just to sit where they put me, was a real kick in the teeth. It was a horrible, horrible feeling and my heart was truly shattered as I knew things would never be the same. But, as much as I despise them, thank the heavens for ticket touts!

Another low point which kind of relates to the last one was Arsenal v Norwich at the start of the 1992-93 season. I'd never stood in the Clock End before. It just didn't feel right. And *that* mural! What had they done? Even the skydiver mistiming his landing and ending up behind the mural in the rubble, and The Prodigy sticking their middle fingers up at us all, couldn't put a smile on my face. And then the result . . . ay, yay, yay. That was one crap day.

The lowest I've ever felt, purely because of a game, was after the League Cup defeat to

Manchester Utd in November 1990. I just stood on the terrace looking out onto the pitch wondering what the hell had just happened, until a steward had to ask me to leave. I really didn't wanna' go. I had this weird feeling that if I stayed there long enough, the result would change. It certainly did four days later. I also remember it was the first time I'd ever stood on the left side of the North Bank. I never stood there again.

Peter Coombs: My very simple answer to the lowest feeling was that sad day in May, 1992 when the old North Bank closed. Over the years I had stood in other parts of the ground: when pocket money was dwindling, in the boys' section (sounds dated now); when I had an extra shilling you could transfer in from either end to standing in the lower tier of the West Stand. Seats were put in at some point, leaving a narrow strip of terracing at the bottom, but 99.9 per cent of the time I watched from the North Bank.

Although there were truly some great years at the refurbished Highbury, I missed the old North Bank. How you could stand on the right-hand side at the top of the stairs, awaiting the final whistle, before quickly heading down to join the queue for the tube?

Over the years a group of 12 or so of us from all parts of the south-east would meet up on the same spot on the terrace and have good laugh. We used to run a lottery – 50p or a pound per ticket with a player's number on for the first goal scorer – and, looking back, there never seemed to be many rollovers. This all changed with the introduction of allocated seat/season tickets.

But while I was sad to leave Highbury, I was also happy. The only way to compete with the rest of Europe was a new, bigger ground, and because it was just round the corner you could maintain many of your match day rituals – from waking up on a Saturday morning until you arrived at The Emirates. But whatever happened to Saturday afternoons and Tuesday evenings, the predictability of the fixture list? To me it's sad how football has gone, including the loss of terracing.

James Miller: The minute's silence for David Rocastle (31/3/2001), which even the Spurs fans respected.

James Smither: I've always described Arsenal as a team that tends to find the most exciting ways to win and the most heart-breaking ways to lose, so there should be no shortage of candidates in this category – but actually, most of our most heart-stopping highs and lows alike during my time following the club have taken place away from the comforting surroundings of Islington, London, N5 – at Anfield, Old Trafford, Copenhagen (twice), Wembley, Cardiff, Paris (twice) and Villa Park, to name but a few). As it turns out, my best and worst feelings at Highbury were separated by three days and inextricably linked.

The lowest was watching us get ourselves knocked out of the Champions League on our own pitch by that vilest embodiment of nouveau-riche football-gone-bad, Roman Abramovich's recently-acquired Chelsea (6/4/2004). To make the defeat even harder to take, we'd already beaten them home and away in the league and knocked them out of the FA Cup that season, and secured a hard-fought 1-1 draw in the first leg at Stamford Bridge two weeks previously that seemed to make us slight favourites to progress.

Initial doubts whether that would be the outcome

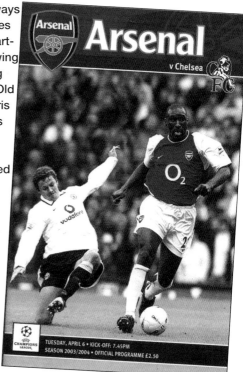

175

must have been present, as our previously flawless unbeaten season had been despoiled just three days beforehand in a desperately poor 1-0 defeat to Manchester Utd in the FA Cup semi-final at Villa Park. The concern was that resulting tiredness and new-found mental fragility at the prospect of our silverware prospects suddenly unravelling would impact our performance level in what was arguably the most important European match in our history.

It's almost too painful recounting what eventually happened but we looked intent on dispelling those doubts straight from the kick-off in what was a brilliant first-half performance. Major concern was the lack of a finishing touch being applied to all our attacking brilliance, until José Antonio Reyes (whose best moments in an otherwise disappointing career in north London tended to be reserved for these opponents) prodded in to put us ahead almost on the stroke of half-time. "It's a good time to score" is a well-worn cliché but, leading in the tie for the first time, we subsequently proved unable to sustain our performance level.

As the second-half wore on, a combination of tension and physical exhaustion started to show and it wasn't a real surprise when Lampard opportunistically drew west London's billionaires level once more. I can't have been the only one fearing the worst as our fresher opponents looked stronger and stronger, and sure enough, the killer blow came just as extra-time was looking likely through the unlikely figure of left-back Wayne Bridge on 87 minutes (another in a long line of Arsenal-killers whose career never really hit another height again – see also Nayim, Danny Rose, David Bentley and others).

The hollow feeling at the end while Chelsea fans cavorted in the Clock End was like nothing I've ever felt before or since at an Arsenal home game. Only Cardiff in 2001 and Villa Park in 1999 (also cup eliminations where we'd had ample chance to prevail) come close. This was regarded as our best-ever team, and with Monaco, Porto and Deportivo La Coruña the other clubs left to get past at the semi-final stage, probably our best-ever chance to win the one trophy that continues to elude us to this day had been grabbed from us by one of our most loathsome rivals.

John Hilditch: The sheer shock of being beaten, 2-1 (3-2 on aggregate), after Wayne Bridge's 87th minute winner. It was the first time we'd lost to them in many years. We all know we could have won the coveted trophy that season.

Alex Morrow: Losing to Chelsea and then finding out we would have played Monaco in the semi, not Real Madrid. That was the Invincibles team – we should have been European champions that year as well.

Neil Payne: I am sure in younger years I was more visibly upset when every defeat used to hurt like hell, as if the world had ended, but I would say probably the Champions League quarter-final v Chelsea. Simply because I thought at the time, and have seen nothing to change my mind since, that we missed the biggest single opportunity of winning the Champions League for the first time in our history.

I say that for two reasons: the quality of the team at that time, with the majority of players at their peak; and the standard of the teams left in the competition. I doubt we will ever see a final between sides of the calibre of Monaco and Porto ever again. It was a massive opportunity missed.

Michael Cherrington: v Manchester City (22/10/2005), the game that featured the infamous Pires-Henry penalty incident after Pires had earlier scored from the spot. It was my personal low because it was the last time I visited Highbury and I remember sitting in my seat remembering all the great times I had there (until I got kicked out).

Tom Humphrey: The last game I saw live was against Wigan Athletic. Not the one you're all thinking of, though. It was the League Cup semi-final (24/1/2006) and Jason Roberts scored in the last minute of extra-time to send Wigan to the final in Cardiff on the away goals rule.

The other low point was losing 4-2 to Charlton Athletic (4/11/2001). A really disappointing day, one of the few blips in a wonderful season for the club.

Ben Sharpe: There's only one game that can answer this question. It has to be the last one at Highbury, v Wigan Athletic (7/5/2006). I was lucky enough to be able to have a ticket and the whole day was very emotional.

On approaching the ground, there was a cordon which I had to go through. This was such a big occasion for Arsenal. The whole build-up involved talking through old memories of Highbury with anyone that was in your immediate vicinity.

The game itself was incredible. We won 4-2, pipped Spurs to a Champions League spot, Thierry got a hat-trick and the final goal was scored within 10 yards of my eyes!

The atmosphere was electric, everybody got together and made it special like I've never experienced at Highbury before. From minute one until the very end, everyone sang their hearts out knowing that this was the end.

Once the final whistle went, the celebrations were over and it was very sad. There were a few tears shed by me and others around me; the realisation hit home that we were leaving but nobody wanted to go.

Keith English: Leaving Highbury was the lowest point.

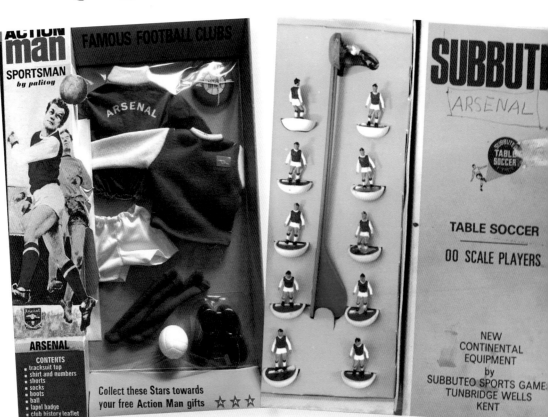

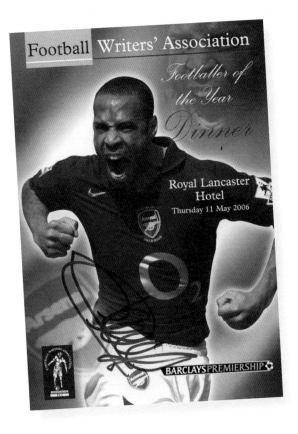

Mʀ HERBERT CHAPMAN

T. DRAKE (England)

R. Gould *(Arsenal)*

RICHIE POWLING

JOHN MATTHEWS

ARSENAL
JOHN
LUKIC

FOTY MENU: Menu for the 2006 Footballer of the Year dinner, hosted by the Football Writers' Association and signed by award winner Thierry Henry.

BIRTHDAY CARD 1: Bobby Gould bursts between two Coventry City defenders.

BIRTHDAY CARD 2: Willie Young gets the point from team-mate David O'Leary and Spurs' Chris Jones.

ALEX FORBES: Famous Footballers, Series A.2, No.41 of 50, issues by Barratt & Co Ltd, Mayes Rd, Wood Green, London, N22.

OGDEN'S CIGARETTES: AFC Nicknames, No.1 of 50, issued by Ogden's.

HERBERT CHAPMAN: Sporting Personalities, No.5 of 48, issued by Gallaher Ltd, Virginia House, London & Belfast.

TED DRAKE: The Sun Soccercards, All Time Greats No.248.

BOBBY GOULD: My Favourite Soccer Stars, No.13, presented free with *Scorcher*.

ALAN BALL: No.5 in set of 22. Issued by A&BC.

BOB WILSON: The Sun 3-D Gallery of Football Stars, set of 20.

RICHIE POWLING: No.189, issued by Topps Chewing Gum.

JOHN MATTHEWS: No.218, issued by Topps Chewing Gum.

JOHN LUKIC: Panini's Football 87, No.8.

'I used to love watching him lead the team out with his chest puffed full of pride - you could tell that wearing our shirt and the captain's armband meant the world to him'

8 FAVOURITE PLAYERS

OVER the course of 93 years and more than 2,000 first team matches at Highbury that featured 450-plus men in red-and-white shirts, none of our contributors were old enough to witness the exploits of heroes such as Buchan, Drake, Hapgood, Bastin, Brain, James, Jack, Hulme, Logie, Compton, Lewis, etc.

But many others that came after joined the pantheon of greats, revered players that earned a special place in Gunners fans' hearts.

Not all of those from the post-war era featured in this chapter can be considered true Arsenal 'greats' but they all left an indelible mark on supporters. We present them in appearance order (with their Highbury first team debut/final game years in brackets).

Q: Name your three most favourite players and say what made each of them so special to you?

WALLY BARNES (1943-56)

Richard Boyes: I go back some 80-plus years as a supporter and I'm going to nominate players who obviously loved the club first and money second, so they may not be the greatest but always gave their best effort. From the 1950s I would select Wally Barnes, a Welsh international who could play at both right and left-back. He was very quick, a good tackler in an age when tackling was a real art and that is what full-backs did in those days. A good leader, he was also the penalty-taker – I don't think he ever missed one. A team player and one-club man.

JACK KELSEY (1951-63)

Paul Harris: The Welsh international goalkeeper is a first choice. My dad bought me his autobiography, *Over The Bar*, published in 1958, which was the first football book I read. I recall his lantern-jawed appearances in an impossibly thick green jersey, his restrained acknowledgements to the crowd behind the goal – and his sheer bravery. I thought at first that he was called 'Agile Jack', as I heard him described that way by many standing around me. I was delighted that he was retained on the staff after his retirement. There was much in him that was 'transferred' to Bob Wilson. Both, as I recall, used to do a little foot shuffle before completing a goal-kick.

TOMMY LAWTON (1953-55)

Bernard Chaplin: During those "years in the wilderness" there were a number of players brought in to try and spark the team, including Tommy Lawton (right). Signed in his twilight years and although past his best at 35-years-old, he was a legend. He scored two goals that I particularly remember: a thumping 30-yard drive and a towering header in which he seemed to float in the air above his marker before planting the ball in the net.

GEORGE EASTHAM (1960-66)

Graham Lister: As a nine-year-old I was thrilled when Arsenal finally signed George Eastham in November, 1960, and even more so when he made his long-awaited first-team debut three weeks later, scoring twice in a 5-1 win at Highbury against Bolton Wanderers.

Rebel with a cause, George Eastham was a renowned midfield schemer.

Eastham's transfer from Newcastle Utd had been protracted and bitter. He'd declined to sign a new contract with the Magpies in 1959 and asked to leave the club. But Newcastle rejected his transfer request and, like all clubs at the time, were able to keep a player's registration, preventing him from moving, while refusing to pay him. Eastham responded by going on strike. Newcastle eventually relented and sold him to Arsenal, although Eastham took his case to court, arguing that the retain-and-transfer system was an unfair restraint of trade. His landmark legal victory in 1963 succeeded in reforming the transfer market and tilting the balance of power in players' favour.

All of that was somewhat academic and beyond my immediate concern. I wanted heroes in red-and-white shirts who could help make Arsenal winners and give me some leverage against the hordes of kids now jumping on the bandwagon of Tottenham's sudden success. The fact that Eastham had proved himself a bit of a rebel was cool but of greater importance was his contribution on the pitch. And over the next five-and-a-half years he orchestrated Arsenal's attacking play quite brilliantly, especially when Joe Baker joined the club and made the most of Eastham's scheming. Unfortunately our defence at the time leaked like a sieve, which must have frustrated a creator like George.

In the footballing sense, the frail-looking inside-forward was one of the most intelligent players Arsenal ever had, with the awareness to spot an opening and the footwork to thread the ball through the eye of a needle to exploit it. He had such balance and poise that he often seemed to dance across the Highbury mud, slipping astute passes through to Baker or Geoff Strong.

In a less protected age, Eastham was inevitably a target for opposing teams' hatchet-men – never more so than when Don Revie's brutish Leeds United visited Highbury in February, 1965 and, having identified George as the danger man, had the likes of Bremner, Collins and Hunter taking turns to try and incapacitate him.

On the other hand, there was a memorable occasion in September, 1963 when Joe Baker took exception to a tackle perpetrated on Eastham by Denis Law and chased his former Torino team-mate and flat-mate across the Highbury turf to remonstrate. Yet Eastham was no pushover, and in fact scored for Arsenal in both those games.

I never succeeded in my ambition of getting his autograph but was the proud owner of *Determined To Win*, his autobiography, and *Soccer Science*, a sort of training manual for aspiring footballers.

It was a black day for Arsenal fans when manager Billy Wright responded to FA Cup defeat at the first hurdle in January, 1966 by making Eastham and Baker scapegoats and dropping the pair. Within months both of Arsenal's best players had left the club.

Bernard Chaplin: He signed under controversial circumstances; his first match was against Leicester City reserves at Highbury in front of more than 10,000 spectators. He had not played football for some time because of his dispute with Newcastle but had a hand in all goals in a 3-1 victory. After another few games for the reserves he made his Arsenal debut, at home, when he scored twice against Bolton in a 5-1 win.

Bernard Kiernan: George was our playmaker god before Liam Brady came along. Everything went through Eastham who was an exceptionally skilful player in, frankly, a mediocre team. He was recognised by England and Alf Ramsey with 19 caps but didn't play in the 1966 World Cup despite his inclusion in the squad.

JOE BAKER (1962-66)

Chris Welstead: Joe Baker was my first real Highbury hero. Signed from Italian club Torino in 1962, I saw his first game at Leyton Orient when, of course, he scored and that was it for me. He was very quick, genuinely two-footed and his strike rate would bear comparison with ANY modern day footballer in this country. Sadly, he left Arsenal before his time but I'll treasure those four years.

Bernard Chaplin: A short but dynamic centre-forward who would mix it with the best. He will probably be best remembered for a Cup match at Highbury v Liverpool. He was up against their giant centre-half Ron Yeats. They had been battling against each other and then had a final clash in which Joe thumped big Ron. They were both sent-off. The problem during the lean years was the defence. We would score four but concede five!

Jeff Owens: He was a brave, skilful centre-forward always battling for the team. Sometimes he seemed to be a one-man forward line.

Keith Weedon: As hard as nails.

GEORGE ARMSTRONG (1962-77)

Chris Welstead: George was the most consistent player that I can ever remember. Not only was he a brilliant winger who could play on either side of the pitch and cross the ball superbly well with either foot, he also did his shift in a defensive capacity when we didn't have the ball. An absolutely whole-hearted trier who never gave anything less than his best. It was unfortunate for George that he played in the England era of Ramey's 'wingless wonders', otherwise he would have won many caps for his country.

Keith Wilsher: He never stopped running, either coming back to defend or, as the song goes, "Georgie, Georgie Armstrong on the wing". He could cross a ball with pinpoint precision. John Radford and Ray Kennedy owe him big-time.

Paul Harris: My second choice is George Armstrong – a winger's winger, if you like. Diminutive and industrious as well as loyal, he was a model professional. He was never in the news for anything other than being a professional footballer. He had an excellent temperament, covered an enormous amount of ground and never 'showboated'. In the playground I only ever wanted to be George Armstrong who, to me, was a great traditional winger and an understandably automatic choice during his long and distinguished career at Highbury.

I would like to add that I did get to meet George at Dunstable Town FC. He was manager of Arsenal reserves who came to play Luton Town reserves (who had hired Dunstable's ground). I was able to speak to him to thank him for all the pleasure he had given me as an Arsenal supporter and to tell him how much I had admired his style of play and attitude. He looked just a little nonplussed but shook my hand and told me he appreciated my words and how I treasure this. "Thanks," he said, "it really does mean a lot to me."

James Miller: He was truly Arsenal through and through.

Keith English: A real Arsenal player, he never gave up.

Lester Allen: Always gave 100 per cent, played on both wings and a perfect crosser of the ball. So sad that he never got an England cap.

Wayne Flatman: He played all the time I watched Arsenal in the 70s. I had the pleasure of meeting George several times and he always had time to talk and sign.

BOB WILSON (1963-74)

Wayne Flatman: Never met him but loads of respect for Bob. Just read his autobiography and the most moving piece of radio when he was talking with Billy Bragg and Simon Mayo.

JOHN RADFORD (1964-76)

Robert Thaine: When I was younger he seemed to be the ultimate No.9: strong and powerful in the air and a great finisher with his feet.

Dave Randall: My favourite player from the early years. No-nonsense, big-hearted centre-forward. Scorer of so many important goals and a real team player.

Lee Pritchett: As a boy, John Radford was my absolute hero. My first match watching Arsenal was his first-team debut and I felt we started our Arsenal life together.

John Morley: My boyhood Arsenal hero. I had always dreamed of playing centre-forward for Arsenal one day and 'Raddy' was our No.9 when I first started going as a kid.

Nobby Ralfe: My boyhood hero.

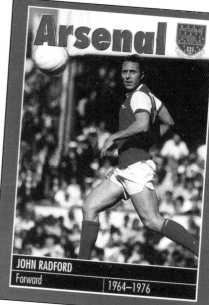

JOHN RADFORD
Forward   1964–1976

FRANK McLINTOCK (1964-73)

Keith Wilsher: He is Arsenal through and through. He's now 75 and last year, when Spurs scored first and the box next to his was full of Spurs supporters giving Arsenal stick, he steamed into them and had to be pulled back! Bertie Mee broke up the Double team too early. He sold Frank to QPR, who nearly won the league the following year, and bought Jeff Blockley to replace him.

Emilio Zorlakki: Purely because he is still the best captain I have ever seen. The sheer will to win, grit and determination was always etched on his face.

I met him in a book shop in Enfield Town, when he launched his autobiography *True Grit* in 2006. The shop had been closed for 20 minutes but after I had made a frantic phone call to the shop he waited for me and was having a cup of tea when I arrived. The shop manager said to me that Frank had rang his wife Barbara and told her to take her time to collect him, as he was waiting for a "friend". Wow! I felt quite humbled.

"Hello Frank, I've waited since March, 1973 to say sorry to you," I said as we shook hands. He looked puzzled.

"You played your last match for Arsenal on March 31, 1973 against Derby County and as you were being stretchered off the pitch the whole stadium rose as one to applaud you – all except one stupid 10-year old boy! You see, I was still cross with you over the mistake you had made that led to Jeff Bourne scoring Derby's goal in the 1st minute!....

"Please allow me to put that right. I'm so sorry, Frank!"

We had a good laugh and chatted for quite a while. He asked me where I was from and I said that I lived in Welwyn Garden City (Herts).

"Oh! I'm there next Friday doing another book signing."

I replied: "I'll see you there."

CHARLIE GEORGE (1969-75)

Bernard Kiernan: Our very own local hero. The same age as me and another Islington-bred lad like me. A phenomenal talent. Whenever Charlie took off from the halfway line in one of his crouching, weaving runs there was a hum throughout the crowd. His crowning achievement, of course, was the 1971 FA Cup-winning goal, plus all his other contributions to the 1970-71 Double. I had the great privilege to meet Charlie on the Emirates Stadium tour in 2017. He was absolutely delightful as a host, so unassuming and professional. Proper 'old school'.

Derek Barclay: The absolute hero of my youth. His look, his hair, the way he played with flair and that trademark celebration of falling onto his back, all made him unique and very much the embodiment of 1970s football.

I met him at an Emirates Stadium tour a few years back and he was brilliant. After that, whenever I'd see Charlie around and about Highbury, I'd say "hello" and he'd always reply: "Hello, how are you?"

What a genuinely brilliant guy; a total legend.

Robert Thaine: For his flair, powerful shots, long hair, arrogance, brilliance and the fact that he was/is an Arsenal supporter.

Peter Lewis: A fellow Islington schoolboy and my first hero.

James Miller: He's one of us.

Keith English: My hero. I once went to a reserve match just to watch him play. Always expect the unexpected when Charlie had the ball.

Stephen Simson: Charlie was one of the players we all emulated in the flats playing football as a kid. Scorer of great goals who also got stuck in where it hurt; he loved a fight. Lived local to me, a born and bred Gooner. That's 'King Charlie'.

John Hilditch: Although before my time, I grew up hearing about him, his goals and the *Charlie George Calypso*. What a song! Also, my mother Laura, a hairdresser, did his mother's hair for a bit. A wash and set I believe.

And then, a Norwegian girlfriend of mine, Silje Marie Aukland, spent her entire time in London calling him 'George Charlie'. She just couldn't get his name the right way around. She met him on a tour of Highbury in 2006, was not disappointed and spent the entire time calling him 'Mr Charlie'.

ALAN BALL (1971-76)

Marvin Berglas: A glamour signing to add to our 1970-71 Double-winning squad. His authority and skills in midfield were admired greatly, along with his white boots. He would balance the ball on the back of his neck in the warm-up and occasionally wind up the opposition by going down on one knee, to feign tying his bootlaces, to show how much time he had on the ball.

LIAM BRADY (1973-80)

Graham Lister: The announcement that Liam Brady was stepping down in May, 2014 from his highly productive role as Arsenal's Head of Youth Development and Academy Manager was sad news for the club, but nothing like as devastating for fans as his previous departure in 1980. At that time he was without doubt one of the best midfielders in the world, a glorious talent and the creative heartbeat of Highbury. That Terry Neill's Arsenal team brimmed with rich potential, which it never quite fulfilled, can be largely explained by Brady's decision – understandable at the time, although no less bearable – to experience football in Italy's Serie A, then unquestionably the world's strongest league.

Brady enthralled a generation of Gunners fans, many of whom – including me – would say he was the best they ever saw in Arsenal colours. The slightly-built Dubliner was a waif with

'The slightly-built Dubliner was a waif with a wand of a left foot, a sublimely gifted playmaker with the skill and vision to dictate the pattern of a game through his own inventiveness'

a magic wand of a left foot, a sublimely gifted playmaker with the skill and vision to dictate the pattern of a game through his own inventiveness.

He burst onto the first-team scene as a 17-year-old substitute for Jeff Blockley in a 1-0 win over Birmingham City in October, 1973, and started the next match at White Hart Lane. Although Arsenal lost that derby 2-0, and fighting between fans on the terraces grabbed a lot of the headlines, Brady – on the too few occasions his team-mates passed to him – was a shaft of sunlight piercing the gloom.

We wanted to see more of him but were denied that opportunity until after New Year, as Bertie Mee – managing the decline of the Double-winning team that he'd broken up too quickly – carefully chose which matches his young starlet could start. But so anaemic was Arsenal's challenge in the doldrum years of 1974-76 that Brady featured in most games during Mee's last two seasons in charge.

By the time Neill was appointed manager in summer 1976, Brady was more than ready to take over the role of chief playmaker from his early mentor Alan Ball. And the return to Highbury a year later of Don Howe as coach accelerated Brady's ascent to greatness.

As for Neill's Arsenal as a whole, they were just short of greatness during Brady's time at Highbury – one FA Cup triumph, three losing cup finals but no sustained challenge for the league title. Yet for many, just watching Brady at work was a reward in itself. He was superbly entertaining with a mesmerising array of attributes: great balance, exceptional close control, an infinite range of passes and the ability to disguise his intentions until the ball was played.

His decision to move to Juventus at the end of the 1979-80 season left a cloud over Highbury that took years to disperse but he was a great success in Italy, winning consecutive titles with Juve and also playing for Sampdoria, Inter and Ascoli with distinction. It was only right that he returned to Highbury in 1996 to look after the youngsters from whose ranks he himself had sprung so excitingly a couple of decades earlier.

Wayne Flatman: Came on as sub against Birmingham City and was a shining example on a wet afternoon. We went the next week to see his full debut v Spurs.

Marvin Berglas: 'Chippy' came in as a 17-year-old in 1973-74 and was the most naturally gifted player I had seen. He was even more special because he came through our youth system. His left foot sprayed magical passes across the pitch and opened up defences. He also scored some special goals along the way.

Paul Manel: The heartbeat of our side in the late 70s, the team I watched in my early years at Highbury. When he played well, Arsenal played well. I used to love watching him spray passes all over the pitch. There was also nothing like a 'Chippy' dribble. He used to beat players with sheer skill. The North Bank idolised him. "Bray-dee, Bray-dee, Bray-dee, Bray-dee . . . Born is the King of High-ba-ree."

Jeff Owens: Skill in abundance, with the ability to score decisive goals and influence the course of matches.

Stephen Simson: A god to many. "Born is the King of Highbury" we all sang on the terraces. By far my favourite all-time player, he had everything a midfielder thrives to be. I was at my happiest being a young kid watching my childhood hero.

He had passion for the game and skills no other player on the pitch could match. His style of play and passing were breathtaking. He would twist and turn opponents inside-out, then lay a beauty of a pass with ease. He also scored some crackers.

Tom Eldridge: Left foot, curling shot, never got fussed or hurried. Part of that amazing Irish contingent playing great football in tough times. 'Chippy'. Genius.

Tony Daisley: Because he was the one world class player we had in the late 70s. It was just a joy to watch him drop his shoulder and glide past people as if they weren't there.

Lee Pritchett: A little genius with a wand of a left foot. And yes, we did all agree he was better than Hoddle.

Yasir Matloub: The first superstar and what I consider to be the only world class player Arsenal had before Wenger's French protégés.

Kelvin Meadows: He was a breath of fresh air in a stale team. I'm sure he could peel a potato with his left foot.

Gary Jones: The man was just a genius and such a special talent.

Peter Coombs: "One Liam Brady, there's only one Liam Brady."

Mark White: Wand of a left foot. "We All Agree . . . Liam Brady is Magic!"

FRANK STAPLETON (1974-81)

Bernard Kiernan: Frank was our courageous Irish striker with a heart of a lion and another one of my heroes. Dublin-born, too, like myself. Brilliant in the air. I will never forget the day when Frank, on the touchline, won yet another do or die challenge right in front of us and an Irish man next to me roared: "Good man, Frank, you are worth three of any of those Englishmen!" Absolutely true. Huge laughter all around us. Priceless.

DAVID O'LEARY (1975-93)

Paul Harris: I know the temptation is to choose a more recent star but I will still go for a player who was a byword for steadfastness and professionalism and who played even more games than George Armstrong – namely David O'Leary. When I used to go to Highbury with my nephew David, we always watched O'Leary's almost ritualistic warm-up routine. It was purposeful and concentrated and seemed to symbolise him. Every move had a purpose and here was a man who took the right advice and knew how to look after himself.

His longevity was simply because he was a class act and thoroughly reliable and successive managers automatically included him and knew they would get a thorough performance each time. He was a model professional and adapted to the styles of each manager.

Both Armstrong and O'Leary showed that ability, training and professional discretion are among the hallmarks of truly great players.

PAT JENNINGS (1977-85)

Andrew Whitnall: I played in goal at school, so Pat Jennings was my first Arsenal hero. I got a signed photo from him for my 10th birthday. I still love it!

Gary Jones: For me, Pat is our greatest keeper. So calm and assured and I loved the green keeper's top he wore with the big cannon in the centre.

John Hilditch: My dad Brian was a goalkeeper back in the day in Northern Ireland, so he educated me about Pat Jennings. I remember seeing him on either *A Question of Sport* or *This is Your Life* and thinking he must be important. Anyway, soon after, I caught the ball on the Junior Gunners' terrace and he came over to collect it, held the ball in one of his big shovels of a hand and in that deep Northern Irish accent said: "Thanks, son." I was awestruck.

Mukhtar Khan: I admired him when he played at the other place and he was world class. I was gobsmacked that he came to us.

CHARLIE NICHOLAS (1983-88)

Paul Manel: The early 80s were barren ones for Arsenal fans. After the departures of Liam Brady and Frank Stapleton we needed a new hero. In the summer of 1983 Charlie arrived from Celtic. He chose us ahead of Liverpool and Manchester Utd, so he was already a hero before he even pulled on the red and white shirt.

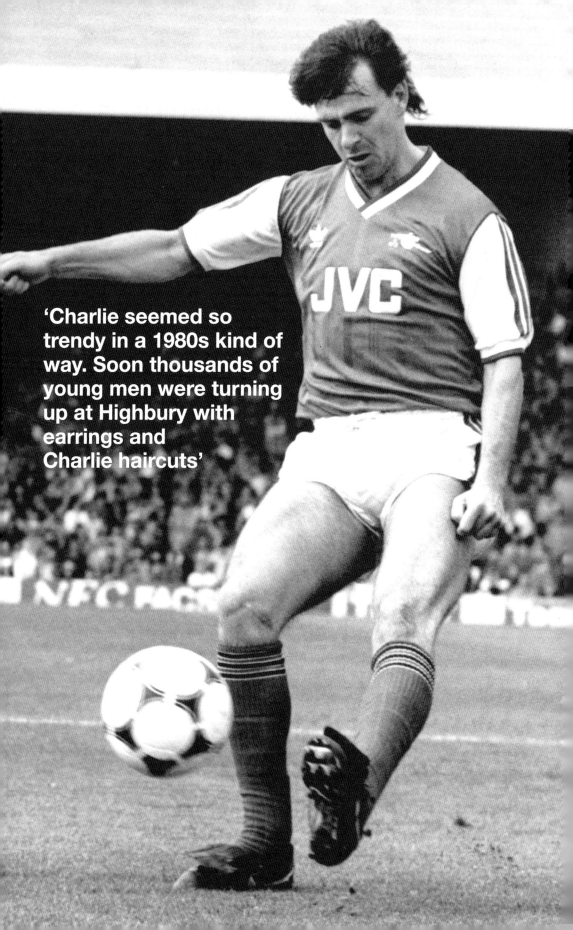

'Charlie seemed so trendy in a 1980s kind of way. Soon thousands of young men were turning up at Highbury with earrings and Charlie haircuts'

For young, impressionable fans on the North Bank Charlie seemed so trendy in a 1980s kind of way. Soon thousands of young men were turning up at Highbury with earrings and 'Charlie haircuts'. Highbury warmed to him immediately. There was a Highbury eruption when he score his first league goal against Birmingham City from the penalty spot.

He probably underachieved in his career at Arsenal but we loved him for his little flicks, feints and above all else, those goals against Spurs.

When he came back to Highbury with Celtic for the Paul Davis testimonial he got a wonderful reception. I remember he ran to the North Bank and threw his shirt to the crowd.

Guy Thompson: The furore surrounding his signing and the anticipation of him playing for us was enormous. It was like 'pop star' status. And this was before the days of the internet and mass media.

For a young player, coming down from Scotland, the weight on his shoulders must have been incredible. The media went absolutely mental about it all. It was like the new George Best was coming to town.

I know he didn't quite hit the heights we were hoping for but he was one player who could change a game in a split second with one moment of magic, which he did quite a few times. Usually against Spurs! Good old Charlie. I'm glad he'll be forever in our history books after his two goals on that sunny afternoon in April of '87. He deserves to be.

And shouting "Charlie Charlie, Charlie Charlie" from the stands was always a blast. He certainly was the new 'North Bank Darling' for a while.

Jon Lawlor: I remember stories from my dad, who watched Celtic every week, and here he was signing for The Arsenal – probably the first big money buy at Arsenal at the time. Remember him being given a hard time because he didn't like getting his hair messed up.

TONY ADAMS (1983-2002)

Neil Payne: Big Tone's career started not long after I was in the early stages of becoming an Arsenal regular. A mistake in a 2-1 loss to Sunderland on his debut (5/11/1983) was hardly the most auspicious start but, typical of the man, he quickly overcame that to show the type of leadership qualities that led George Graham to make him captain in 1988.

To say Tone had great character, presence and tremendous willpower would only be telling half the story. Never was there a more deserving player to be leading the club on that unforgettable night at Anfield in 1989.

Matured as a player and man under Wenger, and his use of the ball in later years left you wondering if he had underachieved as a player.

A true Arsenal legend and a pleasure to watch throughout his career. Never did he shirk a challenge on or off the field.

Ian Tredgett: His arrival in the side coincided with my more regular attendances at matches, so I felt I watched him develop.

I was lucky enough to meet him, purely by chance, with some (Arsenal-supporting) friends in a restaurant in London in 1998, the week after we had won the Double. We ended up spending most of the evening in his company. Naturally, we talked football, at least for some of the time, but a whole host of other things too (travel, films, etc) as you would on an evening out with friends. We all know he was a great player but in my experience, also a very nice guy.

Richard Boyes: Mr Arsenal. Our best-ever captain, a real leader of men, he ignored Manchester Utd who chased him for a long while and would have paid him far more than he got at Arsenal. But he stayed at Highbury, The only player to win the championship in three different decades. He also loved playing for England.

Guy Thompson: What more can anyone say about him? The fact he's now known worldwide as Mr Arsenal says it all. I was there for his debut in '83 and witnessed first-hand how he overcame the awful barracking from opposition fans, as well as his highly publicised personal issues, to become not only a club, but also a national team legend.

The lynchpin of the greatest back line the game's ever seen and the only man to lift a league title in three different decades. There's no argument about how important he was.

There's a reason George Graham called him a 'Colossus'. He was, and still is, the epitome of our great club. And he was one of our 'own'. Nuff said.

Paul Manel: Captain supreme. I remember seeing Tony make his debut. Even as a gangly 17-year-old you could see that Arsenal meant everything to him. He developed into a wonderful captain and leader of men who inspired fellow players and the fans.

Tony spanned eras. He made his debut at a Highbury with North Bank and Clock End terraces. The team he played for had mainly British players and a British manager.

He said 'goodbye' in his farewell match against Celtic (13/5/2002) in a smaller capacity, all-seated Highbury with executive boxes. We had a large number of oversees players and a French boss.

For 19-odd years Tony had been a constant amidst major changes on and off the pitch. After winning four league titles, three FA Cups, two League Cups and a European Cup Winners' Cup, Tony Adams bowed out. Farewell to Mr Arsenal. I still think he will return one day to our new home as manager!

Robert Grainger: Possibly the greatest captain for Arsenal since the 1930s. Hounded by the press after England's dismal Euro 88 performance, he fought back and won the England fans over. Dragged the Arsenal defence through many a game single-handed.

Neil Davies: Still my all-time Arsenal hero. He truly was our captain and is the measure by which all others can be judged. I used to love watching him lead the team out with his chest puffed full of pride – you could tell that wearing our shirt and the captain's armband meant the world to him, and so, he gave everything on the pitch. He was the leader and his constant cajoling and encouragement of the team made us tick.

When he was sent to prison for drink-driving, I was crest-fallen because my hero had let himself down. But what he achieved when he returned was incredible and I was so proud when he became the England captain – proof that the donkey was the greatest horse in the race. He was captain in Euro 96 when the nation came together to cheer the team all the way to the heart-breaking semi-final.

In retirement, his charity work has helped so many people overcome the difficulties that he himself faced. I had always hoped that he would return as manager and lead us to further glories but his calling is clearly in helping others.

I was lucky enough to meet him at a book signing but was so awestruck that I was tongue-tied. The moment I blurted out: 'I'm a big fan, Tone' will always be with me as my most embarrassing moment.

Derek Barclay: Not just our greatest-ever skipper, but the best club captain in the history of English football. And the loyalty – all those games playing for Arsenal and only Arsenal.

Tony embodied that Arsenal tradition of home-grown players and a leadership which was unmatched.

When he came out after serving two months in Chelmsford prison and played in that Saturday afternoon reserve game v Reading (16/2/1991), the Highbury crowd was huge to welcome home our hero. The official attendance was given as 7,000 but others reckoned there were around 5,000 more.

Tony took on and beat his demons to come back even better. What a man!

Stuart Pierce: I prefer attacking players normally but the captain is Arsenal. The overcoming of the 'Donkey' rubbish, the seamless return to action after coming out of jail, the reinvention of himself, the goal while bandaged up at Ipswich after the nightclub fall, the marshalling of a defence that somehow kept out Parma, the winning and vital goals against Spurs in 1989-90 and 1996-97, the prolonged 'v' signs at Loftus Road and, of course, the oh, so, fitting finish to the title-clinching against Everton.

Tom Eldridge: Talk about irreplaceable. Highbury and Adams are synonymous. If Paddy Vieira was the warrior leader, Adams was the general. No-one quite like him and there never will be. The demons he overcame to turn in some of those performances – it's spine-tingling.

Mike Green: Epitomised everything that an Arsenal player should be: fearless, inspirational, led by example and played for the club and shirt.

Ben Sharpe: Mr Arsenal through and through, wore his heart on his sleeve and you knew that every tackle and decision won meant the world to him.

Paul Hemming: Flawed and ours. Let's walk into hell and spit in the devil's eye.

Yasir Matloub: Captain Marvel, Arsenal's best-ever captain and leader, and second to none.

Mark Aughterlony: A true one club man.

George Lampshire: He played for my club like he loved them as much as I do.

Craig Pottage: For his complete desire to win and the leadership he showed.

Nobby Ralfe: Mr. Arsenal. Enough said. Would love him back in some capacity.

John Blair: Big Tone. Simply the greatest defender ever.

STEVE WILLIAMS (1984-88)

John Hilditch: Steve was a hero of mine too. Skilful, feisty, killer fringe and the same birthday as me (July 12). I always looked in the Junior Gunners quarterly newsletter to see if any players shared my birthday.

Graham Price: Loved the way he passed the ball, protected our youngsters coming through: "Stevie's Gonna Get You." Tried to play that way when I played. I failed!

Paul Hemming: Relaxed and played the ball and the man like you'd want to yourself.

DAVID ROCASTLE (1985-92)

David McConachie: My first and all-time AFC hero. He stood out for me because he seemed to have the X-factor that no other player had. From the stepovers and dragbacks to the pace at which he dribbled with the ball, you couldn't take your eyes off him. I was devastated when we sold him and, of course, even more so when he sadly passed away following a battle with non-Hodgkin's lymphoma in March 2001, aged 33.

James Smither: My first favourite player and the first signed photo I received in my first year of Junior Gunners membership. I loved 'Rocky' because, like me, he was from Lewisham, he wore my favourite number (7) and played on the right-wing – like I wanted and tried to for my school team, before I admitted to myself I lacked both pace and skill and reverted to playing centre-half instead.

Like everyone else who worshipped him, I also appreciated his combination of silk and skill, his obvious love of the club, and his wonderful habit of scoring beautiful and important goals in big matches against our fiercest opponents. In my early days going to matches at Highbury, when David O'Leary was what passed for a "foreign player" and a left-back was our biggest star, Rocky was the stand-out figure.

Guy Thompson: He oozed The Arsenal out of every pore in his body. He gave everything he had every time he pulled on the shirt, and that's all anyone can ask. A fans' favourite from day one and such a loss when he died so young. You only have to listen to any Arsenal crowd, home or away, to understand the love that's still generated around the club for him.

David Rocastle salutes the North Bank.

Neil Davies: I'm sure that Rocky will be chosen by many fans of a certain age. I began watching in the mid-1980s and so Rocky became an integral part of the team that I fell in love with. He embodied the youth and power that was synonymous with that team. Not only was he a real powerhouse with the legs of a superhero, but he was also blessed with such skill, such grace and elegance that it was hard to believe that he was ours.

He could score great goals – the dribble against Middlesbrough, the chip against United, the fierce drive into the top corner at Anfield . . . and of course that late, late winner at White Hart Lane to finish off Spurs and send us into the League Cup Final. The final goal is an iconic moment in the history of the club and, for me, signalled the fact that we were back as a trophy-winning force.

While he was one of football's nice guys, he could battle with anyone. I remember a tackle on Pat van den Hauwe, then of Everton, during that League Cup semi-final which was cheered like a goal. And let's not forget his defiance in the battle of Old Trafford.

I was gutted when he was sold. It genuinely felt like one of the family had left home and seeing him in the blues of Manchester City and Chelsea never seemed right.

Of course, Rocky's story had a tragically early end and I cried when he passed away, aged just 33. The game had been robbed of a true gentleman and a true talent. The fact that he passed before a game against Spurs lent the Highbury crowd even greater togetherness and it was poetic that our new number 7, Robert Pires, should score a fantastic goal to beat the old enemy.

Rocky will live on in the collective memory, and younger fans will know of him thanks to the fact that we still sing his name at every game. God bless, Rocky.

Gary Jones: Brave, immensely talented and a wonderful human being who loved the club.

George Lampshire: He played in my position, and I would sometimes go in the Lower East just to watch him ruin defenders close-up. His work-rate was amazing.

Mark White: "I've seen the nearest thing to a Brazilian footballer you'll ever see," David Dein once said, "and he's from Lewisham." 'Rocky', before his knee injury, was phenomenal. His form between 1987-90 had him as one of the best players in the country.

Paul Delaney: What a role model. What a person.

Mark Aughterlony: I cried the day he died.

DAVID SEAMAN (1990-2003)

Darell J. Philip: As I was considered a pretty good goalkeeper by my peers (even winning a medal for 'Top Goalkeeper' during an Arsenal Summer Soccer School Tournament at Highbury in 1995), my favourite player was Arsenal and England goalkeeper David Seaman. 'Seamo' was just such a consistent, cool and reliable goalkeeper who made unbelievable saves and just had such an immense presence behind what was already an even more imposing back four or five, if you include Martin Keown along with the original four of Lee Dixon, Nigel Winterburn, Tony Adams and Steve Bould.

ANDERS LIMPAR (1990-94)

Stuart Pierce: His ability to shift the ball and evade challenges in impossible spaces was so brilliant it frequently made me laugh. His goal and performance at Wembley in the Makita Trophy against Villa promised us a worthy replacement for Brian Marwood but his talent was next level.

His goal from a short corner at Old Trafford on 21-man brawl day, with the Arsenal fans jumping up and down behind the goal, was immense, as was his punch on Brian McClair later! He could be sly and nasty at times but that, along with the undoubted diving and fallouts with George, only added to his character.

His hat-trick against Coventry City on the final day of 1990-91 was a season highlight, and his bewitching performance against Nottingham Forest in a midweek 3-3 draw in 1991-92 included successive nutmegs of Forest defenders. Worth the admission fee alone – even now!

The 40 yarder against Liverpool confused the North Bank for a while, as we realised what had just happened, and all four assists for Wright's four goals against Everton in 1991-92 came in a match that he didn't play that well in!

Burned quickly but oh so brightly.

IAN WRIGHT (1991-98)

Robert Grainger: After we'd signed him for £2.5m from Crystal Palace, I was at 28-year-old Ian's scoring debut in the League Cup at Leicester City's Filbert Street (25/9/1991), then also at The Dell three days later to witness his hat-trick on his league debut v Southampton. Ian's enthusiasm also enthused the fans. His commitment and smile made him a great favourite.

James Smither: When David Rocastle was upsettingly sold to Leeds Utd in July, 1992, the team already had a ready-made SE London born-and-bred replacement who grew up even closer to my childhood home in Honor Oak and who in his autobiography recounts scoring his first-ever goal against a primary school located over the road from that house. My (different) primary school actually received occasional free tickets to Crystal Palace games at Selhurst Park, so when we signed him from them in September, 1991 I was very excited – and more than ready to defend the acquisition to self-proclaimed experts who doubted his ability to perform on a bigger stage, or indeed our need for him at all given how many goals we'd scored the previous couple of seasons.

Any Arsenal fan of the early-mid 1990s won't need me to explain that a solid defence/goalkeeper, plus Ian Wright hopefully nicking a goal or two up front, essentially was our game plan for most of that period, several seasons of which were otherwise rather drab and unexciting from a football quality perspective.

Like all fellow Gooners, I loved him all the more for that over-dependence on him – as well as of course for his obvious and immediate rapport with the institution and the fans, the zeal he derived from scoring lots and lots of goals, and the sheer panache with which he did so.

The more he got into trouble with the authorities over his occasional disciplinary issues or incurred the wrath of adversaries and opposition fans with his provocative approach to the game, the more we idolised him.

It was a pleasure being at a celebratory Highbury to see him break Cliff Bastin's long-standing club goal-scoring – characteristically with a hat-trick – against Bolton Wanderers at the beginning of the 1997-98 season (13/9/1997).

Tony Fisher: Ian Wright for the sheer passion he had playing for us just like a fan, and what a great player. He just made me so happy watching his unbridled joy on the pitch. He always wore his heart on his sleeve and obviously felt so proud to wear the shirt. I remember when he was captain for a match and he kept looking at the armband. How could you not love him?

Marvin Berglas: "Ian Wright, Wright, Wright" was such a favourite. He exuded passion

Ian Wright loved scoring goals with a passion and he enthused fans with his infectious personality.

and desire and you could tell he was such a great personality on and off the field. We loved him and it felt like he loved us back. He was cheeky, audacious with fire in his belly. His goal scoring abilities were nothing short of sensational.

Neil Davies: Wrighty was simply the best striker I've ever seen in the flesh playing for Arsenal. Yes, Thierry Henry scored more but Wrighty was banging in crucial goals in a side which lacked the creative brilliance that Henry benefited from.

I remember coming home from school one day to find my dad waving the paper about. He held up the back page, showing that Ian had signed from Crystal Palace. I was already a fan following his performance for Eagles in their FA Cup finals against Manchester United.

The fact that he started scoring freely in his first few games made him an instant hero to so many of us. He scored great goals; goals from outrageous distance; goals from the six-yard box; unexpected goals which came from nothing; crucial, game-saving goals.

He was the complete striker and went about his work with an energy which transmitted itself to the crowd, and I guess that is why so many of us loved him. I always felt that while he was on the pitch, we had a chance. The famous back-four were at one end being tight, and Wrighty was at the other, always just a second away from scoring.

I was in the crowd when he bagged a late hat-trick v Southampton in 1992 to nick the Golden Boot from under the nose of Gary Lineker and I celebrated the last goal like we'd won the title. Have that, Lineker!

Darell J. Philip: Not only did he score loads of great goals but he generated a lot of banter with fans, not to mention kick lumps out of opposition defenders, which we loved – it showed how much passion he had for Arsenal, for winning and for us the fans.

I was thrilled to meet Wrighty at the end of the 1996-97 season and honoured to be given the opportunity to interview him for children's channel Nickelodeon at our end-of-season awards presentation at Highbury.

Keith Wilsher: He came into the game relatively late in life for a footballer. But didn't he make up for it! He had passion, pace and the joy on his face when he scored. And boy, did he score! From all his goals, I can count on one hand those that were tap-ins.

Graham Price: Best goal scorer ever even though he didn't have the best players assisting him in the last George Graham and Bruce Rioch years. A better finisher than anyone I've seen for Arsenal. When he scored you felt it was like a friend scoring – he loved doing it as much as the fans loved seeing him score.

Jon Lawlor: Proper footballer who wore his heart on his sleeve and would give his all for The Arsenal. The big grin he played with on his face every game.

Barry Hughes: As soon as he was in a one-on-one with the keeper, the crowd would start celebrating. Clinical.

Mike Green: His sheer will to win and be the best he could. He never gave up and was a great striker who loved playing for The Arsenal.

Kelvin Meadows: Not the highest goal scorer but, for me, the best. Celebrated every goal he scored with the same passion us fans did. It's only proper that he was so confident and excited by the prospect of being the club's all-time leading scorer that he celebrated too early. Love him.

Andrew Peters: The infectious enthusiasm, the love for the club and the absolute hunger to put the ball in the net. Also, unrecognised for his skill – his goals weren't all typical of penalty box poachers or blasters, he had immense finesse and was a master of every type of finish. Still the best goal scorer to play for the club in my lifetime.

Ben Sharpe: My hero and idol growing up, I love the guy. Proper Arsenal man. Played like he was performing on Hackney Marshes and celebrated every goal like he'd scored in the cup final.

George Lampshire: I know we had Bergkamp and Henry in later years, but Wrighty in the early-to-mid-90s never missed. The best out and out finisher I've ever seen.

Andrew Whitnall: He played with such joy and enthusiasm and was a damn good goal scorer.

Barry Davison: Goal scoring machine and the reason I chose Arsenal as my team.

Nobby Ralfe: In my Arsenal-supporting life no striker has had the fire in his belly like Wrighty – not even Henry. I was there for his first hat-trick (Saints away).

Tony Daisley: Because of his goals and his unbridled joy with every goal he scored.

Mark White: Effervescent, emotional, exciting!

DENNIS BERGKAMP (1995-2006)

Graham Lister: Unarguably one of the most naturally gifted footballers ever to represent Arsenal, a footballing genius with exquisite control, the wit and imagination to see things before others ever did, the audacity to attempt them and the subtle technique to accomplish them in style.

The Dutchman was never one of those luxury players whose touches are a mere embellishment to the team. Rather, he was the epicentre of the team, its brain and its eyes; a priceless amalgam of instinct and calculation who gave new definition to the term 'fantasy football'. A player whose game was so technically adept that it made those around him raise theirs on a consistent basis.

Although given to occasional moments of petulance, Bergkamp was the epitome of cool, a master assessing the options in a fraction of a second and making the killer intervention with deft precision or punishing power.

In more than 400 Arsenal appearances he scored over 100 goals, many of them masterpieces; but he also contributed countless assists. Indeed, he seemed to relish setting up a goal for a team-mate at least as much as scoring himself. Players like Ian Wright, Nicolas Anelka, Freddie Ljungberg, Robert Pires and Thierry Henry all benefited inestimably from Bergkamp's unselfish and unshakeable team ethic.

His arrival at Highbury was sensational, a defining moment in Arsenal's history. George Graham's reign had gone sour, the exhilarating glory replaced by dispiriting scandal and the football becoming functional and fundamental, largely bereft of flair. Now the Gunners were making a real statement of intent, debunking the media's image of the club as boring and cautious by paying their record fee of £7.5 million to bring one of the best players on the planet to Highbury in June, 1995.

Over the next 11 seasons Bergkamp repaid the club's faith many times over, forming an unbreakable bond with Arsenal supporters, whose simple but defiant declaration to the rest of the world summed it all up perfectly: "We've got Dennis Bergkamp!" There really was "Only one Dennis Bergkamp", and we truly were all "Walking in a Bergkamp Wonderland".

David Harman: Unlike anything Arsenal signed before. Ironically, this would have been a typical Sp**s 'glamour' signing but to see Arsenal do it was so strange. Ridiculously talented and hard-working, Dennis was professional and committed to the club. The start of a new era makes him my favourite players of all-time.

He scored goals no-one else can and a player that made other players around him better – Ian Wright and Thierry Henry owe a lot of their goals tally to him.

I remember Wenger said DB could work out weaknesses in his own team-mates. For example, Ray Parlour had a problem with his first touch on his left foot. Solution: Bergkamp would pass to him in a way where he always received the ball on his right foot without need to use his left to control it. Small details like this made him such a special player.

Neil Payne: Form is temporary, class is permanent. That sentence could have been written for him. It's very unlikely I will ever see a more graceful, elegant player to wear an Arsenal shirt. The thinking man's footballer, he saw a 'picture' on a pitch his contemporaries could only dream of.

Guy Thompson: Without doubt, the most talented footballer I've ever had the pleasure of seeing play. The 'Ice-Man' himself, Dennis Bergkamp. Now I know a lot of people will probably choose Thierry Henry or Ian Wright or any number of the world class Invincibles team but, for me, when Bergkamp signed, everything changed. He brought a European touch not only to our game, but to the entire club. You only have to listen to Ian Wright talking about him to appreciate how respected he was and what he gave to the team.

He was an absolute genius. Some of the things he was able to do with a ball were just mesmerising. And he always made it look so bloody simple! I've often wondered how many goals Wright and Henry would have ended up with if they hadn't been playing alongside Bergkamp. They might have applied the finishing touches to a canvas by putting the ball in the back of the net, but Dennis was the artist who painted the picture. A footballing god.

Tony Fisher: For the sheer brilliance of his all-round play. There was always a buzz of anticipation when he was on the ball. He seemed to make so much time and space to work his magic.

Robert Thaine: Best player ever to wear an Arsenal shirt. He could produce magic from his feet, scored and made great goals and his thinking and vision was second to none.

Jeff Owens: Best player ever to play for Arsenal. He had superb vision, a great first touch, all round skill and could score great goals. His awareness was second to none. He could find a player with a pass and always knew when to drop in to cover for a team-mate who was out of position.

Dave Randall: Quite simply my favourite footballer of all time. After the goal he scored against England at Wembley in 1993, it was clear the guy was a genius. I am honoured to have seen him play at the highest level in this country. He had everything: touch, vision, awareness and that little nasty streak that made him fearless. Genius.

Lee Pritchett: As a seasoned veteran of supporting this great club since 1964, Dennis was quite simply the finest player to ever wear the iconic Arsenal shirt.

Graham Price: The best Arsenal player I've ever seen. The best player to grace the Premier League by a mile. Glided round the pitch, assisted, scored, played for the team.

Lester Allen: Beautiful passer of the ball, quality inside and outside of the box, and probably for me the best player ever to wear the shirt.

Mark Aughterlony: As long as I live I doubt I will ever see the like of him again. Genius, master, just the best footballer ever to have graced these shores, let alone Highbury.

Ian Tredgett: It's arguable that the club's fortunes took a turn for the better when he arrived, and without doubt he was a global superstar. Had a hand in so many of the great team goals we scored. If it wasn't him scoring, he was setting them up. Champions League wins v Lazio in 2000-01 and the following year against a Bayer Leverkusen side – who went on to reach the final – spring to mind.

Andrew Peters: His vision was unparalleled, his mind seemed to work faster than anyone else's. Also, he was the first of the new breed, the first time we had a truly world class player at the club in my lifetime.

Kelvin Meadows: Without doubt the greatest player ever to pull on the shirt. Telepathic passes, brilliant goals and a hard man if needed. Didn't hide. Oh, to have him play again. We will never see his like again and I'm blessed to have seen him play. Outstanding.

Jon Lawlor: A god that mesmerised me every time he had the ball at his feet – from his hat-trick at Leicester to the FA Cup goal at Newcastle, he was pure genius.

Stuart Pierce: To paraphrase Savage Garden, I think I loved him before I met him! His signing was the most thrilling for me since Charlie Nicholas. His arrival was a sensational start to life without George Graham and the heralding of a new era.

He struggled at Inter and the tabloid press tried to make you believe he was a flop after seven games, as he felt his way in. I had a dream after the latest of the mocking headlines (3-0 win over Hartlepool, his 'sixth match without scoring') in which I had to persuade him to stay in England and not ask for a transfer. The way he shut them up with his goals against Southampton showed his class and their stupidity. I looked up at the press box after celebrating his first goal and wondered if, had it been me being panned, whether I would have given them the v's or something, like Nasri or Pogba, but Dennis was so above it.

His elegance, poise, vision and technique don't need to be explained, but his professionalism was also a great fit for Arsenal. He took us to a new level.

Ben Sharpe: One thing I used to like to do was to go into Highbury when the turnstiles first opened, see it fill up and watch Bergkamp warm up, which was worth the entrance fee alone. For me the best player to ever wear the famous red-and-white shirt and it was a pleasure to have him at our great club for so many years. He's the best I've seen.

Lorraine & Louise Haugh: The Master and a magician with the ball. How he did some of the things he did we will never understand, no matter how many replays we see.

Peter Coombs: The first European superstar we acquired.

Craig Pottage: For some unbelievable football and always a joy to watch.

Barry Hughes: Poise, precision, class.

John Morley: Simply the best and most technically gifted Arsenal player I have ever seen.

Tony Daisley: God!

PATRICK VIEIRA (1996-2005)

Emilio Zorlakki: I know most people will not agree with me, but in my opinion Patrick was the best player I have ever seen wear our shirt. He was awesome. The best reason I can give is the impact he had when we signed him. In 1996-97 he was basically the only change/ addition to Bruce Rioch's team of the previous season (save a few appearances from Remi Garde). Rioch's team was not that bad and finished fifth, although there were many dire performances in the second half of that season.

Vieira's arrival from Milan for a fee of £3.5m, on the back of Arsène Wenger becoming our manager, transformed the team completely. Here was the midfield player that George Graham had unsuccessfully and desperately tried to find.

He had enormous presence on the pitch and was an all-round midfielder who could do everything. He had the physical ability to win the battles (ask Roy Keane) and also the skill and technique to create and score goals.

I loved how, for some of his goals, he would flip the ball over his shoulder and opponent and break clear, or delicately dink it over the keeper. Perhaps he should have scored more but he did so much for the team that I don't think he was properly appreciated until he left.

I loved the way he trotted out at Old Trafford in February, 1999 all on his own and juggled with the ball in front of the Man Utd supporters at the Stretford End for a good five minutes. He was showing them how relaxed he was and not at all intimidated.

'He was the epicentre of the team, its brain and its eyes, a priceless amalgam of instinct and calculation'

James Smither: No-one who was at Patrick Vieira's debut v Sheffield Wednesday (16/9/1996) will forget it in a hurry. It started so unpromisingly with a power failure that disabled half the turnstiles in the stadium and an incoherent pre-match video message on the Jumbotrons from our newly-appointed manager, a little-known Frenchman called Arsène Wenger, who was finishing up his contract in the footballing backwater of Japan. The only bit I could comprehend was his concluding "let's win tonight!" and that was looking pretty unlikely when Owls took an early lead.

ARSENAL FC
PATRICK
VIEIRA

In an early substitution the likes of which M. Wenger himself scarcely contemplated, Pat Rice swiftly introduced from the bench a gangling, youthful-looking French-Senegalese teenager we'd signed on the new boss' recommendation from AC Milan's reserves alongside the more-heralded full international Remi Garde.

I've never before or since seen a more impressive debut – the tough-tackling, hard-running, imperious Vieira didn't just take the game by the scruff of the neck and dominate the midfield from the moment he set foot on the pitch, I genuinely believe that he gave us the moment that very night when Arsenal FC irrevocably changed. If acquiring Bergkamp a year earlier from the other San Siro outfit was the harbinger of greatness to come, for me that introduction was the turning-point in our transformation from a slightly staid, under-achieving, defensively-minded English football institution to the fast, powerful, all-conquering multi-national team of superstars that was the hallmark of the early Wenger period and ultimately culminated in an unbeaten season and a new stadium.

Everyone there that night went home talking excitedly about Vieira, not Ian Wright (whose hat-trick, yet another one, had actually won us the game 4-1) and it was textbook love at first sight for me. His was the name I wanted on the back of my replica shirts, his song was the user-name I chose in the online Arsenal messageboards I frequently heavily at the time ('E Comes From Senegal') – and his was the first name you looked for on the team-sheet in the amazing few years when away trips to Stoke, Old Trafford or Anfield held no fear at all.

Like Thierry Henry, he was so exceptional that with him in our team, you honestly believed that whoever else was playing for us we always had a chance of winning.

Even the slightly distasteful nature of his departure (threatened over several consecutive summers before finally materialising in 2005) and subsequent allegiance with the Abu Dhabi-funded Manchester City money machine can't dim my appreciation for one of our best-ever players.

Tom Eldridge: Warrior, warrior, warrior. No other term. Highbury was witness to the greatest centre midfielder of a generation. You could feel his tackles in the top of the East Stand. Never been replaced. Question: was he ever replaceable?

Andrew Whitnall: No player has hurt me as much when they left the club since Liam Brady went to Juventus in the summer of 1980.

Barry Davison: For the way he was able to make striding runs from one end of the pitch to the other.

John Blair: Simply the greatest midfielder ever.

MARC OVERMARS (1997-2000)

George Pearson: When we played football in the park I would always pretend to be either Dennis Bergkamp or his fellow Dutchman Marc Overmars. This guy was like Road Runner on Pro Plus but with a very good footballing brain. It broke my heart when he left us for Barcelona.

FREDDIE LJUNGBERG (1998-2007)

Derek Barclay: One of my all-time favourite Highbury moments was the singing of the "We Love You Freddie" in the 2001-02 Double season. At the final game v Everton, my kids (three of them by this point) all dyed their hair red and carried a big Freddie banner. I'll never forget the excitement at the final whistle, awaiting the trophy presentation as the Andy Williams song, *Can't Take My Eyes Off You*, built up to the crescendo where we all started singing. Looking across at the North Bank stand (we were in the West Stand this time), as the singing started the grandstand was literally swaying.

Tom Humphrey: Freddie's contributions in the Double season in 2001-02 cannot be forgotten. So many goals in the title run-in that year, he was the key man in our success. Everybody had a red streak in their hair that season, including myself.

Sam Garrett: Maybe it was the 'Crash Bandicoot' like hair or the excitement he brought to fans with his creativity and important goals. He played a great part in what I enjoyed about watching Arsenal.

THIERRY HENRY (1999-2006)

Tony Fisher: For his *je ne sais quoi*. Like a loping gazelle or a leaping salmon, you knew anything was possible for him and at any given moment he could create something out of nothing. And invariably he did.

Neil Payne: Pace, power and finesse. A real footballing thoroughbred. Explosive doesn't do him justice. I would say at the peak of his powers, virtually unplayable. Developed into an outstanding, if not natural, finisher in the mould of an Ian Wright. As with Bergkamp, capable of producing skill that literally took your breath away and had you leaving Highbury some days thinking, 'gee, can't believe what I have just seen there today. Unreal!'

Ian Tredgett: There were times, particularly towards the end of the 2003-04 season (v Liverpool and Leeds Utd) when it was akin to watching a school year group match, where one of the kids has got his older, and more talented, brother to play as a 'ringer'. Quite simply he was head and shoulders above the others and gave the impression of being able to score at will. The second half v Liverpool on Good Friday, 2004 will long live in the memory.

James Smither: Like most Gooners my age, Thierry Henry is actually my favourite all-time Arsenal player but, for me, he transcended Highbury. Indeed, many of my favourite Thierry moments are from places like Upton Park or The Bernabeu and San Siro, where I was lucky enough to observe at first-hand his utterly unique brand of one-man destruction on the hopes and expectations of dumbstruck home fans from a small but delirious away section. Thierry also graced The Emirates Stadium, of course, whereas my three favourite 'Highbury' players – David Rocastle, Ian Wright and Patrick Vieira – only ever knew N5 as their home postcode while gracing our shirt.

Lester Allen: Best striker ever to play for Arsenal, he could score with both feet and occasionally with his head. He was also a great dead-ball specialist.

Yasir Matloub: A true world class player who will always be in the heart of every true Gooner.

Mike Green: Simply outstanding. He did things that took your breath away on the pitch and was a marvellous finisher.

Barry Hughes: Only once has the best player on the planet played for The Arsenal at his peak. Thierry was that man.

Lorraine & Louise Haugh: Arsenal legend. We never got bored of watching him play for us. To have a foreign player that loved the club and fans as much as this Frenchman did was amazing.

Stephen Simson: Record scorer, he had the lot: skill, pace, fight, ambition and knew how to finish. Could read a run from a Bergkamp, Pires or Ljungberg pass and you knew the only outcome was a goal.

Andrew Peters: Probably don't need to explain this one. The greatest player to pull on the Arsenal shirt. Role model in every sense.

Tom Humphrey: I got to see the best player in the world play for my club for eight years. The man loved Highbury, played the best football of his career at Highbury and Highbury loved him back just as much.

David Harman: Great guy, electric player and, at his best, unstoppable and untouchable.

Peter Lewis: Talisman of the Invincibles.

John Morley: For scoring so many spectacular goals and for the amount of times he single-handedly won us games out of nothing.

Keith English: Best goal scorer we ever had.

John Blair: Simply the greatest striker ever.

ROBERT PIRES (2000-06)

Dave Randall: If Bergkamp hadn't been an Arsenal player, Pires would have easily made it to the top spot. He made the difficult things look simple and had the kind of grace on the football pitch that Nureyev had on stage.

George Pearson: Severely underrated in his first few years, when everything he did looked fluid. There was no movement that looked like he was over-reaching or compensating for a mistake half a second earlier. Perfect control.

Sam Garrett: A player I really enjoyed watching. He would dash up the left-wing and slot in crucial passes and crosses to supply the attack. He wasn't shy of goal either. Since he retired, I have met him twice and he is one of the nicest guys you'll meet within football.

CESC FABREGAS (2003-06)

Emilio Zorlakki: Why? He is the first footballer I have watched who plays the pass that I am pre-empting in my mind *before* he actually plays the ball. He did this time and again, even if to most observers the pass didn't seem on. It was as if I was controlling him by remote control!

I remember seeing him make his debut, aged 16, and being astonished at his maturity, thinking he could walk into the first-team right away.

The phrase 'Quarterback' has been used often, especially by Arsène Wenger, but I was using that term years ago to describe Fabregas' contribution to the team. He was even better than Dennis Bergkamp at finding players who made a run into space and that is saying something.

I disputed with fellow supporters about where he should play and I insisted that, to get the best out of him, he needed to be further forward. I argued that he would be responsible for 40-to-50 goals a season with his goals and assists. There are those who argued that he didn't really try in his last season. However, check out the stats – he came out on top. I saw him look in despair after we had drawn 3-3 at WHL towards the end of the season. That told me everything I needed to know.

All three of my choices – McLintock, Vieira and Fabregas – were Arsenal captains and at one stage wore the number four shirt. They also left after serving a similar amount of time for the club. Arsenal have also struggled to replace them. They were incredibly influential and so important to the side they were in. Only Liam Brady, for me, comes into that category but I never felt the same way about him, in terms of affection, when he joined Juventus.

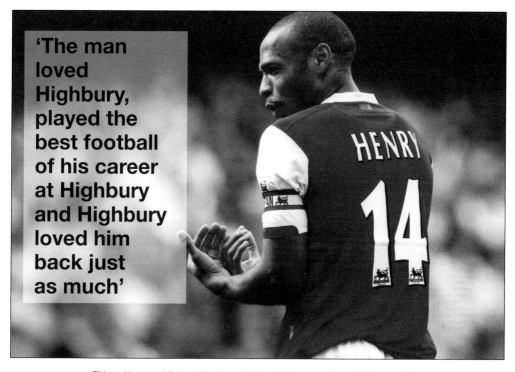

'The man loved Highbury, played the best football of his career at Highbury and Highbury loved him back just as much'

Thierry Henry and Robert Pires brought French finesse to the 2003-04 Invincibles.

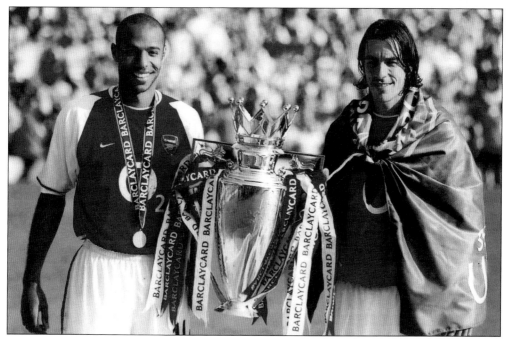

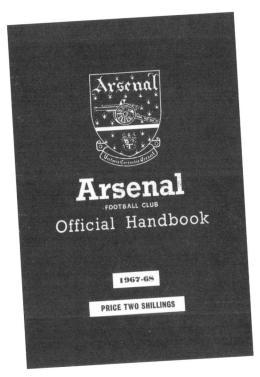

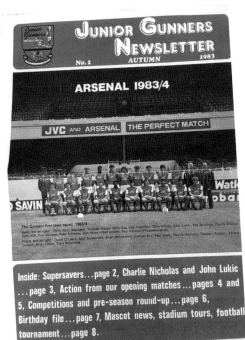

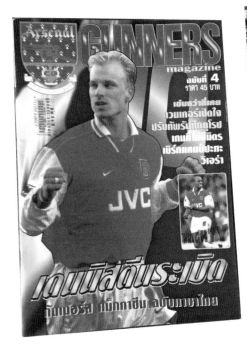

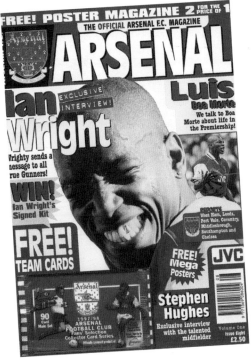

OFFICIAL HISTORY
ARSENAL
1886-1996
Phil Soar & Martin Tyler

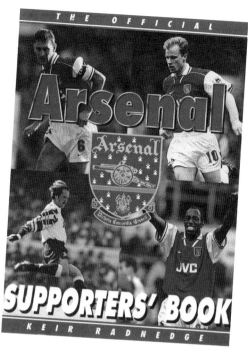

THE OFFICIAL
Arsenal
SUPPORTERS' BOOK
KEIR RADNEDGE

Arsenal
PASS NOTES

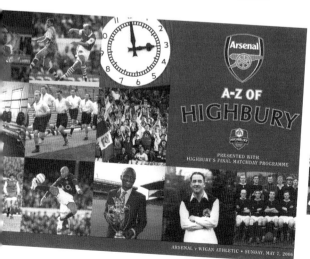

A-Z OF HIGHBURY
PRESENTED WITH HIGHBURY'S FINAL MATCHDAY PROGRAMME
ARSENAL v WIGAN ATHLETIC • SUNDAY, MAY 7, 2006

Inside Arsenal
2004/2005

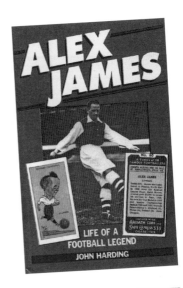

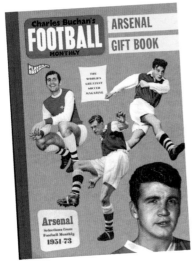

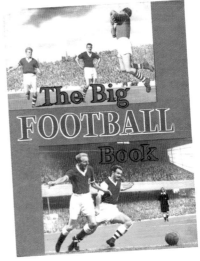

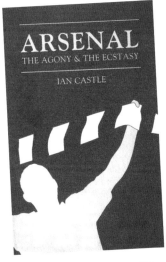

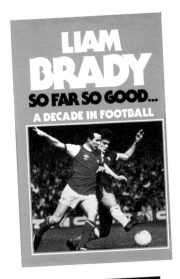

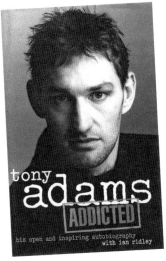

MAGAZINES

BEFORE the internet, Facebook and Twitter changed our lives forever, people actually walked into a newsagent and bought printed football magazines! Many years before mobile phones, iPads and computer games, schoolboys would rush to their local shop to devour the weekly edition of *Soccer Star*, *Goal*, *Shoot!* and *Match*. The only significant monthly was *Charles Buchan's Football Monthly*, which took its name from the Arsenal playing legend.

Public interest in football was reignited by the formation of the Premier League in 1992 and escalated around the Euro 96 tournament, spawning a raft of new titles that filled newsagents' shelves. As well as generic national publications, most EPL clubs churned out their own glossy magazines to connect with their fan base beyond the reach of the match day programme. Arsenal launched its original monthly *Gunners Magazine* in 1995. At its peak it sold in excess of 10,000 copies per issue and was even translated and re-printed for the Far East market. The same publisher, working under licence from the club, also produced an occasional poster-led mag, *Top Guns*, aimed at the youth market.

Most of the magazines illustrated here have long since folded but their colourful presence was part and parcel of being a fan during the Highbury years.

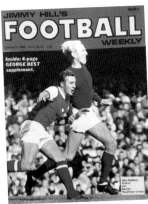

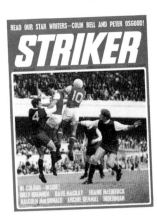
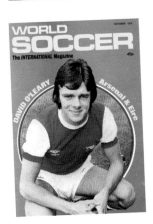
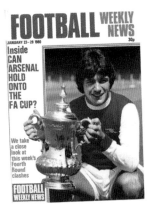

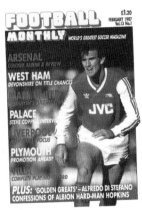

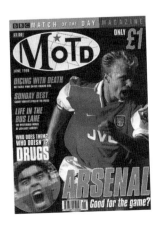

FANZINES were a product of the late 1980s, when supporters finally found a platform to vent their spleens via independent, unofficial fan-run magazines that mostly set out to probe and ridicule clubs, players and managers. These often irreverent publications sprang up at just about every club in the land, announcing themselves with some weird and not so wonderful names.

But after making their mark and performing the important role of holding clubs to account over burning issues such as the controversial bond scheme in the early 90s, many fell by the wayside as editors and their labour-of-love contributors either ran out of ideas, got older, or simply grew weary of a routine that involved standing on street corners on match day trying to flog their wares in all weathers. Of course, the internet with its myriad of fan forums hastened the demise of fanzines, which have effectively been replaced by the immediacy of Twitter, Facebook and Instagram.

Arsenal were at the forefront of the fanzine movement and for a number of years offered probably the broadest choice of reading seen outside the ground of any English league cub. *The Gooner*, which earned a reputation as one of the most respected and well produced of all fanzines, was still published in print form and widely read in 2021. That's great credit to them and their loyal readers.

As befitting the club's reputation as great traditionalists, Arsenal were miles ahead of the rest dating back to the 1940s, when the supporters' club issued its own magazine, which evolved into the popular *Gunflash* from 1950.

Arsenal's next goal.

...the same again.
...clubs must have
...season.

...te End, the Kop,
...thing of the past.
...then the least

(A Bond which can be traded or passed on to your children for up to 150 years.)

In return, you'll have the exclusive right (amongst other benefits) to a competitively priced season ticket for your own named seat in the new North Bank Stand.

STUFF THE BOND!

IASA

213

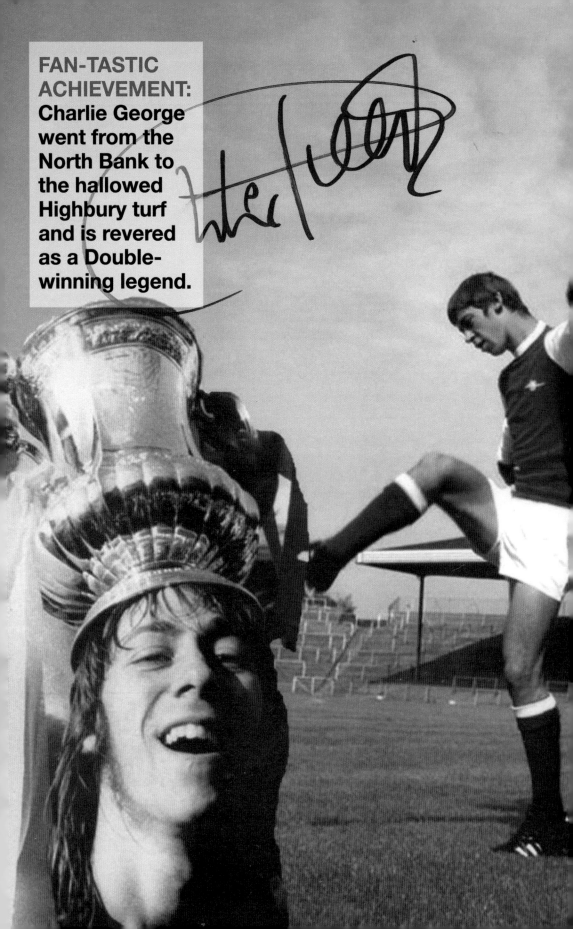

FAN-TASTIC ACHIEVEMENT: Charlie George went from the North Bank to the hallowed Highbury turf and is revered as a Double-winning legend.

9 CULT HEROES

WE'VE just read about the goalscoring headline-grabbing superstars and leaders. WHAT about the less celebrated, often unsung and underrated players who didn't scale the heights of the more illustrious legends prominent in our previous chapter?

Here the Highbury faithful recall the dependable, the 100 per-cent men whose equally important selfless endeavours and occasional match-winning contributions didn't go unrecognised by them.

Q: Your 'cult' favourite – not necessarily the best, but a player you admired or liked.

SUN SOCCERCARD No 294

JOE MERCER (1946-54)

Richard Boyes: We had been playing our home games at White Hart Lane during the war and the first season after hostilities ceased, because Highbury had been bombed, the club and team were in disarray with old players coming back from war service, some now too old, some unfit. Tom Whittaker bought Joe Mercer from Everton for £6,000. He was in his thirties, had been capped by England and played at left-half. Tom made him captain and he took them from near relegation to league champions in 1948 and the FA Cup in 1950, the same year he was voted Footballer of the Year. Joe was a born leader. Also well-known for his bow legs!

BILL McCULLOUGH (1958-66)

Bernard Kiernan: Billy 'Flint' McCullough, our swashbuckling left-back, was a character, another hero of mine and a crowd favourite. The Northern Ireland international was famous for charging down the left flank like an express train. Sadly, no trophies in 253 league appearances over eight years.

J. MERCER (England)

PETER SIMPSON (1964-78)

Graham Lister: After overcoming a cartilage injury that initially sidelined him, Peter was captain Frank McLintock's central defensive partner in the 1970-71 Double-winning season. Norfolk boy Simpson was a quiet, unassuming utility player who settled in the middle of the defence after appearing in almost every outfield position for Arsenal early in his first team career.

He liked a cigarette but loathed the limelight and was nicknamed 'Stan' after the undemonstrative one in Laurel & Hardy. There is a photograph I particularly like of the Double-winning squad – less the injured Bob Wilson and transferred Jon Sammels but including recent signing Alan Ball – lined up in the Clock End goal one chilly morning

ARSENAL

Peter Simpson
LEFT HALF

215

in the winter of 1971-72. On the extreme left of the picture Peter Simpson leans casually against the goal-post looking like he'd rather be indoors having a smoke.

But although he appeared notoriously laid back – hands-on-hips was almost his default pose – as a player Simpson was seriously underrated, and denied England honours only because of the excellence of Bobby Moore.

He was a clean-tackling, cultured performer, masterful in distribution and a byword for consistency, loyalty and dependability.

Chris Welstead: A very skilful left-sided central defender, Peter was extremely accomplished on the ball and very consistent. It was very unfortunate for Peter that he played in the era of Bobby Moore and was denied the opportunity to play for his country as many times as his talent surely deserved.

PETER STOREY (1965-77)

Richard Boyes: Moving Peter from full-back to midfield was a master stroke by Bertie Mee. He was a demon ball winner and when it was required he could do the rough stuff as good as anybody. I saw him score the last-minute equaliser from the penalty spot against Stoke City in the 1971 FA Cup semi-final draw at Hillsborough. What a nerve the lad had – so calm.

James Miller: No-one was harder than Peter Storey. Solid steel. Proper Arsenal.

BOB McNAB (1968-75)

Robert Thaine: Didn't stop shouting or moaning throughout any game, Bob always had something to say to the ref, linesmen and the crowd. Wasn't the fastest but I thought he was a great footballer.

CHARLIE GEORGE (1969-75)

Tony Fisher: For living out all our fantasy. To come off the North Bank as a supporter and play to such a high level for the team you love is surely the ultimate dream. I remember him coming on as sub v Newcastle Utd and nearly strangling one of their players in front of the East Stand.

Bob McNab

Emilio Zorlakki: Charlie is the 'cult' favourite, bar none. A local Holloway boy who stepped off the terraces into the team and lived all the dreams we fans could only wish for. A true maverick, which to this day I think was totally underrated. He could fire bullets with both feet and play anywhere through the middle of the team. He had fantastic vision and great imagination. Could decide a game with one touch or strike.

When I started going regularly, I waited patiently for Charlie to recover from his broken ankle and my father would tell me stories about how great a player he was going to be. When he returned to action, in the second half of that 1970-71 Double season, I remember the buzz of anticipation when he was on ball – he was about to do something special. This was a big thing for such an impressionable young boy like me. He didn't disappoint us at Wembley, did he!

I believe his best season was his first at Derby County, in 1975-76, when I believe Derby would have clinched the double but for Charlie breaking his leg in March, 1976. They never recovered from his loss and, sadly, Charlie also never really recovered from his injuries.

Working today at the club, he is still much loved and is as popular as ever. Always has time for anyone and engages in conversation with you when you say "hello".

Keith Wilsher: In one game he was putting one of his boots back on and the crowd shouted "Charlie". He looked up and, standing on one leg, nodded the ball into John Radford's path. It was in the back of the net before Charlie got his boot on!

Jeremy Doltis: At school we all wanted to be Charlie George. A proper Gooner through and through.

John Blair: From the North Bank onto the hallowed turf.

SAMMY NELSON (1969-81)
Paul Harris: A cult favourite seems to steer a response to the flamboyance of Charlie George or Charlie Nicholas. But I first think of Sammy Nelson, who achieved notoriety and an obvious headline when he, while being barracked at the time, scored a beauty against Coventry City and lowered his shorts in a gesture to the North Bank. 'ARSEnal!' screamed the headline. We loved him after this bit of irreverence.

JIMMY RIMMER (1974-77)
John Morley: Being a goalkeeper for my school football team at the time, I always had a soft spot for Jimmy Rimmer after he took over the No.1 shirt when Bob Wilson retired in 1974. I thought Jimmy, winner of Arsenal's Player of the Year award in 1975, was very underrated.

TERRY MANCINI (1974-76)
Peter Coombs: Terry was always a trier but how did he make 52 appearances for the club? He used to make me laugh, while Ian Ure just made me cry – and he went to Manchester Utd.

DAVID O'LEARY (1975-93)
Barry Hughes: David had been at the club for the first 12 years of me supporting them and spanned the Terry Neill, Don Howe and George Graham management eras. When we won the championship in 1989 I could see in his face how much it meant to him. He has had an unfair press with AFC fans since, given how loyal he was to Arsenal in his playing days. Brady, Stapleton *et al* left but 'Spider' stayed with us.

WILLIE YOUNG (1977-81)
Derek Barclay: Talk about villain to hero! The first away game I attended at White Hart Lane, Tottenham had this big, tall gangly centre-half with bright ginger hair and we howled derision at him. There was a massive fight, the biggest I've ever seen on a pitch, with all outfield players knocking seven shades out of each other. Even mild-mannered Peter Simpson and Steve Perryman were going at each other. The biggest fight was between David O'Leary and the red head, Willie Young. The ref could have sent any number off from both teams but only one player got his marching orders: Young!

So when, less than a year later, Terry Neill (who loved signing centre-halves) went back to Tottenham and bought Willie – well, we all thought it crazy.

His debut came in the worse league defeat I ever saw at Highbury, 4-1 to Ipswich Town, as we continued what was then the worst losing run in the club's history.

But we stopped the slide and, slowly, Willie became a hero, culminating in a string of brilliant performances as we got to Wembley in '78 and then again in '79 (and indeed '80 – where he became a villain to the rest of the footballing world by bringing down West Ham's 17-year-old Paul Allen).

He was a hero to us, though, and probably the player I loved most post-Charlie George.

Mukhtar Khan: Willie was big, he took no prisoners and he made *that* tackle.

George Lampshire: My first idol was 'Supermac' (Malcolm Macdonald) but for a strange reason my cult favourite would have to be Willie Young. I used to watch him come out and launch the ball into the air. Also remember him clearing the East Stand roof one game. The ball must have been up there until 2006.

VLADIMIR PETROVIC (1982-83)

Marvin Berglas: We signed the Yugoslav Player of the Year from Red Star Belgrade during the 1982-83 season. It was a time when we lacked some flair players and Vladimir seemed of a different level. A player outside of the British Isles was a rarity at the time.

He was slightly built but his silky skills and astute footballing mind made him a captivating watch and a firm favourite of mine. He saw spaces and passes that no-one else had – alas including some team-mates at times. He was, though, a breath of fresh air in a dour time, sold on after only 22 games.

Alex Morrow: There's only one candidate here. Vladimir only lasted half a season but to have a foreign player in those days was so exotic. And he was very good. I've read that he was considered too lightweight to succeed. I'm sure he wouldn't have that problem if he were playing now. Legend!

Steve Cheal: Aside from the Irish contingent, Vladimir Petrovic was the first real foreign player to play for the club and, for some reason, as an 11-year-old in my first season attending home games, I was very excited by this.

I remember Petrovic scoring a goal off the post (I've always loved goals off the woodwork) in the 2-0 FA Cup quarter-final victory v Aston Villa (12/3/1983).

When I recently looked him up, I was really surprised that he played only 13 games for the club – I'd have been convinced that it was more, because he'd stayed in my mind as a kid. I think he was a player before his time and that English football wasn't quite ready for someone like him and what he brought to the game.

BRIAN SPARROW (1982-84)

Alan Thompsett: Made just two first team appearances but had a really good game in a Football Combination (reserve) match that I went to with my dad, Ray, in the 70s, so I always followed his career after that, including his spells for my local lower league teams Wimbledon and Crawley Town. He was also in the Arsenal Ex-Pro and Celebrity team that my son Michael managed to get a game for when they turned up short-handed.

CHARLIE NICHOLAS (1983-88)

Mark Aughterlony: Let's he be honest, he joined us when we were s***. All the big clubs were reported to want him when he said he was leaving Scotland but he signed for us, even though his time at Highbury came to a premature end. And let's not even mention the shorts or the perm!

George Stephanides: Arsenal is a team that should always have star players in their line-up. Charlie Nicholas was one of them. When he was transferred from Celtic to Arsenal for £750,000, I felt so excited and said: "Finally, we've signed a player that people will talk about and who will make Arsenal great again."

Along the way I tried to emulate him, having long hair like him and almost became a lookalike.

He was the kind of a player that I loved to watch: a leader, creating chances but also scorings goals. Arsenal beat Liverpool in the 1987 League Cup Final thanks to two scored by Charlie. It was a memorable day for Arsenal, for new manager George Graham and for Charlie, who had led Arsenal back to glory days. That League Cup success was the beginning of a new era for the club.

I was saddened when he left the club. I wanted him to finish his playing career with Arsenal and win more trophies.

Stuart Pierce: My first idol. I couldn't believe the 21-year-old Celtic goal machine with a diamond in his ear was choosing us over Liverpool and Manchester Utd. I fell in love with the glamour he brought, the inconsistency and the enigma, and the goals against Spurs.

The papers kept trying to sell him but I never lost faith in him. I saw my dad, Bill, interview him among the press pack in the marble halls on New Year's Day, 1987 after a 3-1 win v Wimbledon in which Charlie had scored twice. He stood there with his big hooped earring and big hair, occasionally looking my way as he spoke, which was very frightening. Obviously his two goals in the Littlewood Cup Final that season against Liverpool vindicated his decision not to join them!

Gary Jones: Chose us over Liverpool and Manchester Utd and loved scoring against Spurs. Epitomised the early 80s: bling, long hair and leather trousers .

STEVE WILLIAMS (1985-88)

Mike Slaughter: I liked his nasty side. He was fully committed, skilful, yet tough at the same time with a flair for a good pass and a good shot but always a yellow card waiting to happen. I remembering reading how he got sent home from an official club event for turning up in a mohair jumper. My rebellious side approved of that!

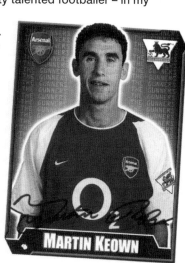

Steve Williams with one of his youngest admirers.

Robert Grainger: Secretly a tough guy in centre midfield. Very firm with a great pass. Chopped Ossie Ardiles in half at The Lane. Proper player.

MARTIN HAYES (1985-90)

John Hilditch: 'Whoops-a-daisy Martin Hayesey' was a pretty talented footballer – in my 13 year-old eyes anyway. I remember that FA Cup match v Millwall when they said they were going to take the Clock End. Anyway, we clear the ball, Hayesey hurtles down the line, over half-way, looks up to play a ball (probably in to 'Smudger'), sees about 30 Millwall on the pitch fighting and performs the most exquisite Cruyff turn ever . . . and heads back towards the North Bank. Can't say I blame him. That day was carnage.

MARTIN KEOWN (1985-86 & 1993-2004)

Neil Payne: Certainly in his second spell at Arsenal, Martin Keown was a massive favourite of mine. As he got older he seemed to embellish the Arsenal never-say-die spirit more than most. Total honesty, commitment and passion to the cause could never be underestimated. In my opinion, when in his prime he would be first on my team sheet, particularly if you knew the game would first need to be won via a physical battle. As an out-and-out defender, very few could match him at his peak.

He also gave me an abiding funny memory from Highbury. I think it was the FA Cup defeat of Liverpool in 2002 when he eventually received his marching orders – but not before he had literally frightened the life out of the little mercenary that is Michael Owen. Clearly Martin was intent on showing Owen who exactly "The Rash" was, and he proceeded at every opportunity to, shall I say, make Owen aware he was around.

So much so, I can remember a freekick being awarded to Liverpool and Owen getting ready to make a run into space close to Keown's path, before realising and quickly readjusting to tread another route in a completely different direction. Hilarious when watching it in the North Bank that day. Fear factor doesn't do it justice.

Ian Tredgett: Martin broke into the side just as I was going more regularly and I felt I saw him develop. I was one of a few hundred hardy souls who saw his debut in a goalless draw at West Bromwich Albion on a soaking wet afternoon in November, 1985.

In April, 1986 he and Tony Adams (both 19 at the time) were paired at centre-back against champions Everton, who boasted England striker and league top scorer Gary Lineker in their ranks, at Highbury. They kept him under control superbly and despite a lucky goal by Wayne Clarke giving Everton the points, I felt then that the future of our defence was in safe hands. I was right, it was, albeit not Martin's (at least not for a few more years). I was sad when he left and delighted it was only a temporary absence.

He had the same attitude as Adams. You wonder what he would have achieved had he stayed with us between 1986 and 1993; he would almost certainly have won more medals with the club than any other player.

Rob Macdonald: An animal of a player. I was so happy when he got on the pitch in his last season to achieve the number of appearances (10) needed to pick up a league winner's medal. His testimonial match – Arsenal XI 6, England XI 0 on May 17, 2004 – was great, just a shame that a sheepish Keown stepped up and had his penalty saved by Norwich City's Robert Green!

Darell J. Philip: Martin Keown just edges out the 'Romford Pele', Ray Parlour. Keown was such a tough no-nonsense defender who I believe was as much an influence at the back in his second spell as the original four – Adams, Bould, Dixon and Winterburn – were under George Graham. I loved Keown's tenacity, passion and never say die attitude. He epitomised the true spirit of what it means to represent Arsenal, 'victory through harmony', and with him in the side you just knew that opposition attackers would be embroiled in a bruising encounter where Keown would often come out on top.

DAVID ROCASTLE (1985-92)

Craig Pottage: I saw his debut against Newcastle Utd and he was the best player on the park. He just exuded quality on and off the pitch, was such a nice person and just seemed to fit Arsenal like a glove.

PERRY GROVES (1986-92)

Lee Pritchett: For his jinking run v Liverpool in the 1987 League Cup Final, the red hair, his song, and the fact that a player with capable, although limited, abilities could be in one of the greatest Arsenal squads of all-time. He deserves his cult status. I still love listening to him on talkSPORT. He loves The Arsenal. Once a Gooner, always a Gooner.

Mike Green: What a trier, what a character. Never gave up nor hid during a game not matter how much stick he was getting from the crowd.

Jon Lawlor: Mr Dependable did what was asked of him, played where the boss wanted him to play and just seemed to get on with it.

Alan Whitnall: "Number one is Perry Groves, Number two is Perry Groves . . ."

Perry Groves wore his heart on his sleeve for Arsenal..

PAUL MERSON (1986-97)

David McConachie: Bit of a rascal but with the ability to do things that others couldn't in a team that was lacking a bit of creativity at times.

KEVIN RICHARDSON (1987-90)

Tom Eldridge: I loved Chris Whyte – I really wanted him to play for England. And in that era I loved Brian Talbot too. Although he was getting on a bit by then, he got around the pitch like the kids did and didn't ever give up anything. But my all-time cult favourite is Kevin Richardson – just for that shift he put in during the 1988-89 season. I thought he was awesome, and when 'Rocky', Michael Thomas and co. were getting all of the headlines, he just turned out week in, week out and nailed everything in his path.

NIGEL WINTERBURN (1987-2000)

James Smither: Arsenal have been particularly blessed at left-back for the entire time I've supported them (Sansom, "Nutty", Silvinho, Cole, Clichy and Gibbs). Nigel wasn't just the dictionary definition of dependable and an indispensable part of the best club defence of all-time, he loved a tackle, was an underrated contributor in more advanced areas of the pitch, and would every so often score the most sensational goals.

Sitting in the Junior Gunners/Cannon Club enclosure in the first five-to-10 rows of the East or West lower as I did for much of my time at Highbury, you got a particularly good view of the effort and talent he displayed with quite brilliant consistency every single game.

Everyone remembers the last-minute screamer to cap a 3-2 win at Stamford Bridge but arguably the similarly long-distance goal he implausibly got with his right foot against

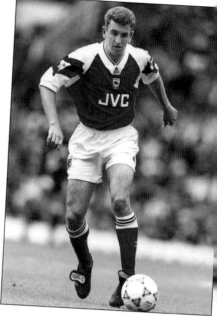

Nigel Winterburn's goal against his former club proved vital.

Wimbledon, from whom we'd signed him the preceding summer, in the last league match before 'that game' in late May, 1989, should be his greatest legacy. After all, without it any sort of win at Anfield wouldn't have been enough to win us the title.

SIGGI JONSSON (1989-91)

Neil Davies: The Arsenal has a rich history of cult favourites but I remember being fascinated by a certain Icelander who arrived in July, 1989. I was so excited by the arrival of an overseas payer that I was convinced that he would become an Arsenal legend. We all know that injuries put paid to that but I managed to bang on about him so much that, for a short time at school, I gained the nickname of 'Siggi'. On reflection, also having my haircut to match his wasn't my greatest coiffuring choice.

ANDERS LIMPAR (1990-94)

Ian Mills: He eventually fell out of favour with George Graham. However, he was sensational in his first couple of seasons and topped off the 1991 title-winning campaign with a hat-trick at home to Coventry City.

JOHN JENSEN (1992-96)

Alan Thompsett: I WAS indeed there when Jensen scored. Played like me, scored as often as I did, loved the Arsenal nearly as much as me.

RAY PARLOUR (1992-2004)

Dave Randall: Ray started out disastrously and none of us thought he was going to make it to the next level. However, he stuck at it, never failing to give 100 per cent and of course culminating in that never to be forgotten 'Its only Ray Parlour' moment at Cardiff in 2002. Very worthy of the 'Romford Pele' nickname.

David Harman: I saw his first few games at Highbury. On first look he seemed like a winger with pace and energy, and always dangerous on the ball (that's how I initially saw him). My dad though he was wonderful. As he got older it was obvious he didn't have the talent to match the more technical players but his hard work and love for Arsenal always make him one of my favourite players. A special mention to Andy Linighan and Perry Groves too.

Ray Parlour giving his all in an FA Cup tie against Port Vale in 1998.

Graham Price: Mr 100 per cent. "Ooh Ahh, Ray Parlour", "It's Only Ray Parlour".

DAVOR SUKER (1999-2000) & GIOVANNI VAN BRONCKHORST (2001-03)

Tom Humphrey: I have two 'cult favourites' from Highbury. The first was Davor Suker, who joined us in 1999, when he was probably just past his best. I loved Suker because the first World Cup I watched was France 98 and he was a star for Croatia in that tournament. When he signed for us, I was very excited. A young Thierry Henry developed into a goalscorer that season and of course we had Dennis Bergkamp too, so, sadly, Suker only lasted a year at Arsenal. I also remember him missing a penalty in the UEFA Cup Final against Galatasaray in 2000 – probably his last kick in an Arsenal shirt.

My favourite cult figure, though, would be Giovanni Van Bronckhorst. Gio wasn't the flashiest player around but he always put in 100 per cent for Arsenal and would play left-back when Ashley Cole was injured. It's a shame that he suffered a long-term injury in 2002, which meant Arsène Wenger went and signed Gilberto that summer, limiting Van Bronckhorst's chances when he returned from injury. Gio had a great career after leaving Arsenal, so I just wonder what could have been for him at Arsenal . . .

FREDDIE LJUNGBERG (1998-2007)

Ben Sharpe: In the latter Highbury years, one of my favourites was definitely Freddie, even though I don't think he's a cult figure because he's loved by many. Dennis Bergkamp is the best I've seen and Ian Wright was my hero but Freddie was one player I loved. He always put in 100 per cent and loved scoring against Manchester Utd, which earned him plenty of brownie points from me.

He kind of went against the grain of what a footballer should be. He had various hairstyles, which were wacky, his clothes were a bit out there and, having met him a couple of times, he's a pretty cool guy.

10 KITS

REPLICA kits are now firmly established as a key cog in a multi-billion pound global money-making machine, as fans all over the world rush out to buy their team's latest home, away and third strips and don't get change from £50 . . . and that's just for a shirt.

It's far removed from those distant days when full kits were not even widely available to buy from general sports retailers, while club shops had only a limited choice of home top, shorts and socks but certainly not an away option. If you wanted a shirt number added, that meant a sewing job for mum or gran!

Teams stuck with the same basic design year in, year out. This was an era in which tradition counted – was there anything more iconically distinctive than the white cannon on red? – and fans' loyalty was not exploited to anything like the same extent it is today. It was not until the late 1980s that people started to wear replica shirts to matches in significant numbers, although the explosion of colour and multiple shirt designs – which then changed every two years – didn't fully develop until after the dawn of the Premier League in 1992.

Here's what a number of our contributors – quite representative of the majority view – chose as their personal favourite home strips . . .

Q: What is your all-time favourite Arsenal home strip from the Highbury era?

1950s & 60s

Richard Boyes: Once again I will be on my own for my selection. After we won the FA Cup by defeating Liverpool 2-0, our last home league game of the 1949-50 season was v Portsmouth, who were first division champions. It was a midweek fixture – there were no floodlights then – played four days after the Wembley final (3/5/1950). Arsenal decided to play in the same strip they had used in the cup final: yellow shirts with blue shorts, very similar to the strip used in the 1971 final v Liverpool.

The game was a sell-out and I was one of many locked out. In the area behind the clock is a large block of flats which were in the early stages of being built. It had scaffolding all round it, so I climbed as high as I could. Although I could only see part of the North Bank end, we still enjoyed the atmosphere. So it's yellow-and-blue for me.

Graham Lister: I'm a bit of a traditionalist when it comes to the Arsenal kit. I was distinctly unimpressed when we kicked off the 1965-66 season having discarded the distinctive white sleeves in favour of an anonymous all-red shirt similar to that worn by any number of other clubs. And I haven't welcomed some of the busier designs of recent years, or the commercial motivation behind the frequent changes.

So it's perhaps not surprising that my favourite strip is the classic one worn in the 1967-68 and 1968-69 seasons: red shirt with white cannon on the chest, white crew-neck, white sleeves and red cuffs; white shorts; white socks with navy blue hoops. It was a modern interpretation of the design introduced by Herbert Chapman in the 1930s, stylishly uncluttered and instantly recognisable as Arsenal.

The shirt design survived unchanged until the 1982-83 season, apart from the addition of manufacturer Umbro's diamond logo and sponsor JVC's name, but the socks were switched to red-and-white from 1969-70 onwards.

Paul Harris: I liked the 1968-69 strip that was a proper encapsulation and a respectful nod to the Chapman period. I am talking red shirts with long white sleeves, white shorts and blue-and-white hooped socks – the best and most distinctive and unique kit. No other team had that deliberate mismatch of socks in terms of the main colour. I hated it when, for away games, they switched to red socks when it was not strictly necessary. Chapman had chosen them because, apparently the colour did not run.

1978-81

1970s & 80s

Marvin Berglas: I loved the original plain cotton red shirt with white sleeves and red cuffs with the subtle yet distinctive white cannon badge synonymous with Arsenal all around the world. We wore this from the late 1960s through to the late 70s.

Tony Fisher: Without question, the simple 60s/70s shirt with just the cannon motif. The only replica shirt I have or will ever wear.

John Morley: 1970-71 Double-winning strip. Classic plain red cotton shirt, white round collar and sleeves, red cuffs and NO blue bits or sponsor's name.

Mike Slaughter: The classic 70s strip, never bettered though most of our home kits have been good. My main memory is seeing Liam Brady in that shirt, untucked and hanging loosely by his side. The redcurrant kit was special as well.

Gary Jones: The Umbro shirt, 1978-81 – cannon with the three cannon balls. Pure class.

1984-85

Ian Tredgett: The classic 1970s shirt, with no sponsor's name nor manufacturer's logo, just a simple cannon on the left tit. I also liked the first Adidas kit we had for the 1986-87 and 1987-88 seasons. I guess it signified the change in the club: new management, good, young players and some hope at last. I will forever associate it with the 1987 League Cup run.

Alex Morrow: The classic version that I saw when I first came to Highbury. Round neck, the old cannon on its own on the shirt, and most importantly red socks. Can't abide white ones – it doesn't look right.

1985-86

226

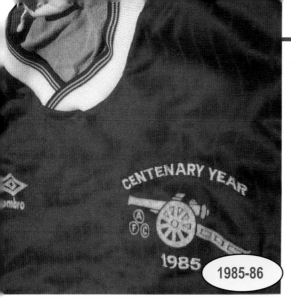

1985-86

1988-90

1990-92

Neil Payne: Always liked the 1982-83 vintage, probably because it holds great memories for me – my first season of going regular with mates. The red-and-black hooped socks, though, were bloody awful.

Tom Eldridge: I absolutely loved the 1985-86 Centenary home strip. It reminds me of some of my heroes at the time – Tommy Caton, Stewart Robson, Kenny Samson. That bright red and the thin white pinstripe – wow! And the 1982-84 first JVC, V-neck, shiny shirt is a real favourite because I wore mine to death trying to be Charlie Nicholas and Paul Davis. The 1989 shirt is always there in any favourite list. Conflicting emotions, though, because Anfield on May 26, 1989 couldn't have been higher but it does always remind of Rocky and how sad that was and still is. But the ultimate for me has to be the old Umbro short-sleeve shirt, 1978-81 – Stapleton, Brady, Rice, Talbot and Rix. The shirt to end all shirts as far as I am concerned.

John Hilditch: The first Adidas one is a classic. My birthday is in July, so a great time of year to get the new kit as a present, which I did every year from Holloway Sports on Seven Sisters Road. I was proper excited about getting that one. In those days, the kit came in its own presentation box, which added to the excitement.

James Smither: I'm sure I won't be the only person to choose the first Arsenal shirt they owned, and in my case it was also the shirt the team wore when I started going to home games in 1987. I still prefer Adidas to Nike as a manufacturer to this day, and this was truly a classic: no gimmicks other than some pretty nifty patterns in the stitching, red shirt, white sleeves, possibly the best collar of any Arsenal shirt since the 1970s, the classic cannon logo facing in the correct (i.e. left) direction and of course our 'proper' long-time sponsor, JVC, with its elegant, minimalist logo. No kit since has come close. In my mind, it will always be the shirt best pictured being worn by a defender with one hand in the air while successfully catching another bemused opposition striker offside.

Mark Aughterlony: 1988-89 Adidas strip. I wasn't old enough to remember the last time we won the league in 1971, so to do so in '89 – my daughter Sophie having been born in the January of that year – means that kit will always live long in the memory. I occasionally wear this replica shirt for five-a-side football with the lads from work, who refer to it as my retro kit. Blooming cheek!

1990s & Noughties

Neil Davies: 1990-92 kit was special. I first saw us in it when we beat Villa at Wembley in the old Makita pre-season tournament and Anders Limpar scored a belter on his debut. I loved the way the white arms arched across the shoulders at the back and it looked every inch like a kit the eventual champions should wear.

Gary Biggs: 1991 Adidas shirt with AFC on the collar and white piping on the shoulders.

Ian Mills: 1990-91 – a classic and we were also unbeaten in the league playing in it at home that season.

Ben Sharpe: 1994-96 kit, mainly because it was the first kit that I got from World of Sport at Finsbury Park.

Darell J. Philip: 1996-97, sponsored by Nike and JVC. It was the first strip I bought and it was during a very special season for me as a member of the Arsenal Ball Squad, as well as being Arsène Wenger's first season with us.

Rob Macdonald: I liked the white and blue strip in 1999. It was also after we had just won the Premier League and played at Wembley in the Champions League. I have the name 'ADAMS' on the back of mine.

Michael Cherrington: The redcurrant strip for the final season at Highbury. It was different from the others and had a collar with goal lettering and number on the back.

Tom Humphrey: I just loved the classy redcurrant kit worn in 2005-06, as it was going back to the club's colours from the first year at the stadium back in 1913.

Many thanks to the following for sending in shirt images: Roberto Puzzi, Aldi Bawazier, Mike Clark, Antony Sutton, Mark O'Toole, John Hilditch, Bas Hamers, Chris Neal, Steve Cheal, Lee Histed, Troy Chandler, James Smither.

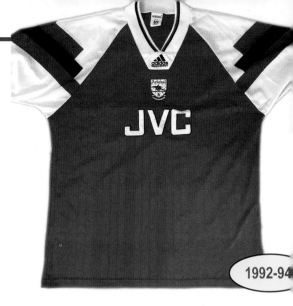

1992-94

1993

1994-9

1996-98

2000-02

2002-04

2004-05

2005-06

HIGHBURY
STADIUM TOUR

Pictures by Lorraine Haugh

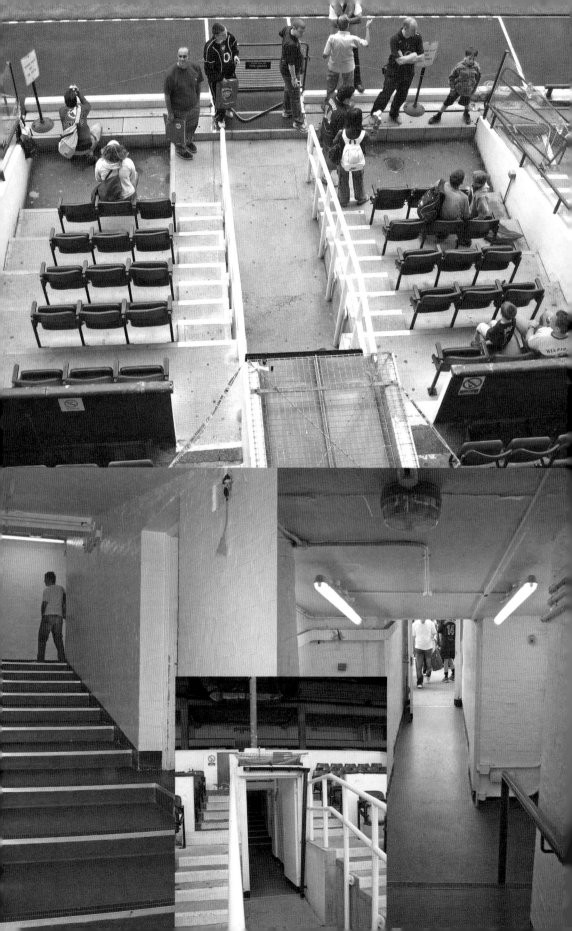

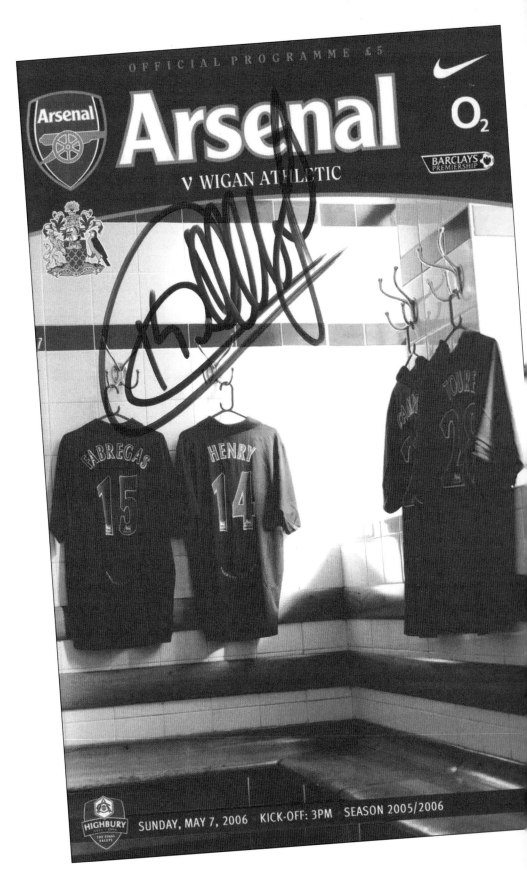

11 SAD GOODBYE

AT 3.00pm on Sunday, May 7, 2006 the club played its final game at The Home of Football in a carnival atmosphere. Managed by Arsène Wenger, Gunners brought joy to an inevitably emotional, sad occasion by beating Wigan Athletic 4-2 to clinch fourth spot in the final Premier League table.

Pipping arch-rivals Tottenham Hotspur to grab the last Champions League qualification spot was the icing on the cake.

Arsenal took the lead when Robert Pires struck from close range in the eighth minute. Wigan hit back when Paul Scharner (10 mins) poked in and then David Thompson (33) curled home.

Henry (who signed the front cover of our programme) scored twice (35 and 56) before slotting a penalty in front of the North Bank after Andreas Johansson was sent off for a foul with 76 minutes gone on football's most iconic clock.

Gunners needed to better Spurs' result to finish above them and Hammers' 2-1 victory – as well as a suspect serving of pre-match lasagne at the Tottenham team's hotel! – did them a huge favour.

A capacity crowd of 38,359 were there on a momentous overcast afternoon but, for one reason or another, not all of our contributors were that fortunate. Some made their last pilgrimage weeks, months or years before the Wigan finale, while others stepped onto the hallowed turf in the days following the last official game.

Q: What do you recall from your last visit to Highbury?

Eileen Clark: My late husband Steven Clark had been an Arsenal supporter since his uncle Bill took him to Highbury at the age of seven (he'd loved them before then but that visit cemented it). I met him at work, Mosercams in Hornsey Road, N19 (he was a draughtsman and I was a clerk/typist) in November, 1971. He was 19, four years older than me. It was, as was once described by an Arsenal-loving priest we met many years later on holiday in Zante, a marriage made in Highbury. After all, I got a boyfriend who was the image of Charlie George (the reason I started supporting Arsenal) and he got a girlfriend who loved football! When I met him he had long hair just like Charlie – very 70s – and had even had a couple of people ask him for his autograph, thinking they were talking to the Arsenal star!"

Steve and I were married for 32 very happy years, having a son Paul and daughter Kelly along the way.

Anyway, back to the end of Highbury. He'd been told earlier that week that treatment for the stomach cancer he'd been diagnosed with the previous year had failed and he only had a couple of months left – news which devastated both of us.

However, he decided that although he was quite weak, he'd love, if possible, to get to Highbury for the final game. So Steve's sister and her husband said they'd drive us from our home in Stevenage to the ground. Timing was an issue: get there too early and he'd never make it through the game; and arriving late, as far as he was concerned, was never an option – you had to be there to cheer the team out onto the pitch.

My brother-in-law drove as close as he possibly dare to the ground, which from memory was the church in St Thomas's Road, and from there me and Steve took a slow, gentle walk to the ground, while the other two drove off to watch the game in a local pub.

Once inside the ground, Steve managed to get the club's complimentary T-shirt on over his coat, which he couldn't take off because he was always cold. He cheered throughout the game as much as he could, savouring every minute.

Once the game came to an end, and even though he was by now reaching exhaustion point for him, he was determined to see as much of the victory celebration as possible. From memory we stayed until the team had gone past us on the lap of honour but I knew, although he would have loved to, he couldn't stay any longer.

I rang my brother-in-law who said, after explaining the situation to a friendly PC, they'd been able to park right at the top of St. Thomas's Road, so just a short walk away, and he was on his way back home with a very happy smile on his face.

Although we had bought our season tickets for The Emirates, sadly, Steve never got to sit in his seat in the new ground.

He passed away, aged 54, just five weeks after the final Highbury game.

Steve may not have made it to The Emirates but his memory did – by way of a stone set just outside The Armoury shop (right).

John Hilditch: I lived at 185 Highbury Hill and, along with some neighbours, decorated the road with shirts and banners for the Wigan game. It was two doors down from the West Stand entrance by the North Bank. A local councillor Theresa Debono stopped the club from decorating the roads but she couldn't stop us.

I had breakfast in the garden that morning and could hear Roger Daltrey rehearsing Highbury Highs.

For the build-up to the game, I had a couple of mates, Richard Pease and Craig Bloomfield, share some beers on our balcony overlooking Highbury Hill and playing the Vieira Boys CDs. People were taking pictures of some properly amateurish decorations I made for the house, including a life-sized cardboard cut-out of Rocky Balboa dressed in the 1985-86 centenary year shirt and red-and-white striped bobble hat. The club put some footage they took of the house in the museum. Sadly for me, I'd popped back in to get more beers when they filmed, so the footage shows just my mate Peasey. He still reminds me about that.

It was a day of mixed emotions. Very sad to be leaving Highbury and a bit surreal to see so many legends walking past the front garden: George Graham, Supermac, Martin Keown, David Seaman and, er, Tord Grip.

Later on, I left the ground with a 'No Alcohol Beyond This Point' sign from the Clock End. It's the only thing I was able to "look after safely" for the club that day.

A week or so later, there was the Islington Schools Crisp Cup Final and soon after that the bulldozers moved in. It was a strange place to live at that time. Looking into the ground from the top bedroom, seeing the place ready to go. The pitch ruined by diggers, half the seats of the North Bank ripped up.

I paid a couple of visits again via my garden wall. It was an incredible feeling, being in a stadium at night, so, so quiet, so full of memories and yet ready to be pulled down. Foxes running around the West Lower and then the flash of the security guard's torch.

I didn't actually know the last time would be my last time but as more and more workers started tearing the place down, the more difficult it got to get in with security and fencing. Maybe that made it easier, not knowing the last time was just that.

Chris Welstead: Of course, I was sad to see the end of this famous old ground but also excited about the move to a state-of-the-art stadium which I could see rising up in Ashburton Grove from my seat in the North Bank upper. It was nice to finish with a victory,

STEVEN G CLA...
GOONER FOREVE...
.·. 1951-2006...

240

a neat symmetry after witnessing a win in my first match over 50 years previously. Unlike many people, I did not feel extremely downcast. It was a case of "Goodbye Highbury – thanks for the memories but let's look forward to a new era at the new ground that will be the envy of many."

Tony Fisher: Such an incredible day, going through every possible emotion with the significance of the event. Sitting in my seats EG129/130 for the very last time after 30 seasons in them. The bitter sweet memories of being with my late son Dean in those seats from boy to man and have him share my passion. Then my youngest daughter Emma taking his place and becoming part of the Highbury family. Also thinking about my late best friend Barry, who used to occupy seat 128, having spent so many years following Arsenal with him all over the country in the old days.

Then to witness the most unbelievably dramatic topsy-turvy match with the Spurs' score constantly being updated. 38,000 Gooners singing "Bubbles". It doesn't get any better than that for football emotion.

The parade afterwards, with all those great players from the past evoking such wonderful memories, especially Derek Tapscott, one of my very first heroes.

It was all just so very special to have been part of such a rich history which will live in my memory forever.

Tony Fisher and his late son Dean with the FA Cup in 1979. Pic taken by goalkeeping legend Jack Kelsey in the club shop.

James Smither: Having never managed to go to every single home game in a complete season before, I was determined to accomplish the feat during our farewell (purple shirts-wearing) year at Highbury.

With the finale against Wigan approaching, and having successfully come through a couple of near-misses (most notably the Champions League semi-final, first-leg, v Villarreal, when a last-minute internet intervention saved my perfect record), I was increasingly nervous about how the club would choose to allocate non-season ticket seats for this most historic of fixtures. With demand set to be unprecedented, a simple 'first come, first served' approach through what were at the time horrendously unreliable postal or telephone application options threatened to be about as high-stakes a lottery as you could imagine.

Fortunately, Arsenal understood this predicament and opted instead for a loyalty-based approach, meaning my sister and I were guaranteed our place at the party due to our attendance throughout the season to date. When it came to selecting our seats, we knew it had to be the North Bank.

As it turned out, of course, the added drama of a head-to-head battle with Tottenham for the final Champions League spot was added to the mix of what already promised to be a supremely emotional final day of not just the league season, but also our almost 100-year tenancy of the world's most beautiful football stadium. Thinking that it could all end unhappily – handing our deadliest rivals eternal bragging rights just two short years since we'd rubbed their faces ceaselessly in our winning the league at their stadium – was almost too much to bear.

I remember arriving at the ground ridiculously early – and immediately noticing how many other people had done the same. I resisted the temptation to wander over to Ashburton Grove (as we called the site of the new stadium back then). Today was all about Highbury, and I'd been avoiding the construction site all year hoping for my first viewing of the finished deal the following autumn to be as impressive as possible.

Instead, I simply wandered around the streets framing the ground that I'd come to know so well: Aubert Park, Avenell Road, Gillespie Road and Highbury Hill, photographing the stadium's exterior, the signs, the stalls and their sellers, the stewards and security personnel, basically all the sights (and smells and sounds) that made up the uniquely Highbury match day experience.

I was thinking a lot about my grandad, Kurt Bromberg – the man who got me into Arsenal, took me to my first game 19 years earlier, and had died almost exactly eight years before that May Sunday – but also about everything else that had changed in my life during that period. While I had transitioned in fits and starts from a nervous primary school child to second school to university, into working life, imminent marriage and a mortgage, Arsenal, and in particular the bricks and mortar and essential 'Highburyness' of our iconic stadium, had remained a constant beacon of stability throughout all that turbulence.

It was an indelible feature of all the years of my life that I can remember with any great certainty: I've never lived outside the south-east of the UK and, as a result, I've been to multiple games every single year since I first caught the bug. I'd passed through its narrow turnstiles literally hundreds of times, from occasional fan brought by elder relatives, to enthusiastic teenager going when I could afford it or I could get back to London from college in East Anglia, through the obsessive phase in my early-mid-twenties when it was all about tallying up as many and as obscure away games as possible, to a (slightly) more balanced and less "all or nothing" psychological arrangement with the club as I approached 30. And now it was disappearing.

I went into the ground as soon as the turnstiles opened, wanting to get tranquil pictures I'd simply never thought to take before of the stands before they started to fill, even of the toilets and their cannon-crested tiling before the influx of fellow users may have earned me some strange looks, of the view from high at the back and low down at the front of the stand – basically as many different vantage points as I could, almost as if I was trying to transport the stadium away from me through the sheer volume of images of it I was capturing for posterity.

I'm sure other people will recount the particulars of the day better than me – the commemorative T-shirts, the parade of legendary former players, the storybook football ending (featuring an unexpected best supporting actor – an East End lasagne), Thierry Henry kissing the North Bank penalty spot, and so on and so on.

What I remember most is trying hard to appreciate every second of the experience rather than complaining or enduring, as I so often do at home games, and soak in every special sentiment Highbury evoked in me.

I didn't leave until the last possible moment after the final post-match ceremonials had concluded, when the stewards really started insisting – and even after that I simply didn't want to leave the streets and go home.

To this day, I still avoid looking at the high-end-housing-shaped hole where it used to stand. Our new stadium is great in many ways, and in the cold light of day an improvement in a number of appreciable and important dimensions. But, for me, it will never be (the) home (of football) like Highbury was.

Dave Randall: Tottenham losing 2-1 at West Ham the day after an Arsenal-supporting chef, working at the Marriott Hotel, West India Quay, had allegedly 'tampered' with their lasagne. They never fail to play a supporting role!

As a result, the Wigan game was joyous. A 4-2 victory meant we yet again finished above the Spuds when everything pointed to the opposite.

My main recollection was that maybe the famous old ground had run its course. Knowing what I know now, this was/is not the case and I miss it to this day.

Jeff Owens: Attended with my son Steven and my father-in-law (Steve's maternal grandfather). Three generations of Gooners celebrating the memories and history of our football club – and, of course, beating Wigan to keep Spurs out of the Champions League.

James (Jim) Miller: Pure sadness, felt like my heart has been torn out. Every goal we scored made me cry. I didn't want to go home. I'm feeling it again writing this.

Arsenal Football club means so much to us as a family: my three grandsons are sixth generation from Dial Square through to today. I have three sisters and one brother all Arsenal, and all husbands and wives are converts. Between us we have eight boys and four girls, while six grandkids all have Arsenal FC in their DNA.

Thank you for doing this book.

Neil Payne: Just taking in the walk from the car, the route via Highbury Fields and that magic moment when you hit the top end of Avenell Road and seeing swarms of fellow Arsenal fans heading towards the stadium for the final time. It just felt so sad and wrong but clearly the club had outgrown what I still call to this day a most unique football stadium. A ground that oozed class, from the marble halls to the East and West stands that, back in the day, were ahead of their time.

We were fortunate to sit near some great fans that became friends over the years as North Bank season ticket holders. It felt more than the end of an era that day against Wigan.

Of course, finishing in style with a Henry hat-trick and nicking a CL spot off our nearest and dearest up the road . . . well, it could not have finished much better.

I miss those days. Highbury will always be home for me more than Ashburton Grove will ever be, and that is not to criticise the job done in the build at the new stadium. Highbury, simply, was something different, a special place with special memories. Real character and charm.

Gone but never forgotten.

Mike Slaughter: As my friends and family left our row in the East Stand for the very last time, I wanted my last view to be memorable and to stay immortalised for ever. I took a photo of the pitch and ground from my seat, had one last lingering look and then stared at the floor as I made my way out for the very last time. I cherish that photo of my last vision inside the ground.

Ian Tredgett: I was lucky enough to attend the game against Wigan, and my only regret

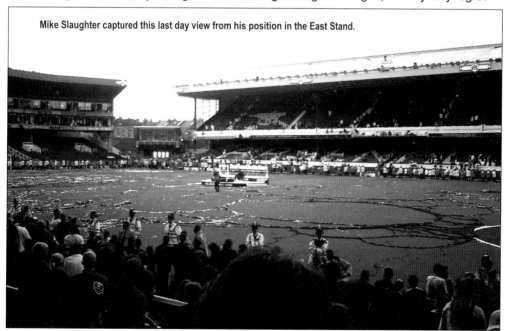

Mike Slaughter captured this last day view from his position in the East Stand.

243

is that my son Ollie, who was two at the time, was too young to attend. Years later he's a regular, I'm pleased to say.

On the day of the game I had two major concerns. Firstly, and like most weeks (but especially the last of the season), hoping for a set of results that put Arsenal as high as they could get in the table after that day's matches. On this occasion it meant us beating Wigan and Spurs losing (or drawing) at Upton Park. Thanks to Thierry Henry and a plate of lasagne this was achieved.

My second worry was that no-one would (especially Henry!) get injured and miss the upcoming Champions League Final. I learnt the previous day that I had got a ticket to the final against Barcelona in Paris and was naturally hugely excited. It felt that it was fate that our first game after saying "goodbye" to Highbury would result in us bringing back the one trophy we could never deliver to Highbury. Just shows what I know!

John Morley: Mainly, the sheer emotion of knowing that I would never attend another football match at Highbury after going for nearly 40 years. The atmosphere outside the ground before the game was special and slightly surreal. Getting into the stadium and seeing everyone wearing their red or white 'Final game' T-shirt was both impressive and special. Obviously Thierry Henry's hat-trick was also special, as was the Highbury 'Closing Ceremony'.

My sons and I were obviously reluctant to leave and waited in the ground long after the ceremony had finished and were among the last to exit the stadium. Walking out of the West Stand and looking over my shoulder at the pitch one last time was very emotional. I ensured I took my camera to record the 'Final Salute'. I'm so glad I did, although nothing will ever replace visiting Highbury to watch The Arsenal.

Emilio Zorlakki: My last visit and match at Highbury was a very stressful and emotional day, which of course was against Wigan Athletic. I deliberately tried to take the whole occasion in slowly, filming and taking photos and just taking my time. I sat on my seat number 84 for one last time observing what different supporters were doing while looking out onto the pitch and all around the great stadium with all its history and memories.

I bought an East Stand apartment in the Highbury Development by accident really (that's a story on its own and for another time). A few weeks before writing this I had visited my new tenants and was with them until virtually midnight. When I left, I decided to go and stand in the communal gardens for a few minutes and remind myself what this great place has meant to me and so many, many people.

Yasir Matloub: The game against Wigan was very sad and emotional. Highbury was my home, something The Emirates cannot emulate, and as Mary Hopkin sang: "Those were the days, my friend."

Paul Harris: When I visit now I always go back to the entrance of the old stand and reflect on the great players from all different teams who have crossed that threshold. It is like having one's past deconstructed to see what remains. But I recall my dad taking me there for my first game and how grateful I am for that. Every year my nephew phones me specifically to thank me for 'making' him an Arsenal supporter. He said he would thank me annually and he does and means it.

I recall there being a minute's silence for the old North Bank before it went (in May, 1992) and one chap yelled out in the silence: "The North Bank should not be remembered for being silent." He had a point but we stayed silent.

But the high emotion of the very last game has been assuaged by our having one of the finest stadiums in the world at Ashburton Grove.

Andrew Peters: Ticker-tape, Thierry Henry bowing down, Ashley Cole looking forlorn at full-time as he realised he was leaving the greatest club he'll every play for. And raw emotion that a big part of me would never experience and see again. A deeply sad day.

John Blair: Watching Thierry do something every Gooner wanted to do: score a goal and kiss the hallowed turf. Magical moment.

Ian Mills: I was present at the final game at Highbury and what an emotional and glorious send-off we gave to the ground.

The game itself was tense as we had to beat Wigan and hope Spurs dropped points at West Ham. We trailed by 2-1 before recovering to win 4-2. Thierry Henry netted a hat-trick, kissing the Highbury turf for good measure once he had completed his treble.

The parade of former Arsenal stars was really good.

On a personal note, 4-2 proved to be a lucky score: my own football team, Rushden United, won their Godbold Cup Final on the same day to become the first team to retain the trophy.

A few days later I was one of several hundred queuing for a piece of Highbury turf as a permanent souvenir.

Lorraine & Louise Haugh: For the final game v Wigan we sat in the North Bank, the same stand we sat in for our very first game. We took pictures of everything that day, as we knew it would be our last chance and we had to savour every minute. One of our most treasured photographs is of Thierry Henry scoring the last-ever goal at Highbury. I can't believe we managed to capture it on camera.

Louise and I stayed in our seat until we got kicked out at about 7.20pm. It was so emotional as we walked down the steps of the North Bank for the last time. As we left we turned around to take a photograph of the Clock End clock one last time.

From her seat in the North Bank, Lorraine Haugh photographed Thierry Henry preparing to take the penalty and then celebrating what was the last-ever goal and his 135th at Highbury.

From his elevated view in the West Stand, Rob Macdonald captured Henry netting the final goal. The Frenchman is one of 269 Arsenal players to find the net in league games at Highbury.

Lee Pritchett: The joy of the colour and happiness of the celebration of all the wonderful times that were had at that majestic stadium, tinged with a sadness that I wasn't going to come and see her anymore. To me, she was home and the greatest football stadium in the world.

Lester Allen: Sadness, end of an era and so many great memories. I sat with my youngest son Jamie, remembering all the happy memories our family had at Highbury.

Marvin Berglas: As Arsenal's resident match day magician at Highbury, the final game there was also my farewell to the stadium I knew so well since coming regularly as a fan from the early 70s and then getting my dream job – being booked to entertain the VIPs and sponsors in the hospitality suites since 1993. In the final season I did a stand-up show before each game for the sponsors in the Executive Lounge, off the Executive Suite, in the West Stand.

One of my sons, Jack, was just five-years-old but already a very keen, young Gooner. I managed to get him an extra ticket and rather poignantly we watched this historic game together from near the front of the North Bank. Ironic, as that was where I regularly first stood back in the day. To round off a truly memorable day, Jack got to meet all the players in the Highbury car park and still treasures his pictures with them and the very special memories to this day.

Graham Price: Before the Wigan game we had a few beers at The Woodbine. My thoughts that afternoon? . . . packed down Avenell Road, narrow turnstiles, beautiful day, not wanting to lose, free T-shirt, redcurrant shirts, pitch looking fantastic, the ground looking pure class (we should never have left!), the final whistle, the parade of past players, Roger Daltrey, fireworks, lingering at the end, feeling disappointed when we left, packed in Avenell Road again, off to The Woodbine to drown our sorrows.

Andrew Whitnall: Sonia, then my girlfriend, now wife, came with me to the last game v Wigan but as she didn't have a ticket she decided to go shopping at Camden Lock. When I eventually left the North Bank for the last time I found her in Elwood Street with a large heavy pub sign she'd bought for me (I collect beer/brewery stuff) at the market and lugged all the way on the tube back to Highbury. Nothing to do with football but I think of that day when I look at it.

Nobby Ralfe: Sad day against Wigan. I watched it from my seat in the West Stand, where

I could see straight down the tunnel. Midweek games under floodlights was like sitting at home in my armchair.

I would like to add the worst thing in my Arsenal life was losing all my Arsenal memories in a suitcase to an old girlfriend from the 70s. Too much to remember but these included silk scarves, pennants, a mug from the '71 Double, programmes.

Peter Coombs: Just wanted to go when the whistle went, having already done a long goodbye. Kept thinking, 'last game in the pouring rain', 'last game under floodlights', etc.

Alex Morrow: I'd been going to Highbury for more than a quarter of a century. I remember feeling sad after that last game against Wigan when they played the montage of players that had passed away and then had a parade of ex-players. The end of an era. Things just aren't the same at The Emirates.

Craig Pottage: I remember thinking how sad it was that we would never play there again and while The Emirates might be a nice new stadium, Highbury was a proper football ground.

Stephen Simson: We lost our true home that day. You stood there thinking about the history that was around us, the players that graced the famous turf. It was such a sad day.

Kelvin Meadows: The feeling that the club I fell in love with had changed and nothing would ever bring it back. I still feel that way.

Paul Hemming: At the Wigan game I felt a sense of apathy, because my love of Arsenal and football changed after the bond scheme. The club could and should have led the way in fighting the ramifications of the Taylor Report. They helped fight the ID card idea because it would have cost them money; but all-seater was a chance to make money from a "new type of customer".

I don't miss Highbury since it closed its terraces in 1992. I used to feel I belonged, I made a difference, I was part of something. I don't feel that now. The ethnic cleansing of working class support, the transition of our typical supporter is beyond recognition. Arsenal was a football club and I was a supporter. I'm not interested in global franchising and the middle class entertainment industry.

Arsenal always had posh support – actors, musicians, sports people – but they didn't go on the North Bank or the Clock End. The new fans wanted the cheap seats and demanded that those that were already there changed.

The atmosphere at football was created by working class men, letting off a bit of steam after a few pints maybe. That was the lifeblood of the game that grew out of the industrial revolution. The post-Euro 96 Sky TV era is not what I fell in love with; PSV at the bowl with no soul and a woman asked me: "How long is the interval?"

I gave up my season ticket after coming out of Wembley after the 2014 FA Cup Final v Hull City and two blocks had 'Verminator' and 'Bosscielny' on their shirts. I'd just had enough. My backstory and background and outlook just doesn't belong anymore, it seemed? I'm pleased I now spend my money on my kids. It's obviously up to the individual. I'm no-one but I'm just not part of that. I still go once a month or so but would rather watch squad players v Rotherham Utd in the League Cup than, say, Manchester City.

✳✳

The following were unable to attend Arsenal's last-ever Highbury match

George Stephanides: It was the evening of May 2, 1990, v Southampton. What I remember was that I once again bought the club's Adidas home shirt for the seasons 1988-89 and 1989-90. The match ended victorious for Arsenal and I watched the team from the East Stand upper, block Z, row V, seat 165.

I vividly remember the North Bank, which came alive after Arsenal went behind, pushing the players to turn the match into a 2-1 victory. Once it happened, the whole of the crowd erupted in celebration – like winning a cup final.

The following day I went again to the Gunners shop to buy the new outfit for next season and was surprised to see that the cannon emblem on the shirt was gone and had been replaced by the club crest.

Bernard Kiernan: Last visit was in May, 1998 – Arsenal 4 Everton 0 – on that famous day when we wrapped up the title. Quite a finale for me.

Keith English: v Manchester Utd (20/9/1998), just before I left to live on Australia's Gold Coast. Great match with Adams, Anelka and Ljungberg scoring our goals. Great day but sad that it would be a while before I could go back. Unfortunately, that wasn't to happen – we moved to The Emirates.

Wayne Flatman: A big win v Aston Villa, managed by David O'Leary, and sat at the Clock End for the first and last time.

Mark Aughterlony: My mum's first-ever game at Highbury was also my last. My mother, Patricia Long (nee Westwood), and late father, David Aughterlony, are both Islington born and bred, married in Thornhill Square, but soon after moved to Bucks for work, where they brought up my brother Lee and me. Anyway, in all the years my parents lived in Islington, Mum never went to Highbury to see The Arsenal. So, for her 60th birthday my daughter Sophie and I arranged tickets for the home match v Sunderland. We also secretly arranged to meet her brother Jim and brother-in-law Chris, both lifelong Arsenal fans, before entering the ground.

Not only was she over the moon when we announced to her a few days before that for the first time in her life would she be seeing The Arsenal, but the look on her face when we met my uncles outside the ground is something that we shall never forget.

John Lawlor: My last visit was very special because it meant I had watched at least one game from every stand at Highbury. I always stood on the North Bank but had managed somehow to watch the Benfica game in the Clock End and a cup-tie against Palace from the East Stand.

I managed a petrol station in Dover, Kent and one afternoon I received a phone call from GlaxoSmithKline that my garage had won four tickets to a Premier League game and before she could finish, I said: "Any Arsenal one would do."

So in due course four tickets arrived that entitled us to go to the players' lounge for a pre-match meal and drinks, followed by the game sitting in the West Upper v Middlesbrough (10/1/2004).

And what an experience it was listening to the two guys sitting behind us talking the whole way through the game as to whether it was handball if the keeper handled it outside the penalty area if his feet were still in the area. They never did come up with the answer.

As for the game, it was a 4-1 win that put us top of the table, with Thierry Henry scoring a pen, Queudrue (O.G.), Robert Pires and Freddie Ljungberg getting the others.

After we went back to the players' lounge for another couple of drinks and to meet some of the players. I had bought a cap for a young neighbour and Bobby Pires signed it for him.

David Harman: It was the Palace game on Valentine's Day (14/02/2004), and guess who I took! I hadn't been to Highbury for a few years due to Uni. Therefore I didn't have many points on my membership and because Arsenal had been so successful, it was becoming harder to get tickets. Midweek game on Valentine's Day? I saw my chance and bought two tickets.

I told the girlfriend I had booked two nights in London, although I deliberately wasn't specific about the trip. But because it fell over Valentine's Day, she logically thought a romantic evening was in store.

Once in London I told her I'd got my dates mixed up and we were going to the football on Valentine's night instead. I apologised and promised her the next night we would do something. Hmm, that didn't go down too well but she just about bought my story.

We went to the game, she was pretty chirpy to start with, enjoying the atmosphere, but that faded quickly when we sat on the North Bank and it was about minus three degrees centigrade. She lived in South Africa, where anything below 10c is considered arctic.

It was a fantastic game, which Arsenal handsomely won 5-1. Lots of great goals and for my last match at Highbury, it was a good send-off.

Good thing that came out of it was that my girlfriend (now my wife) refused to go to a game ever again! So I have never had to deal with the "I want to go with you stuff" and she just lets me get on with it. Result.

Stuart Pierce: It was the 49th match of the 49-game unbeaten run (16/10/2004). I wasn't going as much by then but I went out in style.

I remember Ian Hendrie giving Aston Villa the lead in just three minutes and running nearly the full length of the pitch to celebrate with the Villa fans. Robert Pires soon equalised from the spot and after Thierry Henry put us ahead just before half-time he wagged his finger at the Villa fans, as if to say "you won't beat us." Pires made it 3-1 midway through the second-half.

I recall an unknown Villa keeper, Stefan Postma, saving nearly everything, and nothing going right for Jose Antonio Reyes. A regular in his upper tier East Stand seat tried to convince his guest of the Spaniard's ability. "He is brilliant, just not today!"

Tom Eldridge: Funnily enough, I have just found the programme in an old shoe box. It was v Fulham on Boxing Day, 2004 with my cousin Luke Keay standing in the Clock End. I was living in Dubai at the time and had been there for a year. We didn't return until the end of 2006, so I missed the whole move to The Emirates.

I didn't ever think that that Fulham game would be my last at such a significant place in my life. Work, fatherhood and a load of other things conspired against me for a long time and I didn't see nearly enough football at Highbury for the last 10 years. But, that day, I did get to see Henry and Dennis score, and that was pretty special.

Sam Garrett: My last visit to Highbury was v Sheffield Utd in the FA Cup fifth round (19/2/2005). I don't know what I was more disappointed about – the red card 10 minutes before half-time for Dennis Bergkamp or the 1-1 draw which forced a replay.

It was a heated afternoon on the pitch in what I would call a grudge match because of our previous fixture against Neil Warnock's side at Old Trafford in the FA Cup semi-final a couple of years before. After going ahead 12 minutes from time through Robert Pires' tap-in, we conceded a 90th minute penalty and had to play a further 120 minutes a couple of weeks' later, ending in a 4-2 win on penalties at Bramall Lane. We made it hard for ourselves but it was the character we showed, and the way we bounced back from the tough times we endured, that led us to FA Cup glory against Manchester Utd that season.

Mukhtar Khan: I didn't realise that it would be my last visit. I was living overseas at the time. Was back for a visit in March, 2005 and the only home game during that time was v Norwich (2/4/2005). It was a resounding 4-1 win – a Thierry Henry hat-trick, plus one from Freddie Ljungberg.

Neil Davies: I took my seat for the final time for a League Cup match v Reading (29/11/2005). This visit was notable for several reasons. For one, I was sat in the North Bank for the first and only time, meaning that the Clock End was the only stand I never cheered from.

From that lofty position, I could see the new ground taking shape in nearby Ashburton Grove. This in itself was both exciting and moving, as I knew that this could well be my last visit; all those memories with my dad Vic and grandad Fred were woven into the fabric of this beautiful, historic stadium. I always felt that the ground crackled with history and the actions of the greatest players and those moments of dramatic triumph and heart-breaking defeat added to its majesty. And my story, which I shared with Dad and Grandad, was a part of it.

This would also be the one and only time I would go to a match with my wife-to-be, Angela Davies (nee Pleydell). This isn't remarkable in any way but the fact that she was from a Spurs-supporting family was a bit of a coup! Nothing says that you've been accepted by the woman in your life more than her being prepared to go arm-in-arm to the home of the club that her father and brother consider to be the most hated enemy.

I did have to drag her out of her seat, however, when the cry went up to "stand up, if you hate Tottenham." Once she was stood, I proudly reminded her that she was now a Gooner! I also took the opportunity to remind her that she was related to the great George Male (albeit that he was her great aunt's brother-in-law) so, in fact, I had returned her family to the true path.

The game itself was memorable for the performance of some of our brightest talent, such as Cesc Fabregas, Robin van Persie and Mathieu Flamini. They strutted their way to a 3-0 win and marched on into the quarter-finals of the cup.

I left that night with a heavy heart, deliberately walking along Drayton Park Road, where we had parked so often with Dad and Grandad. My days and nights at Highbury were and are a special, magical part of my life and I am proud to have been a part of the story.

Guy Thompson: I'm pretty sure it was the 7-0 win v Middlesbrough (14/1/2006). I remember tickets were so hard to come by at that time. Everyone and their cat wanted to go. The touts were boshing their prices right up, so it was a real struggle finding any but I managed to get hold of one about 10 minutes before kick-off. I'm glad I did, even though it worked out at just over £17 per goal.

I did manage to get hold of one of the crush barriers while they were demolishing Highbury. I guess it came from the right side of the North Bank, at the back. That's the area we picked it up from anyway. I really wanted the one I used to lean up against, right at the back and in the middle by the gangway that led up to that little place where you could get a crap cup of tea. But you couldn't really get that far in. The place was a bloody mess when we got there. I was crying inside.

I was working in the Garrick Theatre in the West End and called the club up to see if I could grab one. They advised me to speak to the demolition men when I got there. Me and my mate Seb went up there, I had a word with the guys knocking the place down and they said if I can lift it, then I'm welcome to it.

We grabbed one that was in two pieces, one 'V' shaped leg and another with the bar still attached across it. Heavy as f***!

Hilariously, and to quite a few strange looks, we then carted it on the tube down to Leicester Square and stored it in the theatre until I could arrange to take it home.

Shame a future landlord thought it was junk and chucked it in a skip while I was away. I could have killed him!

Tom Humphrey: The last game I saw at Highbury was v Wigan in the League Cup (24/1/2006), which, as mentioned earlier (chapter 7), was rather painful viewing. But my last visit to the stadium came on the final day of that historic season, coincidentally against Wigan again. We tried to get tickets but they were like gold dust and we missed out. Overhearing touts outside, they must have made a killing at the prices they were charging.

Even so, for one last time, me and Dad went to Cockfosters and caught the tube in on an emotional day. We got ourselves a programme as a souvenir and bought other things such as scarves and merchandise, as well as merchandise for the upcoming European Cup Final. So we said our 'goodbyes' to the stadium for one last time and headed back home before kick-off.

On the way home, we heard the news of Tottenham's food poisoning as they prepared to play West Ham, with the majority of their team ill due to some dodgy lasagne at their hotel! There was briefly some talk about Arsenal's game possibly being postponed, as well as Tottenham's, because of the race for Champions League football being decided in that game.

When we got home, news that both games were going ahead reached the radio and me and my family watched on the TV as we said goodbye to the stadium that we'd all been to at one point in our lives. A very sad occasion but the move was something the club had to do.

Looking back, I am so thankful I was able to go to Highbury as often as I did. I saw some of the best Arsenal teams in the club's history at a young age and can only thank Dad for taking me. I hear so many people around my age group that didn't get to go there once.

I was spoiled by the football Arsenal played in the early-to-mid 2000s and Highbury will forever be in my heart. Highbury or The Emirates, one thing will always stay the same. My love and passion for The Arsenal is just as strong as it was back then, win, lose or draw.

Dan Hill: Dad and I went up to soak in the atmosphere of the final game even though we couldn't get a ticket. We bought a programme as one last souvenir and saw people selling Champions League trophy balloons. As we came out of Arsenal station we heard the news about Tottenham and their infamous lasagne and had a good laugh about it.

We then paid a visit round the corner to look at our newly-built stadium before heading back home in time to see the end of the Wigan game and farewell celebrations.

Graham Lister: For reasons too painful to recount I was unable to attend Highbury's Final Salute that brought the curtain down for good on the venerable old stadium. So although I didn't realise it at the time, my last visit to Highbury for a match was on April 15, 2006, when Arsenal hosted West Bromwich Albion. It was particularly significant for two reasons.

Firstly, the fans had designated it Dennis Bergkamp Day and complimentary orange T-shirts with 'DB10' printed on the front were given to those attending.

Secondly, a season ticket holder in Block J of the lower East Stand, I was finally able to obtain the use of the seat next to mine for this match, so it was also the first time I'd been able to bring my son Alex, then aged 10, to a game. We travelled down from Leeds to King's Cross by train and got the tube to Arsenal underground station, emerging onto Gillespie Road where he was immediately assailed by the sights, sounds and smells of a Highbury match day, as I'd been some 50 years earlier.

The Arsenal team line-up before facing West Brom on April 15, 2006 – designated DB Day in honour of Dennis Bergkamp.

Manager Arsène Wenger with the Dutch maestro, who came off the subs' bench to help secure victory.

He absolutely loved the day, and I loved showing him the stadium and seeing him absorb the history, taste the atmosphere and experience the excitement. The fact that Arsenal won 3-1, and that Bergkamp scored (having come on as a 71st minute substitute along with Robert Pires, who also netted) made it even more special.

Steve Cheal: Sadly, I couldn't go to the final game but I'll always remember my last visit, v West Bromwich Albion. I'd not have remembered the score (3-1) had I not looked it up but I'll always remember being there for the great Dennis Bergkamp's final Arsenal goal in the last minute. As an adult, he's remained my favourite Arsenal player.

The day was all about Bergkamp – they sort of dedicated the game to him – and the goal he scored summed up everything about him: his positioning, two touches and then a lovely finish.

Tony Daisley: It was the 2-0 Champions League win v Juventus (28/3/2006), when Fabregas completely outplayed Vieira, who had left us the year before. Went with fellow staunch supporter Mark Jocelyn.

Derek Barclay: It was the day towards the end of the final season when they gave out balloons and you had to write the name of a departed person on the label and let it go. I put my late father Leslie's name on there. After originally going with my sister as a child, Dad had assumed the mantle of taking me to Highbury – and he quickly got the bug. I remember he'd feign the fact that he only went because I wanted to go but then when I went off to university in 1978, he carried on going to all home games on his own without me! I was really proud of him for doing that.

The last game he went to at Highbury before he passed away was when we beat Coventry City 6-1 and were presented with the league trophy (11/5/1991). He was in my thoughts at my final game at Highbury, for sure.

Mike Green: My last visit to Highbury was for the penultimate home game, v Spurs (22/4/2006). It ended 1-1 and I recall getting there early, having a good walk round the ground, buying some memorabilia and simply trying to take everything in, as I knew it would be my last visit to the famous ground. It was a funny experience and very emotional as I savoured all the thoughts of the highs and lows over a big part of my life and of the days and nights I had enjoyed there with so many different people, some who were no longer with us but would have loved to have been there.

As a footnote, I have a gorgeous Labrador and his name is . . . you guessed it, 'Highbury'. And by god does it suit him.

Keith Wilsher: With great sadness. It's been the home of football since I was five-years-old. I can still smell the plastic souvenirs from the little kiosk on the top floor of the West Stand.

Mike Green's pet Labrador named 'Highbury'.

Gary Jones: On my last visit to Highbury I ventured into the marble halls and just stood there and took it all in. So many memories haunt that place, it's magical.

Barry Davison: The last time I was at Highbury wasn't for a game, it was for a stadium tour. I remember thinking that I wanted to remove a blade of grass to take home with me but my morals wouldn't allow me to steal from someone I love (how I regret it now).

Bernard Chaplin: My last visit to Highbury was in fact to the 'End of an Era Auction' held at the ground. Unfortunately, the prices realised were out of my price range, although I did manage, after the event, to buy an art deco tile on eBay!

My contribution to this book is dedicated to my good friend Arthur Booth, who passed away 27 years ago. We attended matches together for more than 35 years, on the terraces and then as season ticket holders. He is still sorely missed.

Robert Grainger: I'm a London black cabbie and recently dropped someone off at what used to be the East Stand. I couldn't help popping in for a nostalgic look. Wish I'd never, as all my hundreds of Highbury memories seemed a distant past while looking at the flats and gardens.

I miss Highbury, big time.

Richard Boyes: I have no special memories of the last game I saw there. The stadium was like home to me and my mates, an architectural masterpiece which was unique. Highbury had a soul which no club has ever had.

We migrated to Brisbane, Australia in 1973. We have cable TV and see every Arsenal game in the small hours, and still sulk when they lose. Unfortunately we have sulked a lot in the last few years. I will be 90 on July 11, 2021 and my Lady Gwendoline is a very young and spritely 80. We have nine grandchildren who support the Gunners, as do their partners. This is not negotiable!

****

A few went into 'extra-time' to pay their last visit . . .

George Lampshire: I was lucky enough to be in steward training for The Emirates in the summer before it opened. We did our first training sessions at Highbury after the 2005-06 season had finished. We did one big session under the North Bank and then walked out onto the pitch before we left. Was quite emotional knowing that I'd be one of the last to tread on that pitch before it was gone forever. I stood in several locations where I remembered watching games from the stands. Emotional.

Mark White: My last visits to Highbury were in the same week. I applied to be a steward at the new ground, half a mile down the road; at the same time I attended a seminar for selling the flats at the old ground. The interviews and induction sessions took place in the North Bank and East Stand; the property seminar was held in the boardroom and directors' box. Bob Wilson, the goalkeeping legend, gave a brief guided tour. It was a nice way to say goodbye.

George Pearson: I was fortunate enough to get tickets for the Nike Joga Bonito five-a-side tournament that was held there in the summer of 2006. Although not an Arsenal event, it was genuinely the last-ever bit of football played at that famous stadium. I remember walking out feeling sad that we'd never walk up the steps to our seats, never see our heroes celebrate goals there again.

At the auction of stadium items and memorabilia, Daniel Goldring bought this sign which used to be located in the West Stand upper tier concourse – he always sat in Block W, Row D. It now has pride of place above Daniel's front door interior at his home in Bushey, Herts.

They think it's all over . . .

THREE days after Arsenal played their final game at Highbury, Andrew Ballard recalls how he and a group of mates experienced the treat of a lifetime . . .

2006 was a memorable year for me, with fantastic highs and incredible lows. It was the final year that my beloved Arsenal, who I had followed over land and sea for the previous 20 years, were to leave their home and travel the short journey to The Emirates.

The good fortune started in March, when I entered a competition to write a piece about David Rocastle. Our match against Aston Villa was to be David Rocastle Day and there was a prize of match tickets for the winners. I wrote about his winner against Spurs at White Hart lane which took us to Wembley in 1987. It won!

The prize was two tickets to the Villa game (1/4/2006), a chance to meet Arsène Wenger and David O'Leary (Villa manager at the time but also my all-time Arsenal hero) and the job of putting in the scores in the half-time scoreboard. As I remember it, Spurs were losing 3-1 at Newcastle at half-time, so it got a massive cheer.

My good luck continued. Arsenal's shirt sponsor, O2, held a competition to play a match on the Highbury turf AFTER Gunners' final game of the season. The competition was to guess a team that Dennis Bergkamp had listed as his all-time top XI Arsenal from those he had played alongside. With 10 correct answers out of 11 (who wouldn't have picked Tony Adams over Martin Keown!), I was chosen as one of the eight winners.

After ensuring that the call from Arsenal telling me to assemble seven friends to make a team up was not a hoax, I started the process of ringing round my Arsenal chums. Sadly, my best mate Paul had booked to go on holiday that very week and wouldn't be able to join us. His place was taken by one of my lads at work (a Spurs fan!) to play in goal.

Within a couple of days an enormous holdall was delivered to my home containing eight complete kits, plus other goodies, with instructions. Our team was called the Cambridge Gooners. It was happening!

We boarded the train on the Wednesday morning after the final match against Wigan, along with some family members and friends who were allowed to watch from the stands. Sadly, my father Gerald was not well enough to join us. It would have made my day to have him with us. We lost him to cancer later that year.

We arrived at the stadium and enjoyed a cooked breakfast in the North Bank. The event was hosted by Bob Wilson, Charlie George and Sammy Nelson. A touch of glamour was added by compere Kelly Dalglish.

After breakfast we were taken out of the stadium, along Avenell Road and into the Marble Halls. We were then sent to the home dressing room so that we could get prepared to run out onto the pitch. What a feeling to leave the dressing and run out into the sunlight through the tunnel which we had seen our heroes emerge from for many years.

For half an hour we ran around on the pitch like excited five-year-olds, taking practice penalties into the North Bank goal, still unable to believe our luck. It was at this point that one of our group ran onto the pitch from the East Stand to take some photos. He was swiftly sent back, as spectators were not allowed on the field of play. Even at the end, with bulldozers poised to move in, standards had to be upheld.

Eventually the games started: eight teams pitted against each other to see who would compete in the semi-final and final. We had a few good players in our side but we were older than most and not particularly fit. Luckily, there were physio teams on hand to offer massages and injury support.

Our first match started controversially when Barney, a no-nonsense firefighter and our right-back for the day, went in hard on the opposition striker and was admonished by Charlie George. Barney has dined out on that story ever since.

We went on to play four games: won two and lost two, the highlight of which was a 4-1 win. Ultimately, we were beaten late on in a 1-0 defeat against the favourites and ultimate winners of the competition which led to our elimination.

After the matches there was a penalty competition with Arsenal mascot Gunnersaurus in goal. Our top striker Neil Loughnane begged to take our penalty. There was a Samsung phone to be won for the scorers. Imagine our glee – and his horror – when Gunnersaurus saved his spot-kick with a swish of his giant foam tail! We have never let him forget it.

There was still time for more wonders. After team photos with the legends, we retreated to the home dressing room where I stationed myself at Dennis Bergkamp's peg. After emptying the entire contents of the bubble bath cupboard into the giant bath, we bobbed around and sang our favourite songs.

Having left the stadium (frisked on the way out – no 'souvenirs' allowed), we decamped to The Gunners pub to drink the afternoon away and swap stories of our greatest day. Although we were not quite the last team to play on the pitch, it was close enough for me.

Cambridge Gooners enjoying their big day out, with lucky competition winner Andrew Ballard in the foreground.

Andrew emerging from the Highbury showers.

FINAL COUNTDOWN: More photos from Lorraine Haugh capturing the reat sense of anticipation and raw emotion of the last-ever Arsenal first team game at Highbury, on May 7, 2006 . . .

NO PLACE LIKE HOME: Sorry, we couldn't really avoid acknowledging what became of the site where one of the greatest football cathedrals proudly stood for 93 years. Amid the ghosts of past Arsenal greats is Highbury Stadium Square, where, in 2021, "an extremely spacious (680 sq ft) 1 double-bedroom apartment set on the 4th floor within the historic East Stand, benefiting from a truly outstanding uninterrupted view of the landscaped communal gardens" cost £500,000.

MARKETING SUITE

EAST STAND

ARSENAL STADIUM

HIGHBURY STADIUM SQUARE

"The soul and spirit of Highbury is non-transferrable. It is not physical, you can't pick it up and move it. It was a club with a huge sense of tradition, where behaving with class was important, but which was also open to innovation. Arsenal was firmly embedded in the local community and had very solid, working-class foundations. The fans espoused the club's values. This visceral attachment, from childhood, to a club and a team is something I have ever seen anywhere else with such fervour. Every supporter's first match at Highbury was like a baptism."

Arsène Wenger

The most successful and decorated Arsenal manager in Highbury history. In his 10 seasons at Highbury (1996-2006), Gunners won three Premier League titles and four FA Cups. They also reached the Champions League Final once. His team remained unbeaten throughout the league season in 1998-99 and 2003-04. The Frenchman won 187 matches at Highbury – more than any other manager – in his 265 games in charge.

"With each step and the higher I got, the more I could see. The splendour of the East Stand came into view. Then the famous clock. And then the pitch. It was an unbelievable sight and feeling. I'm not a religious person but if there really was a heaven, then I'd just stepped right slap bang into the middle of it. I just stood there for a moment and took it all in. I'd made it. I was finally on the North Bank. I was home."

Guy Thompson

"All that anxiety, energy and hope was being transformed into a wall of noise which I'll never forget. I remember not being able speak for a couple of days afterwards. After waiting 17 years, Arsenal had turned it all around in less than two minutes. I remember thinking my heart was going to explode amid the euphoria as people went crazy, jumping and hugging each other, perfect strangers brought together in one marvellous moment."

Steve Cooper

"I jumped off the stretcher and ran back to the North Bank. I was in agony watching our incredible 3-0 win. Next day I had my appendix out!"

John Powell

WE would like to thank the following 200-plus Arsenal supporters who took the time and trouble to respond to our original questionnaire, or contacted us via social media, and/or sent photographs for possible inclusion in the book. There simply wasn't enough space to include every single submission in full (it would have led to much repetition), while some images weren't of sufficient quality required for publication, but the following all played a huge part in making *Highbury Memories* possible. Special thanks must go to Lorraine Haugh, Roberto Puzzi, Gary Jones, Barry Sargent and Masahide Tomikoshi for the volume and poignancy of images they kindly made available to us.

A
Mark Adams
Edward Aiko'bua
Lester Allen
James Anthony
Jill Armstrong
Dave Ashby
Philip Ashman
Mark Aughterlony
Bryan Austin
Richard Averillo

B
Tom Badger
Andrew Ballard
Derek Barclay
Tony Bateman
Marc Beaumont
Marvin Berglas
Gary Biggs
Mike Birch
Steve Birch
John Blair
John Bowles
Gwen Boyes
Richard Boyes Snr
John G. Bugden
David Button
Mark Briggs

C
Ian Castle
Bernard Chaplin
Steve Cheal
Michael Cherrington
Eileen Clark
Malcolm Clayton
Harry Clowser
Peter Coombs
Jacqueline Cooper
Steve Cooper
Daniel Coyle

D
Tony Daisley
Paul Dargan
Neil Davies
Barry Davison
Brian Dawes
Michael Deasy
Paul Delaney
Jeremy Doltis
Paul Donohoe
Ewan Drake

E
Tom Eldridge
Stefano Enepi
Keith English
Nigel Evans
John Exley

F
Tony Fisher
Wayne Flatman

G
Sam Garrett
Kayne
Goddard-Knell
Daniel Goldring
Richard Gosling
Robert Grainger
Mike Green
Peter Gregory
Rob Griffiths

H
Lorraine &
Louise Haugh
David Harman
Paul Harris
Dave Heath
Paul Hemming
John Hickford
Dan Hill
John Hilditch
David Hillyard
Richard Holmes
Chris Hudson
Barry Hughes
Tom Humphrey
Mike Hunt
Christopher
Hylland

J
Nick Jackson
Robbie Jericho
Gary Jones
Richard Jones

K
Steve Kell
Paul Kelly
Brian Kendal
Mukhtar Khan
Bernard Kiernan
Julian Kirkby

L
Gregg Lamb
George Lampshire
John C. Lawlor
Gary Lawrence
Tom Leaney
Peter Lewis
Graham Lister

M
Rob Macdonald
Simon
MacMichael
Jem Maidment
Paul Manel
David Marks
Daniel Marsh
Steve Martin
Jamo Masterton
Yasir Matloub
Tim McCarthy
David McConachie
Alex McGarry
Kelvin Meadows
James Miller
Ian Mills
John Morley
Pete Mountford
Alex Morrow
Phil Murphy
Iain Murray

N
Dave Nathan
Peter Norton

O
Paul O.
Joe O'Connor
Stephen Orr
Jeff Owens

P
Paul Padfield
Vince Pardoe
Neil Payne
George Pearson
Adam Pembrey
Kieron Pennie
Andrew Peters
Darell J. Philip
Stuart Pierce
Tony Porter
Craig Pottage
John Powell
David Pretlove
Graham Price

Lee Pritchett
Roberto Puzzi

R
Pat Rainsford
Nobby Ralfe
Dave Randall
John Reeve
Paul Robertson
David Roche

S
Chris Saltmarsh
Andy Selby
James Seymour
Del Sharkey
Ben Sharpe
Tracy Sharpe
Stephen Simson
John Skinner
Mike Slaughter
Barry Smith
Cecil Smith
Kerry Smith
James Smither
George
Stephanides
Nick Stephens
Jeff Stevens
Andrew Stewart
Richard Storey
Richard Stubbs
Andy Strouthous

T
Robert Thaine
Alan Thompsett
Guy Thompson
Sandra Thulambo
Ian Tredgett

V
Bob Varney

W
Simon Wadey
Chris Welstead
John White
Mark White
Colin Whitehouse
Pete Wilday
John Williamson
Keith Wilsher
Mark Wilson
Andrew Whitnall
Paul Woodley
Nancy Wright

Y
Layth Yousif
Danny Young
Rhiannon Young

Z
Emilio Zorlakki

Photographs
Albert Allen, Mark Andrews, Paul Bates, Aldi Bawazier, Steve Blowers, Robert Boyling, Wayne Brown, Andrew Bullen, Steve Carey, Mike Clark, Ian Crane, Tim Crane, Les Easterbrook, James Elkin, Duncan Essex, Bas Hamers, Lee Histed, Gary Lawrence, Kevin Martin, Daniel Marsh, Chris Neal, Antony Sutton.

Bibliography
The Essential History of Arsenal by Rab MacWilliam and Kevin Connolly (published in 2003 by Headline) was a tremendous resource for checking dates and match details. A nod also to the *A-Z Of Highbury* (published by Arsenal FC, presented with Highbury's final match day programme, May 7, 2006) and *Arsène Wenger: My Life in Red and White* (published in 2020 by Weidenfeld & Nicolson).